to the Library of
Goshen College
from
Charles Merrill
Boston 2001

IN THE GRIP OF STRANGE THOUGHTS

RUSSIAN POETRY IN A NEW ERA

~

In the Grip of Strange Thoughts

Russian Poetry in a New Era

SELECTED & EDITED

BY J. KATES

ZEPHYR PRESS

Brookline, Massachusetts

Project Editor: J. Kates
Project Coordinators: Ed Hogan, Leora Zeitlin
Book Design & Production: Dan Carr and Julia Ferrari

Cover: *Window in Moscow,* by Eric Bulatov. Reproduced by permission of
Eric Bulatov and Galerie Berndt, Cologne, Germany.

"A Union of Lone Wolves," by Mikhail Aizenberg, translated by Nathalie Stewart.
Translation copyright © 1999 by Nathalie Stewart.

"Introduction," "Between Zukofsky and Zhukovsky," and "Notes" to the poems copyright © 1999
by J. Kates.

Further credits, which constitute an extension of this page, appear on pages xvi–xvii.

ISBN 0-939010-57-7 [hardcover] ISBN 0-939010-56-9 [paperback]
Library of Congress Catalog Card Number: 98-89440

The paper used in this book meets the minimum requirements of the American National Standard
of Permanence of Paper for Printed Library Materials Z39.48-1984

Printed in the United States of America by
Quebecor Printing Vermont

First published 1999 by
ZEPHYR PRESS
50 Kenwood Street
Brookline, MA 02446, U.S.A.
and simultaneously in the United Kingdom
by Bloodaxe Books Ltd.

*The editor and publishers gratefully acknowledge the generous support for this
project by the Witter Bynner Foundation for Poetry, the Bydale Foundation, the
Massachusetts Cultural Council, and the National Endowment for the Arts.*

MASSACHUSETTS CULTURAL COUNCIL

NATIONAL
ENDOWMENT
FOR THE
ARTS

In memory of
Nina Iskrenko (1951–1995)
Bulat Okudzhava (1924–1997)
and
Ed Hogan (1950–1997)
Founder of Zephyr Press

Table of Contents

x

Table of Contents

Acknowledgments

In the Grip of Strange Thoughts was originally conceived by June Gross in 1990, when she was still one of the directors of Zephyr Press. For me, her suggestion began a long course of study that is not likely to end. Had it not been for June, I would have spent the last seven years very differently.

Meanwhile, the anthology has continued through marriage, birth, divorce and death among its compilers. In short, *In the Grip of Strange Thoughts* became part of life as it is lived. And, like all life, it has endured only through the collaborative effort of so many people that it is impossible to acknowledge them all without simply celebrating the world.

To begin with, Ed Hogan, the founding publisher of Zephyr Press, pushed and pulled over several years to make this anthology not only conceivable, but to insure its quality. It is as much his as mine, and stands as a memorial to his commitment to Russian literature in English. The difficulty in acknowledging others has been underlined by Ed's loss; he died, shortly before the book went into production, in a canoeing accident that also took the life of his invaluable assistant, Helena Lisovich. There are many people whose contributions to *In the Grip of Strange Thoughts* were known to Ed and Olenka alone. But, in addition to the poets and translators we publish, we would like to thank as many as we can by name, and express our gratitude for a multitude of services to those otherwise not mentioned:

Maryna Albert, Giles Anderson, Grigory Benevich, Tom Birchenough, Nadezhda Burova, Jamie Byng, Ekaterina Cherkassova, Arkadi Choufrine, the Citizens Exchange Council, the Club Dolet, Natasha Derevianko, Denise DesRochers, Thomas Epstein, Adrian Flatgard, Dr. Gilbert Fuld, the Galerie Berndt, Helena Goscilo, David Greene, Andrey Gritsman, Anjali Gupta, Mike Guyette, Marie Harris, Clem and Doris Hogan, Tamika Hughes, Elena Kai, Alla Kashtanova, Helen Kates, Peter Kates, Michael Katz, Stuart Kelter, Alexandra Kirilcuk, Richard Kostelanetz, Denis Maslov, Olga Maslova, Lilian Meltzer, Arsen Mirzaev, Anatoly Naiman, Michael Naydan, Natasha Perova,

Valentina Polukhina, Eduard Safronsky, Jan Schreiber, Marian Schwartz, Aleksei Shelvakh, Robert Smyth, Nathalie Stewart, Nomi Victor, Pyongson Yim, Aleksey Zenkevich.

The work that Ed Hogan started has been continued after his death by Leora Zeitlin, whose encouragement, guidance and knowledge of the publishing business in general and Zephyr Press in particular have brought *In the Grip of Strange Thoughts* at last to publication. My personal debt to her at the conclusion of this project is as great as that to Ed Hogan at the beginning.

Also, the project could not have been started or completed without substantial support from the Bydale Foundation, the Witter Bynner Foundation for Poetry, The National Endowment for the Arts, and the Massachusetts Cultural Council.

J. Kates

Acknowledgements

"Here, everything gets eaten…," "Daughter," "A Party on Women's Day," "Seven Beginnings," by Olesia Nikolaeva, translated by Paul Graves and Carol Ueland. Translations copyright © 1999 Paul Graves and Carol Ueland. Russian texts reprinted by permission of the author.

"How the young flutist smiles…," "To me, Muscovites…," "Ah, Nadya, Nadyenka," "Departure," by Bulat Okudzhava, translated by Ronnie Apter and Mark Herman. Translations copyright © 1999 by Ronnie Apter and Mark Herman.

"Among black trees…," "What's left for me to say…," "The curve of your lips…," "Lay your head in my lap…," by Olga Popova, translated by J. Kates. Translations copyright © 1999 J. Kates. Russian texts reprinted by permission of the author.

"Imagine this: a mighty giant asleep…," "It's better not to live in Moscow…," "In the Desert," "Entry into Jerusalem," and "Dialogue No. 5" from *Texts of Our Life* by Dmitry Prigov, translated by Robert Reid. Translations copyright © 1995 by Robert Reid. Reprinted by permission of Edinburgh University Press. Russian texts reprinted by permission of the author.

"I will live and survive," "Like Mandelstam's swallow…," and "For the cry from the well…," from *No, I'm Not Afraid* by Irina Ratushinskaya, translated by David McDuff. Russian texts copyright © 1986. Translation copyright © 1986 by David McDuff. Reprinted by permission of Bloodaxe Books Ltd. Russian texts reprinted by permission of the author.

"Nanny Tanya," "The Return," "The Moscow Station," "The Secret Agent," by Evgeny Rein, translated by Judith Hemschemeyer. Translations copyright © 1999 Judith Hemschemeyer. Russian texts reprinted by permission of the author.

"From an Album," "Psalm 1," "Psalm 137," "Dionysus," by Genrikh Sapgir, translated by J. Kates. Translations copyright © 1999 J. Kates. Russian texts reprinted by permission of the author.

"Still-life," "The Stepmother," "Eros Poesis," "The whole city…," by Tatiana Shcherbina, translated by J. Kates. Translations copyright © 1999 J. Kates. Russian texts reprinted by permission of the author.

"Female Figure," "The Grasshopper and the Cricket," and "Fifth Stanzas" from *The Silk of Time* by Olga Sedakova, translated by Catriona Kelly. Translation copyright © 1994 by Catriona Kelly. Reprinted by permission of Edinburgh University Press. Russian texts reprinted by permission of the author.

"The Dump," "Remembrance of Strange Hospitality," "Elegy on an X-ray Photo of My Skull," and "A Parrot at Sea" from *Paradise* by Elena Shvarts, translated by Michael Molnar. Translation copyright © 1993 by Michael Molnar. Reprinted by permission of Bloodaxe Books Ltd. Russian texts reprinted by permission of the author.

"There it all was…," by Viktor Sosnora, translated by Maia Tekses. Translation copyright © 1999 Maia Tekses. "A Letter," "Crow," by Viktor Sosnora, translated by Mark Halperin and Dinara Georgeoliani. Translations copyright © 1999 Mark Halperin and Dinara Georgeoliani. "The Supreme Hour," by Viktor Sosnora, translated by F. D. Reeve. Translation copyright © 1999 F. D. Reeve. Russian texts reprinted by permission of the author.

"A Leningrad stairwell…," "Herostratos and Herostratos," "The Terrorist," by Sergey Stratanovsky, translated by J. Kates. Translations copyright © 1999 J. Kates. Russian texts reprinted by permission of the author.

"Like Thousands of Others," "An Engraving," "Dynamo Stadium, 1980," "Battle," by Aleksandr Tkachenko, translated by Maia Tekses. Translations copyright © 1999 Maia Tekses. Russian texts reprinted by permission of the author.

"Polyhedral…," "The seamstress stitches…," "The drake pays court…," "Heliopter…," "The house over the garden…," "Street lamp…," by Mikhail Yeryomin, translated by J. Kates. Translations copyright © 1999 J. Kates. Russian texts reprinted by permission of the author.

Quotation in "Introduction" from *A History of Russian Poetry* by Evelyn Bristol, copyright © 1991. Reprinted by permission of Oxford University Press, Inc.

Quotation in "Introduction" from *Seven Pillars of Wisdom* by T.E. Lawrence, copyright © 1962. Reprinted by permission of Dell Publishing Co.

Quotation in "Between Zukofsky and Zhukovsky" from *Catullus* (Gai Valeri catulli Veronensis Liber). Translation copyright © 1969 by Celia and Louis Zukofsky. Reprinted by permission of Addison Wesley Longman.

Excerpt in "Between Zukofsky and Zhukovsky" from "Poetry as a Form of Resistance to Reality," copyright © 1992 by Joseph Brodsky. Reprinted by permission of Farrar, Straus & Giroux, Inc., on behalf of the estate of Joseph Brodsky.

Quotation in "Notes" (to Kenjeev) from *Eugene Onegin* by Aleksandr Pushkin. Translation copyright © 1936 by Babette Deutsch. Reprinted by permission of Princeton University Press.

A Union of Lone Wolves

Mikhail Aizenberg

"SO, how was your literary group created?" A straightforward question would appear to have a clear and coherent answer. Unfortunately, that is not possible. It was never created. And it is not a literary group. For any conscious author of the seventies and eighties, whether or not he/she belonged to any kind of group was a notoriously secondary question. All those who lived in the "underground world" were lone riders, outsiders. I mean precisely "outsiders," and not "members of the opposition": they did not stand against one thing in particular, but against everything at the same time. There could not have been a worse position for creating a group.

But there are motivations, so to speak, on a different level. For some mysterious reason, poets (unlike prose writers) always seem to live in herds. They need to look around at each other, to confront each other, to be jealous of each other, to create surprises and be surprised. And so it happened that gradually the careers, or destinies, of some came to cross the paths of others on the same literary map. A clear description of this situation would require something like an "epic fresco" where dozens of different characters are pictured all at once. Each name irresistibly calls others to mind, and it is difficult to single out any particular number of names and put a frame around it without, indeed, creating a "literary group." But again, this is not a group. It is a hothouse where many subtle relationships breed — personal and artistic affinities, destinies linked together by friendship or artistic rivalry. It would be easier to say what there was NOT in those relationships: flatness and neutrality. And the way of life that we gradually came to follow was the life of those intersecting circles, fairly isolated although not completely closed, of friendships and conversations that often brought us together. Then, over time, these meetings became more regular, their character changed spontaneously, and gradually they developed their own particular etiquette. A clan? We could, in fact, even use the term family, except that in inverted commas it takes on a rather suspicious, Sicilian kind of connotation. A "cosa nostra" — a common cause? But art as a whole is indeed a common cause. The absence of any individual interest is part of its very nature; art is done over and above the author's personal ambitions, over the heads, so to speak, of poets and governments alike. What we were trying to do, perhaps half-consciously, was — as with a heat exchange system — to create the conditions for a normal literary situation. And perhaps for more than that. Anyone's success — even somebody else's — made something open up in one's own space, made some things more clear, and helped one to continue living. Any artistic success became a social event.

Life in Soviet times, as is perhaps the case with anything that is turned inside out, also had its "right" side. And a wonderfully bright, radiant side it was. It was the kind of brightness that blinds a person, for a second, who comes in from a dark, icy winter night and steps into a warm room with a friendly company sitting around the table. The closeness of those friendly conversations is akin to the "closeness of the words in a verse": it transforms the very nature of the circumstances which have created it.

I am convinced that one day, when the old, Soviet-time "kitchen" and all those things that made up our everyday life finally disappear from it, they will immediately turn into the most happy fairy tale of our century, its most lively myth. The past does not, like the Titanic, all of a sudden go down under water with all lights blazing. It disappears gradually, slowly changing its components, replacing memories with more and more recent layers that are created in a totally different kind of light. But the light of the Moscow kitchens is brighter still than that eternal eclipse. It can shine through anything. It is in that light that, even now, we are able to lift the heavy carcasses of our different natures and species, and to look at each other with tenderness.

Our most recently formed society is something like a mosaic. When we were young, we all used to play on different teams. In the mid-1970s the name of Rubinshtein was systematically pronounced in the conjunction "Rubinshtein-and-Monastyrsky," as if that were a single family name. Prigov's friends were almost exclusively artists, which in fact he himself is, too (as well as Viktor Koval). Gandlevsky lived to the rhythm of his "Moscow Time." I always showed my new poems to a few people of my generation (including Koval and Faibisovich) and to three relative "elders": Leonid Ioffe, Zinovy Zinik and Evgeny Saburov. It was in fact Saburov who introduced me to Prigov, and Prigov brought me to Vsevolod Nekrasov. This was the time when a series of long chains of cross-generation and cross-professional links began to emerge. Our associations with visual artists were the most successful: they were the most natural, and they proved the strongest over time. Many artistic works found unexpected resonance in literature, which was most welcome for some of us. From the very start, Semyon Faibisovich was at the epicenter of all these events; Eric Bulatov, Oleg Vasiliev and many others were also among our most frequent companions.

In the mid-1980s Timur Kibirov appeared, followed by Denis Novikov (and today it would seem strange not to mention Ivan Akhmetev, Grigory Dashevsky and Yuly Gugoliev). Although they came from different ends of the literary field, very soon they were all classified together as "Avant-Gardists," or worse — "Conceptualists." But perhaps this was not as inappropriate as it seems. There are not so many radical Avant-Gardists in underground literature, but the unique link, characteristic of the underground world, between a person's art and behavior in life, and the conscious feeling of belonging to a corporation, are precisely one of the distinctive features of Avant-Gardism. This brings the entire underground world close to the Avant-Garde movement, independent of its stylistic differences.

But the first, vague notion of a "common literary ground" began to occur to us only after we became members of the "Poezia" ("Poetry") Club, in 1986: as it turned out, what we shared was stronger than our differences. In the Club everyone was supposed to belong to a group, and we too, in the end, had to declare ourselves as the "Zadushevnaia Beseda" group (*i.e.* "Hearty Discussion," which was indeed what we were engaged in most of the time). Then, in 1988, somehow very naturally and almost instantly, the "Almanakh" performance group came together, with seven poets and one singer: S. Gandlevsky, D. Novikov, T. Kibirov, D.A. Prigov, L. Rubinshtein, M. Aizenberg, V. Koval and A. Lipsky (listed here in their order of appearance on the stage). We performed together for several years, went on a couple of tours, had big arguments about little things, but in fact we were secretly admiring each other all the time. And now that the maturity (or perhaps, on the contrary, the ingenuity) of our relationships has been tested hard, I think it is time to acknowledge that our first impressions had not always been that optimistic.

About twenty years ago, I returned to the philosopher Boris Grois a text which he had lent me to read, Rubinshtein's "Program of Works," with the lapidary comment: "I don't call this poetry." "But what is poetry?" Grois asked with an insinuating note in his voice. "Poetry is ..." I had to stop and think — "Poetry is a strike of good fortune." The philosopher gave me a long look and asked me no more theoretical questions.

But a few years later, Rubinshtein's new works began to inspire unexpected streams of consciousness, make hearts beat, and throw out sparks of joy that had not been foreseen in the scenario. To experience such a feeling is usually a rare privilege in life, but I must admit that we were clearly among the lucky ones. And now, when I hear Lipsky singing a new song with words by Koval, I can feel a heavenly breeze coming through my hair and slightly chilling my cheekbones. "Like a burning rose, a glass of alcohol / Is turning round and round inside my heart," reads Gandlevsky, and the mournful rhythm cramps my breathing, and compels my pulse to the vibration of the verse.

And so on and so forth. There were hard times and good times. And the philosopher is wrong: after all, poetry is a strike of good fortune.

Translation by Nathalie Stewart

Introduction

J. Kates

AS the 1980s turned into the 1990s, the political and social
entity known as the Union of Soviet Socialist Republics
disintegrated suddenly into its constituent parts. The dis-
solution of the Soviet abstraction left the separate *peoples* (as they
were referred to in Soviet terminology) to rediscover their own
historical destinies. One of those constituent parts is something
called "Russia," with deep roots and an uncertain future, but char-
acterized by, among other quirks, a fierce literary identity. "Russia"
has come to signify both a place on a map and a state of mind, like
any national identity. It is unavoidably present in Moscow and St.
Petersburg (even while natives worry about its disappearance) and
deliberately evoked around the world, from Berlin to Paris to
Philadelphia and Chicago and Tel Aviv.

What happened in Russia at the turn of the decade was more
than a political revolution. It was also a cultural earthquake of
unprecedented impact. Not the tentative and quickly retracted
freedoms of expression accorded by Catherine the Great, nor even
the two-year window of chaos opened by the October Manifesto
in 1905, which let in air that artists continued to breathe after the
Revolutions of 1917, begin to come close. Beginning in 1986, all the
roofs collapsed, exposing Russia to all kinds of weather. For the
first time in its entire history, there was no censoring mechanism at
all — not by bureaucracy, not by ideology.

But to say that the roofs had collapsed is not to say that all the
foundations had crumbled. Writers continued to write from estab-
lished positions, not in a free-for-all anarchy. While there were no
more ideological constraints, there were still schools — schools
without texts, you might say — and, outside the schools, still influ-
ences. Writers who had flourished in the climate of official litera-
ture were still free to flourish. And at the same time, a seventy-
year-old tradition of subcultural and countercultural literatures
was also suddenly able to acknowledge itself and be acknowl-
edged in public.

The transformation that overtook and took over the avant-garde of the visual arts in Russia during this handful of years has been chronicled by Andrew Solomon in his account of the visual arts, *The Irony Tower*. Perhaps someday soon we shall see a narrative of the convolutions of literature parallel to his work. But poetry is not expressed in painting and happenings, and can't be talked about in the same way, even when some of the same figures, like Dmitry Aleksandrovich Prigov, show up on both sides of the line. Poems best represent themselves.

Moreover, what happened to poetry in Russia around the year 1990 didn't happen only in the avant-garde. It would be deceptive to focus only on the daring and the experimental. In Russian art, even the most avant-garde works have never lost touch, in technique or in content (if only by parody) with the conventional main line. The story of what was going on with poetry includes at a second extreme even the banal — at a third, what Russians disdainfully call graphomania and what is most echoed in America by so-called "workshop" poetry. The closest the Anglo-American literary world has ever come to this kind of ferment was during the heyday of the bitter "battle of the anthologies" in the 1960s, when different groups of poets were staking out vast claims to be "the new American poetry" in ways that proved mutually exclusive. As the years have settled the dust, good poets from all camps have come to be recognized — and mutually acknowledged. But, in Russia, these camps are still armed and watchful. When I showed Aleksandr Kushner a book of poems by another poet, he glanced at it briefly and threw it down with one scornful remark, *"Vers libre!"* And just a couple of days later, a very different poet, at the mention of Kushner's name, snorted out a pun on the Russian word for "boring": "Skutchner!"

What has been occurring in Russian literary culture can be summed up in two movements: a break-down of establishments and a break-up of language. First of all, let's glance at the break-down of establishments.

Before, there were compartments. Cultures. Literatures. All in the plural.

There was an Establishment of writers and artists sanctioned by the government, rewarded with the perquisites of club memberships, artists' colonies, ease in traveling abroad and in meeting foreign colleagues. On my first visit to the Soviet Union in 1986, we met with Writers' Union members in formal meeting rooms, paper and pencils laid out on the tables alongside soda pop and mineral water. Most of these were men (and a few women) in their fifties and sixties. We dined with them at formal dinners. We exchanged literary opinions constrained by ignorance and politics. Early on, in my own brash American ignorance, I pressed one writer for his knowledge of other, unapproved writers. An interesting, intelligent man, he denied having ever read Brodsky or Sinyavsky. In retrospect, I regret slightly having forced him to lie that way.

When we asked to meet a new generation of writers, the poet who was then urged on us most insistently as the coming young Establishment poet of those years was a former football player, Aleksandr Tkachenko, who has continued writing and editing into the new era, like so many others, with the accommodations of his generation.

And there was a political dissidence of artists who set themselves actively against the Powers That Were, publishing their work in flimsy carbon copies (*samizdat*) and sending it abroad to be smuggled back in to their own country (*tamizdat*). In the West, the best known of the younger poets in this category was Irina Ratushinskaya, born in Odessa in 1954, who enjoyed a brief flare of popularity here. The politics and oppression of the writer, however, who was imprisoned for reading and writing "anti-Soviet" literature, worked to obscure the quality of the poems she wrote. After her expulsion from the Soviet Union in 1986, she has continued to work and write in the United Kingdom. Resistance can take many forms, though, and the play of language is always subversive of established discourse. The playfulness of artists and writers like Dmitry Prigov in Moscow had not always hidden their own subversion, and they would have suffered more for it if circumstances around them had not changed rapidly.

The year 1986 also saw the appearance of *Krug* (Circle), an anthology put out by writers, among them five poets in this

8 anthology, who had loosely organized themselves into the Club 81 in Leningrad. *Ponedel'nik* (Monday) came out in Moscow in 1990, a collection of "seven samizdat poets" (three of whom are represented here) and *Lichnoe Delo* (Personal File) in 1991. These were artists who comprised a "second culture," not so much concerned with politics as just wanting to pursue their own artistic and literary directions, which automatically drew them closer in content and style to the actively politically dissident. We met with these people in their own private apartments or in the semi-protected spaces maintained by foreign cultural attachés. And, of course, there has been a venerable émigré Russian culture, with traditions already half a century old — some would say, a century old — and its own network of cultural associations.

There were doors between these compartments — some more open than others. But if you were standing in one room, you knew where you were, and you were not standing in another. After 1990, there is question and debate whether what prevails is a single culture — one gigantic hall like the Manezh in Moscow — or two or more, or none at all. Significant émigré magazines that used to publish in Paris and New York have moved to Moscow and St. Petersburg. Writer's Unions have replaced their own complacency with committees that act like commercial agents, trying to "place" members' work with publishing houses that now seek the patronage of audiences overwhelmed by translated and home-bred sleaze .

Before 1990, there existed a relationship between the Russian writer and the Russian reader that was legendary in the western world — and legendary partly because it was based on actual cultural phenomena. In Russia, we understood, poets had vast followings, read in stadiums to overflow crowds. Bella Akhmadulina's outthrust jaw was as recognizable then and there as Dennis Rodman's hair is here and now. Books sold out in editions of hundreds of thousands. When a poet like Yevgeny Yevtushenko read out a scathing poem like "Stalin's Heirs," it created the kind of storm that, in those days, couldn't even be stirred up in America by a drunken congressman dancing naked in a fountain with a call girl.

If anywhere, the Russian identification with literary cultural icons was carried on by those poets who sang their work — the Bards, as they have come to be known in English. Among these were the actor Vladimir Vysotsky, revered as a kind of conflation of Hamlet and Bob Dylan who died young in 1980, and Aleksandr Galich, who died in Paris in 1977. But the most enduring, and the one most to be taken seriously by high literature as well as by popular appeal, has been Bulat Okudzhava, a novelist as well as a poet and songwriter.

Whatever had been true among the notions of the exalted reverence of poets among the masses was wiped out among other changes in society. There were deliberate alterations — a new generation of poets eschewed the public style cultivated by their elders and chose, instead, a new intimacy of their own coterie, descended from the necessarily private support groups that flourished under the late Soviet system. Some of the changes were generally cultural. As state-sponsored publishing broke down, and small independent presses sprang up, an entire system of book publication and distribution fragmented. What earlier would have been unpublished or circulated in *samizdat* carbon-copy typescripts now became published editions of a few hundred copies. At the same time, the status of the artist as a folk-hero has diminished, and mere mortals peddle their wares in the new open market.

Meanwhile, the language of literature has been changing. Many would see it as a liberation, an upswing, after a long repression. Long submerged linguistic experimentation from the days of the Futurists and the Oberiuty resurfaced. Peculiar languages of western capitalism — advertising lingo, headline newspeak and more literary styles — rapidly replaced old Soviet sloganeering. In fact, the abandonment of Soviet language left room for the particular problem Günther Grass had addressed in relation to post-Nazi German: What is the writer's relationship to a "damaged" language, one in which words and meanings have been tortured and deformed by pernicious official usage? Visual artists and literary artists struggle with similar problems in Russia, on the one hand laying bare the euphemisms and allegories of earlier discourse, and on another using these same "æsopic" skills of indirection they had honed during harsher times to turn allusion and parody into self-critical tools.

Other changes from the West came sweeping in. While two of the four towering poetic Horsemen of the Soviet Apocalypse were women (Anna Akhmatova and Marina Tsvetaeva, riding alongside Osip Mandelstam and Boris Pasternak) women's voices have been muted in Russian poetry until recently — muted, but not silenced. Now, from all sides, they begin to be heard, even if the new establishments hold them to old standards. "The power of women's poetry in Russia today," Yunna Morits has written, referring to the influence of Akhmatova and Tsvetaeva, "is measured in akhmatsvets."

But poets of a new generation write neither in Akhmatova's shadow nor Tsvetaeva's. Tatiana Shcherbina became an early spokesperson for a cosmopolitan culture, educated in Western classics and drawing her inspiration from French twentieth-century models. As soon as the opportunity presented itself, she experienced Europe first hand, living first in Munich for a couple of years, then in Paris, before returning to her native Moscow to plunge into various editing projects. If she is to be seen as representative of anything, it is of a sensibility that practiced integrating home and abroad, *there* and *here*. Aleksey Parshchikov moved from Moscow to California and Switzerland (and is now back in Russia); Ilya Kutik from Moscow to Sweden and Illinois. For a while, in the words of Anatoly Naiman, "all compasses pointed west," until, as one acquaintance of mine, a conceptual visual artist, sighed, "I never could have imagined I'd turn down a trip to Switzerland. But now I have to stay home, or I won't get any work done."

Long suppressed influences from inside Russia also asserted themselves — notably the experimentation with typography and nonrepresentational language pioneered at the turn of the century by Andrey Bely, Velimir Khlebnikov, Vladimir Mayakovsky and others, questioning the look of the page and the very notion of the page itself. We have only suggested that innovation and experimentation in this anthology, with the talmudic presentation of Viktor Krivulin and the helter-skelter look of Nina Iskrenko. We had planned to include Lev Rubenshtein, whose work exists at the borderline — if there is one — between poetry and performance art. He writes not on pages, but single sentences on index cards packaged in paper boxes, as in this beginning of *Mama Myla Ramu* (*Mama Was Washing a Window Frame*, 1987):

1.
Mama was washing a window frame.

2.
Papa bought a television.

3.
The wind blew.

4.
A wasp stung Zoya.

through to its end:

82.
That day everything was as usual.

83.
I got up, got dressed.

It might be easy just to replicate a number of cards on a page, as Rubinshtein himself has done in a new standard-format book of collected poems (*Regularnoe pis'mo*, 1997) but the easiness is deceptive. Having forgotten to bring his own cards to a reading recently, he read from the book, and the poet himself was not the only one to notice that the rhythm was wrong. To reproduce the text as if it were ordinary verse would be to distort seriously the effect Rubinshtein produces. In the end, we thought it better to provide this note without the text. Those who are interested in reading the words of some of Rubinshtein's poems in translation can find them in *Five Fingers Review*, the editors of which have stood in the vanguard of publishing translations of new experimental poetry, and the 1992 anthology *Third Wave*, which was the first attempt to gather and look at poets of this generation.

The absence of Rubenshtein is only one of a number of absences from *In the Grip of Strange Thoughts*. There are three other reasons for the exclusion of poets who otherwise should be included in this group picture. About a few, very much has been said, and the ready availability in excellent English translation of the work of Joseph Brodsky, Andrei Voznesensky and Yevgeny Yevtushenko has encouraged us to leave them out to make room for others. Their place in the years of transition should be noted, however. By the turn of the eighties into the nineties, Voznesensky and Yevtushenko's worldwide attention had, in ironic effect, contributed to their waning interest at home, while Brodsky, who had begun his transition from being a Russian poet in exile into being an American poet writing in Russian, was at the height of his influence in the Soviet Union.

Other poets have been not so much excluded, as left out because satisfactory translations of their work were not available. The absence of Lev Losev and Anatoly Naiman, among others, are serious holes in this work. Let these absences stand as a kind of hubris mark, a deliberate imperfection to encourage further translation and publication.

I suppose that every editor of an anthology would like to think that his or her own work is actually definitive, and therefore the decision to exclude one writer or another is agonizing, as if there were only so much space in a lifeboat. But anthologies are not lifeboats, and on the wide waters of literature bob all manner of craft. The one arbitrary decision made very early in the selection process for *In the Grip of Strange Thoughts* was not to include poets who had already died before 1990. A more comprehensive collection without this limitation would include Leonid Aronzon, Ian Satunovsky and Boris Slutsky, among others.

St. Petersburg prides itself on being "the window on the West." Paradoxically, that very pride has tended to breed a kind of aristocratic conservatism in contrast to the ferment of Moscow. Mikhail

Aizenberg has acerbically noted that, "in the middle 1970s all verse could have been divided into good, bad, and 'Leningrad.' The distinction of this last was that it was impossible to determine whether the poems were good or bad." But within this milieu, distinctive poetic voices have emerged more and more strongly, and Aizenberg's comment nowadays reads as more aphoristic than just. St. Petersburg holds not only the contrary disciplines of Kushner and Arkadii Dragomoschenko, but also the continuing, developing work of Mikhail Yeryomin, who has written hundreds of tightly controlled eight-line stanzas for more than thirty years. The accumulation of his poems has more in common with the vision of a Pound or a Berryman than with anything else in his immediate surroundings. During the same years, Viktor Sosnora's poetry has ranged from convention to experimentation, from sentiment to fireworks, in a grand profusion.

Still, these diversities are nothing to what we find in Moscow. There, interpenetration of the visual and literary arts has influenced both painting and poetry. Genrikh Sapgir worked with artists in the so-called Lianozovo school. (His "Sonnets on Shirts" was originally part of an exhibition.) Among the Conceptual group, the interpenetration extended to performance. While painters like Ilya Kabakov and Eric Bulatov were incorporating verbal and pictorial icons of Soviet life into paintings that sometimes became concrete poems on canvas, Dmitry Prigov straddled these media with his own reductive language-play. From this center, other poets like Sergey Gandlevsky have been challenging the more ordinary employments of language in their society. For many of these artists, the loss of their "underground" status provoked a kind of crisis, as much because they had to reorient their use of words and picture as for any more superficial reasons.

The role of locality of art in Russia is a little difficult to explain to the English-speaking world, with its myriad of centers of American or British-inspired culture, each with its own accent. In Russia, still, the arts are centripetal, the two centers are Moscow and St. Petersburg, and the word "provincial" retains a strong meaning. And the dangerous category of "nationality" (or, as Americans would say with slightly less political freight, ethnic

background) is not without meaning, too. Fazil Iskander's Cauca-
sian spice, Gennady Aygi's Chuvash barbaric yawp, Jewish sensi-
bilities, Ukrainian pride, and "pure" Russian concerns are all
subtexts in this contemporary poetry.

Recognition of what has happened to Russian poetry in the past
few years can not be complete without acknowledgment of the
Russian diaspora — not the community of exiles that has domi-
nated this century, but a re-integrated international Russian cul-
ture that flourishes from Berlin to Australia. During the decades
after World War II that we characterize as the Cold War, who
could have imagined, except in the course of imagining some di-
sastrous total destruction of capitalism, that New York subway
advertising signs would be printed in Russian?

In addition to Ratushinskaya now in England, Bakhyt Kenjeev
lives in Canada, Dmitry Bobyshev in the American Midwest, Bella
Dizhur in New York, and Elena Ignatova in Israel. These poets are
no less Russian for their residence abroad.

Two common elements of Russian poetry will look very con-
servative, even reactionary, to Western readers unfamiliar with
Russian tradition.

One element is how allusive and culturally rooted even the
most seemingly liberated poetry is. Nina Iskrenko quotes
Pasternak, Sergey Gandlevsky and Bakhyt Kenjeev weave Pushkin
into their verse. In this anthology, we have deliberately selected
three poems by three very different poets that all play with the very
same line from one poem by Aleksandr Blok. And many poems
refer culturally not only to Russia's own classical heritage and the
Bible, but especially to the historical and literary monuments of
Greece and Rome, as well as to other touchstones of Western Eu-
ropean culture, that seem to have disappeared from much of
Western verse. The continuing appropriation of Greco-Roman
mythology can be read in an understanding of Moscow as the
"Third Rome," not merely historically in a religious or imperial
sense, but also in living culture. This is how Genrikh Sapgir, for ex-
ample, explains the flavor of his "Dionysus," but we can look
across our selections here among Sergey Stratanovsky, Olga
Sedakova, Shcherbina — a wide range of poets — and see the same

language of assumptions. Before the liberation brought by *glasnost* and *perestroika*, there was another equation to be made, in that if the analogies between the two earlier Roman Empires could be drawn culturally, then political allusions could be veiled and safely elaborated.

A second element is the persistence of strictly rhymed and metered verse, even among the avant garde. In spite of the experimentation of the early twentieth century, avant-gardism in the content of Russian poetry was never closely linked to revolution in the form of verse, as it was in the West. (This presents its own kind of problem to the translator who wants to convey a progressive effect that in English is contradicted by the strict form of the original.) Gennady Aygi, whose roots are in the Chuvash culture, is often spoken of as the father of modern free verse in Russian, an importer of a kind of shamanistic character that American readers might associate with Jerome Rothenberg. Influences from the non-Russian East of Japan, China and India have made themselves felt as well as those from American and Western European literatures. Needless to say, there is no lack of practitioners for whom the new freedom (as so often in Russia in the last decade) spills over into licentiousness. In 1991, the monumental *Antologiia russkogo verlibra* (Anthology of Russian Vers Libre) appeared, showcasing 360 writers, eight of whom are represented in *In the Grip of Strange Thoughts*.

For a quick, overall survey in English of the history of Russian poetry up to our time, no better book is available than Evelyn Bristol's *History of Russian Poetry*. But she comes to an open-handed conclusion just where this collection begins, with the rather obvious statement that "The younger poets who have appeared recently have not yet achieved the distinction of the older poets." Mikhail Aizenberg's essay "Nekotorye drugie" ("Some Others") charts comprehensively the underground streams in Russian poetry since the Revolution. This appeared in the Moscow journal *Teatr* in 1991 and was translated by Marian Schwartz among a selection of Aizenberg's essays for a special issue of *Russian Studies in Literature*. Aizenberg's chronicles have turned out to be a major guide in my own adventures, even as he pursues different ends. For general introductions to the culture of Russia in transition, Andrew Solomon's *Irony Tower* and Svetlana Boym's *Common Places* are evocative and illuminating.

* * *

Transliteration is a constant vexation, and writing the Russian language in latin letters is like swimming through mud. A system developed by the Library of Congress for academic usage is certainly accurate, but unwieldy to read. All other systems are inaccurate. Russian names, especially, do not slide easily into the roman alphabet: Preferred transliterations differ by wave of emigration — Romanoff or Romanov; by western language of preference — thus, generally, Osip Mandelstam from German, rather than Mandelshtam in English, but Mikhail Aizenberg rather than Eisenberg; or by individual accident. Responding to proofs for this anthology, translator Lyn Hejinian engaged the issue succinctly: "It seems to me, given that he has published in a number of magazines and had two books come out in the U. S. under the spelling Arkadii Dragomoschenko, that he should continue to be known as that. I realize that your alternative spelling is derived from specific rules of transliteration, and you may have compelling reasons for wanting to adhere to them strictly throughout the text."

No, Lyn, there is no compelling reason to be consistent. My own inclination is to follow the example of T. E. Lawrence in transliterating Arabic names for *Seven Pillars of Wisdom*, whose encouragement of inconsistency is a constant reminder that these names are undomesticated, are чужие, "for their consonants are not the same as ours, and their vowels, like ours, vary from district to district. There are some 'scientific systems' of transliteration, helpful to people who know enough Arabic not to need helping, but a washout for the world. I spell my names anyhow, to show what rot the systems are."

Unfortunately, we can't just spell the names anyhow. Still, I hope our system is sufficiently inconsistent to be useful.

(a) We spell personal names in the way the named person prefers, or, failing that, in a way that may have become generally recognizable. Bakhyt Kenjeev prefers to write his name with a "j," but

a wide survey of reference to Bulat Okudzhava's name in print rep-
resents the same cyrillic letter in its more formal transliteration as
"zh." We have followed this convention.

(b) In the notes and supplementary material, we use the Library
of Congress system familiar to the academic world for titles and
other undomesticated Russian words.

(c) Russian words maintained in the text are spelled in the way
best designed to help someone who speaks no Russian to say them
so that they might be comprehensible to a Russian. Call this the
travel-guide system.

With a similar inconsistency that reflects the diversity of writ-
ing in this anthology, most explanatory footnotes — those pro-
vided by the poets themselves, the translators or the editor — can
be found at the back of the book. But in two selections, those of
Mikhail Yeryomin and Viktor Krivulin, the notes themselves are to
be read as part of the texts they comment on, and are therefore
included with those texts.

Bulat Okudzhava
Булат Окуджава

Bulat Shalvovich Okudzhava (1924-1997) was born and raised in the Arbat in Moscow. He studied Russian philology at the University of Tiflis. After receiving his degree in 1950 he worked as a village schoolteacher near Kaluga, where his first volume of poetry, *Lirika* (Lyric Poetry) appeared in 1956. He returned to Moscow in late 1956 and worked for the publishing house Molodaia Gvardia and then the journal *Literaturnaia gazeta*. In 1957 Okudzhava began to recite his poems to the accompaniment of his guitar, at first privately and then publicly. These performances soon brought him enormous popularity and renown. Throughout the 1960s Okudzhava's poetry circulated in samizdat and tape recordings. He published three more shorter volumes of poetry from 1964 to 1967, but his next collection of songs and poems, *Arbat, moi Arbat* (Arbat, my Arbat), appeared only in 1976, after a long hiatus. Although he is best known for his songs, Okudzhava was an accomplished writer of purely literary poetry and prose. He published seven more volumes of poetry in his lifetime and also wrote screenplays, children's stories, and several novels, one of which, *Uprazdnennyi teatr* (Closed Theater, 1993), won the Booker Prize in 1994.

Translations by Mark Herman & Ronnie Apter

~

Как улыбается юный флейтист,
флейту к губам прижимая!
Как он наивен и тонок, и чист!
Флейта в руках, как живая.

Как он старается сам за двоих,
как вдохновенно все тело ...
И до житейских печалей моих
что ему нынче за дело?

Вот он стоит у метро на углу,
душу раскрыв принародно,
флейту вонзая как будто иглу
в каждого поочередно.

Вот из прохладной ладони моей
в шапку монетка скатилась ...
Значит, и мне тот ночной соловей —
кто он, скажите на милость?

Как голосок соловья ни хорош,
кем ни слыву я на свете,
нету гармонии ну ни на грош
в нашем счастливом дуэте.

How the young flutist smiles,
flute pressed to lip.
How trim, clean, and naive he is.
The flute comes alive in his hands!

And how he strives to breathe for two,
the inspiration filling his whole body.
And as for worldly cares,
what, at this moment, are they to him?

Here he stands in the subway station,
baring his soul to the people,
plying his flute like a needle,
probing each passerby in turn.

From my cool palm a coin
has rolled down into his hat …
For sweet mercy's sake,
who is this nightingale to me?

However well he sings,
whatever face I wear in the glare of day,
not a kopek's worth of harmony
informs our happy duet.

Мне москвичи милы из давней прозы
и в пушкинских стихах.
Мне нравятся их лень и смех, и слезы,
и горечь на устах.

Когда они сидят на кухне старой
во власти странных дум,
их горький рок, подзвученный гитарой,
насмешлив и угрюм.

Когда толпа внизу кричит и стонет,
что — гордый ум и честь?
Их мало так, что ничего не стоит
по пальцам перечесть.

Мне по сердцу их вера и терпенье,
неверие и раж ...
Кто знал, что будет страшным пробужденье
и за окном пейзаж?

Что ж, век иной. Развеяны все мифы,
повержены умы.
Куда ни посмотреть — всё скифы, скифы, скифы.
Их тьмы и тьмы, и тьмы.

И с грустью озирая землю эту,
где злоба и пальба,
сдается мне, что москвичей-то нету,
а вместо — толпа.

Я знаю этот мир не понаслышке:
я из него пророс.
Но за его утраты и излишки
с меня сегодня спрос.

To me, Muscovites are sweethearts out of old stories,
recast in Pushkin's verse.
I like their laziness, their tears and laughter,
and the bitter taste in their mouths.

When they sit together in an old kitchen,
in the grip of strange thoughts,
the bitter fate they hear on the guitar
is mocking and morose.

When a mob screeches in the street below,
where then proud honor and intellect?
What's left isn't worth reckoning on
the fingers of one hand.

How I admire their faith and perseverance,
their faithlessness and rage ...
Who foresaw the terrible awakening,
the new landscape outside?

A new age, all right: myths scattered, minds shattered,
and Scythians everywhere,
the scourge of the East, rising within us,
hordes upon hordes upon hordes.

And as I sadly survey my homeland,
its anger, its gunfire,
it seems to me there are no more Muscovites.
Instead, there is a mob.

It is not by hearsay that I know this world —
it spawned me.
And now I must answer for its excesses,
both the profits and the loss.

Ах, Надя, Наденька

Е. Рейну

Из окон корочкой несет поджаристой,
за занавесками — мельканье рук.
Здесь остановки нет, а мне — пожалуйста:
шофер автобуса — мой лучший друг.
Здесь остановки нет, а мне — пожалуйста:
шофер автобуса — мой лучший друг.

А кони в сумерках колышут гривами,
автобус новенький, спеши, спеши!
Ах, Надя, Наденька, мне б за двугривенный
в любую сторону твоей души.
Ах, Надя, Наденька, мне б за двугривенный
в любую сторону твоей души.

Я знаю, вечером ты в платье шелковом
пойдешь по улице гулять с другим …
Ах, Надя, брось коней кнутом нащелкивать,
попридержи-ка их, поговорим.
Ах, Надя, брось коней кнутом нащелкивать,
попридержи-ка их, поговорим.

Она в спецовочке в такой промасленной,
берет немыслимый такой на ней.
Ах, Надя, Наденька, мы были б счастливы,
куда же гонишь ты своих коней?
Ах, Надя, Наденька, мы были б счастливы,
да не гони же ты своих коней!

Но кони в сумерках колышут гривами,
автобус новенький спеши, спеши.
Ах, Надя, Наденька, мне б за двугривенный
в любую сторону твоей души.
Ах, Надя, Наденька, мне б за двугривенный
в любую строну твоей души.

Ah, Nadya, Nadyenka

for E. Rein

Across a windowsill a smell of toasted bread,
behind the curtain lace a woman's hand —
The bus will speed on by, there is no stop in sight,
but driver, let me off, please be a friend.
The bus will speed on by, there is no stop in sight,
but driver, let me off, please be a friend.

And in the evening light, the horses' swaying manes —
This is a brand-new bus — why does it crawl?
Ah, Nadya, Nadyenka, would that the bus fare were
the token granting entry to your soul!
Ah, Nadya, Nadyenka, would that the bus fare were
the token granting entry to your soul!

I know that you will be with someone else tonight —
You dress in silk and out the door you walk.
Ah, Nadya, Nadyenka, you crack the whip too much —
Please slow the horses down and let us talk.
Ah, Nadya, Nadyenka, you crack the whip too much —
Please slow the horses down and let us talk.

She in her overalls, her greasy overalls,
and on her head a ridiculous chapeau.
Ah, Nadya, Nadyenka, we could be happy, but
why are you driving those poor horses so?
Ah, Nadya, Nadyenka, we could be happy, but
where in the world do you want them to go?

But in the evening light, the horses' swaying manes —
This is a brand-new bus — why does it crawl?
Ah, Nadya, Nadyenka, would that the bus fare were
the token granting entry to your soul!
Ah, Nadya, Nadyenka, would that the bus fare were
the token granting entry to your soul!

Отъезд

Владимиру Спивакову

С Моцартом мы уезжаем из Зальцбурга.
Бричка вместительна. Лошади вмасть.
Жизнь моя, как перезрелое яблоко,
тянется к теплой землице припасть.

Ну а попутчик мой, этот молоденький,
радостных слез не стирает с лица.
Что ему думать про век свой коротенький?
Он лишь музыку, чтоб до конца.

Времени нету на долгие проводы …
Да неужели уже не нужны
слезы, что были не даром ведь пролиты,
крылья, что были не зря ведь даны?!

Ну а попутчик мой ручкою нервною
машет и машет фортуне своей,
нотку одну лишь нащупает верную —
и заливается, как соловей.

Руки мои на коленях покоятся,
вздох безнадежный густеет в груди:
там за спиной, — "До свиданья, околица!"
И ничего, ничего впереди.

Ну а попутчик мой божеской выпечки,
не покладая усилий своих,
То он на флейточке, то он на скрипочке,
то на валторне поет за двоих.

Departure

to Vladimir Spivakov

Mozart and I are leaving Salzburg.
The carriage is roomy. The horses match.
My life, like an over-ripe dappled apple,
longs to drop to the tawny earth.

So? My fellow traveler, this youngster,
isn't drying nostalgic tears.
Why should he dwell on the shortness of life?
His life is music, first to last.

And there isn't time for a long drawn-out sendoff …
And perhaps there is no more need for tears,
which were, after all, not shed in vain,
nor for wings not given, you know, for nothing.

So? My fellow traveler waves and waves
a high-strung hand in time to fate,
groping to find the one true note —
and bursts into song like a nightingale.

My hands lie listless on my knees,
A hopeless sigh thickens my chest.
The village recedes — "Goodbye, goodbye!" …
And there is nothing, nothing ahead.

So? My fellow traveler, divinely gifted,
indefatigable, resolute,
now on the piccolo, now on the violin,
now on the French horn, sings for two.

Inna Lisnianskaia
Инна Лиснянская

Inna L'vovna Lisnianskaia. Poet, translator and literary critic. Born in Baku in 1928, Lisnianskaia was forced to fend for herself at the age of 13 when her father left for the front during World War II. She left school in order to work in a hospital for wounded soldiers and finished high school only in 1947. In the fifties Lisnianskaia's poetry came to the attention of Aleksandr Tvardovsky, the influential editor of *Novyi Mir*, who began to publish her work. Four volumes of Lisnianskaia's work were published between 1957 and 1978. After resigning from the Writers' Union in 1980 to protest the expulsion of two younger writers following the *Metropol'* almanac affair, however, Lisnianskaia's work went unpublished in the Soviet Union until 1988. In addition to appearing in numerous literary journals, Lisnianskaia's more recent collections of poems include *Dozhdi i zerkala* (Rains and Mirrors, 1983), *Stikhotvorenia: Na opushke sna* (Poems: On the Edge of Sleep, 1984), *Vozdushnyi plast* (Airy Layer, 1990), *Posle vsego* (After Everything, 1994), and *Odinokii dar* (A Solitary Gift, 1995).

Translations by Judith Hemschemeyer

Ветер дует и свет задувает,
Задувает и сердце мое,
Но не верьте мне, так не бывает!
Это нас, как табак, набивает
Время в трубку и курит ее,

И выкуривает из таможни
В синий воздух родных и друзей,
С каждым часом на сердце тревожней,
С каждым разом мне все невозможней
Дожидаться минуты своей.

Ветер дует и речь задувает …
Но не верьте мне, так не бывает,
Я порю несусветную чушь!
Это время, куря, затевает
Мировую миграцию душ.

The wind blows and makes the light tremble,
It makes my heart tremble too,
But don't believe me, these things don't happen!
It's just time, tamping us, like tobacco,
Into its pipe and smoking it.

And from the customs house it smokes our friends
And relatives into the blue sky,
Each hour my heart feels more anxiety,
Each time is more unbearable for me,
Waiting for the moment that will be mine.

The wind blows and makes my speech tremble …
But don't believe me, these things don't happen,
I am speaking utter drivel!
It's just time, smoking, devising
The worldwide migration of souls.

~

Слыть отщепенкой в любимой стране —
Видно, железное сердце мое
Выдержит и не такое еще,
Только все чаще его колотье
В левое мне ударяет плечо.

Нет, это бабочка в красной пыли
Все еще бьется о сетку сачка …
Матерь, печали мои утоли!

Время уперлось в стенные часы,
Сузился мир до размера зрачка,
Лес — до ресницы, река — до слезы.

To be thought an outcast in my beloved country —
It must be made of iron, this heart inside of me.

It seems my iron heart
Can endure still worse,
Only more and more often I feel its beat
Slamming my left shoulder.

But no, it's a butterfly in the red dirt
Battering itself against the net ...
Oh, Mother of God, relieve my grief,

Time has run dead into the wall clock,
The world has shrunk to a pupil's dot,
The forest — to an eyelash, the river — to a tear.

Два брачных бражника, чьи крылья — нервный шелк,
И первый выстрел почки,
И строчка дятлова, и соловьиный щелк,
И дождика звоночки, —

Весна блаженствует: приспели времена
Раскрепощенья духа,
И речь открытая на улице слышна,
Да я уже старуха.

К беззвучным выкрикам, к житью с зажатым ртом
Я привыкала долго,
Беда под силу мне, а радость не в подъем
И уязвимей шелка.

И вдруг кощунственный я задаю вопрос
В час крайнего смятенья:
Голгофу вытерпел, но как Он перенес
Блаженство воскресенья?

Two carousing hawk moths, their wings like nervous silk,
And the bud's first explosion,
And the woodpecker's rat-tat-tat and the nightingale's whip-crack
And the tinkling sound of small rain.

Spring is in full bloom: the time has come
For the spirit to be free,
And I can hear open speech from the streets,
But I am already an old woman.

Silent shrieks of pain, life with clenched lips,
I have grown accustomed to the yokes,
I have the strength for disaster, but joy I cannot lift
And it is more fragile than silk.

And in a moment of utter confusion
I suddenly pose this blasphemous question:
Golgotha He could endure, but how could He bear
The ecstasy of resurrection?

~

Я в зеркало гляну, бывало —
По горлу прокатится дрожь, —
Там черная совесть зияла
Моими глазами, и все ж

Покамест опалы и смерти
Страшилась я пуще зеркал,
Глагол, как младенец в конверте,
Дремал и пустышку сосал.

Баюкало снежное поле,
Укачивал южный камыш:
Дремли, да не думай о воле,
Дремли, а не то — угодишь…

И вдруг я забыла о страхе
И ведаю, что меня ждет.
Но горло, готовое к плахе,
Открыто и вольно поет.

Нет-нет и приснится конвойный
И чей-то затылок в строю,
Но утром почти что спокойно
Я зеркалу в очи смотрю.

Whenever I looked in the mirror,
A tremor would pass through my throat —
A dark conscience would be gaping there
Through my own eyes, and yet

In those days I feared
Death and disgrace more than mirrors,
And like a new-born babe, The Word
Still slept, sucking a pacifier.

The snowfields sang its lullabies,
The southern reeds rocked it to sleep:
Sleep, and don't think of freedom,
Sleep, if you don't — beware ...

And suddenly I forgot my fear
And I know now what awaits me.
But my throat, prepared for the scaffold,
Is singing out, open and free.

Now and then I dream of a prison guard
And the back of the head of the one before me,
But in the morning I am almost calm
When I look the mirror in the eye.

Aleksandr Kushner

Александр Кушнер

Aleksandr Semenovich Kushner. Poet and essayist. Born in Leningrad in 1936, he graduated from the Herzen Pedagogical Institute in 1959 and taught literature from 1959 to 1970. One of the best-known poets of his generation, Kushner made his debut with his 1962 collection, *Pervoe vpechatlenie* (First Impression). Since then he has published eighteen more volumes of poetry, the most recent being *Na sumrachnoi zvezde* (On a Gloomy Star), which appeared in 1995. Some of his poems have been published in *Contemporary Russian Poetry: A Bilingual Anthology* (1993), translated by Gerald S. Smith and in *Russian Poetry: The Modern Period*. He has also published a substantial number of essays on the nature and history of Russian poetry. He was awarded the Severnaia Palmyra prize for literature in 1995. Since 1993 Kushner has been editor-in-chief of the Biblioteka poeta publishing house in St. Petersburg.

Translations by Paul Graves & Carol Ueland

Как писал Катулл, пропадает голос,
Отлетает слух, изменяет зренье
Рядом с той, чья речь и волшебный образ
Так и этак тешат нас в отдаленье.

Помню, помню томление это, склонность
Видеть все в искаженном, слепящем свете.
Не любовь, Катулл, это, а влюбленность.
Наш поэт даже книгу назвал так: "Сети."

Лет до тридцати пяти повторяем формы
Головастиков-греков и римлян-рыбок.
Помню, помню, из рук получаем корм мы,
Примеряем к себе беглый блеск улыбок.

Ненавидим и любим. Как это больно!
И прекрасных чудовищ в уме рисуем.
О, дожить до любви! Видеть все. Невольно
Слышать все, мешая речь с поцелуем.

"Звон и шум, — писал ты, — в ушах заглохших,
И затмились очи ночною тенью."
О, дожить до любви! До великих новшеств!
Пищу слуху давать и работу — зренью.

As Catullus wrote, a man's voice deserts him,
his hearing flies, and his sight betrays him
near the one whose speech and bewitching person
at a distance are in every way pleasing.

This longing, this tendency—how well I recall it—
to see all in a distorting, blinding brightness:
this isn't love; it's infatuation, Catullus.
Nets: our own poet even chose the word for a title.

Till our thirty-fifth year we follow the models
of the ancient Greek tadpoles and Roman minnows.
How well I recall! From open hands we take our fodder;
we try out on ourselves a smile's fugitive brilliance.

We hate and love, and every bit of it is painful.
We draw lovely monsters in our mental pictures.
But to live through to actual love! Seeing all, able
automatically to hear, to speak between kisses …

You wrote that "ears ring and buzz in their deafness,"
that "over the eyes a nightlike blackness thickens."
But to live through to love! Its exalted freshness
gives food to hearing and new work to vision.

Кипарис

За то еще люблю я черный кипарис,
За то еще люблю, за то еще, что, черный,
Он всех темнее здесь, и сверху смотрит вниз
Один повисший клок, безвольный, беспризорный.

Я черный кипарис за то еще люблю,
Что жесткие наверх зачесывает прядки,
Что вспомню про ларец и запах уловлю
Бессонных тех стихов, разбитых на тройчатки.

Бумажные листы в смолистой духоте.
С бессонницей всю жизнь бороться, задыхаться.
Что видит кипарис? Кораблик на воде,
Как пенится волна и гребни золотятся.

Нам вечность на земле при жизни суждена,
Как если бы в одну вместилось жизней десять.
Но как ни привыкай, когда-нибудь она
Кончается, себя дав ночи перевесить.

Я черный кипарис за то еще люблю,
Что, сделав из него скрипучие носилки,
Несут на них во тьме уснувших к кораблю,
И черная земля, как сон, горит в затылке.

Прощай! В другой стране таинственной очнись,
Где хвоя никогда сухой не будет, пыльной.
За то еще люблю я черный кипарис,
Что лучший обелиск он мертвым надмогильный.

Cypress

For this, as well, I love black cypress; and I love
it also for this, as well: that is, for blackness,
for being darkest of all things here. One drooping tuft
hangs, peering from its great height, abandoned, feckless.

I love black cypress for this, as well: that it combs back
its stiff and wiry locks, the needles of the cypress;
for this: that on recalling a cypress chest, I catch
the scent of sleepless poems broken into triptychs.

Those sheets of paper in the stuffy, resinous air.
All through life to fight insomnia and suffocation.
What does the cypress see? A ship on water where
the great wave spires in foamy curls, where wave crests glisten.

We're destined for eternity in this life on earth,
as though in one life ten could be accommodated.
But the endless ends; no matter how familiar
it is, sometimes it lets the night outweigh it.

I love black cypress for this, as well: that, having carved
out creaking stretchers from the wood, people bring them
to bear the sleeping ones back to the ship through the dark,
and black earth burns the occiput as if dreams linger.

Farewell! May you wake in another land, mysterious,
where drought and dust never assault the cypress needles.
For this, as well, I love black cypress: that the best
of obelisks to raise over the dead is a cypress seedling.

Воспоминания

Н. В. была смешливою моей
подругой гимназической (в двадцатом
она, Эс-Эр, погибла), вместе с ней
мы, помню, шли весенним Петроградом

в семнадцатом и встретили К. М.,
бегущего на частные уроки,
он нравился нам взрослостью и тем,
что беден был (повешен в Таганроге),

а Надя Ц. ждала нас у ворот
на Ковенском, откуда было близко
до цирка Чинизелли, где в тот год
шли митинги (погибла как троцкистка),

тогда она дружила с Колей У.,
который не политику, а пенье
любил (он в горло ранен был в Крыму,
попал в Париж, погиб в Сопротивленье),

нас Коля вместо митинга зазвал
к себе домой, высокое на диво
окно смотрело прямо на канал,
сестра его (умершая от тифа)

Ахматову читала наизусть,
а Боря К. смешил нас до упаду,
в глазах своих такую пряча грусть,
как будто он предвидел смерть в блокаду,

и до сих пор я помню тот закат,
жемчужный блеск уснувшего квартала,
потом за мной зашел мой старший брат
(расстрелянный в тридцать седьмом), светало…

Memoirs

N.V., my girlfriend then, who laughed nonstop
in high school (an S.R., she died in '20),
was with me there; we'd gone out for a walk,
as I recall, through Petrograd in springtime

—this was in '17—and met K.M.
running off to his tutoring; I imagine
we liked him because he was so poor and seemed
grown-up (in Taganrog he died by hanging);

and Nadya T. was waiting by the gate
on Kovensky Prospekt near Chiniselli
Circus, where all that year a crowd would meet
for rallies (a Trotskyite, she perished);

at the time, she and Kolya U. were close;
as he liked singing more than politicians
(he, wounded in Crimea in the throat,
went to Paris and died in the Resistance),

he said we should skip the rally and stroll
to his place, where what must have been the highest
window anywhere looked out on the canal;
his sister (who later was to die of typhus)

recited some Akhmatova by heart,
and Borya K., so funny that we almost
collapsed, betrayed a mournful glance (he'd starve
in the blockade), as if of dire foreknowledge;

and to this day I recall the fallen sun
the pearly sheen spread over that drowsy quarter;
I was retrieved by my older brother (gunned
down in '37) toward morning ...

Петух

Петух, чудовище с кроваво-красным гребнем,
Зубчатым, губчатым, чуть загнутым, в твоем
Зверином облике неотразимо-древнем
Есть что-то гневное, грозящее огнем.

О, как ты топчешься на месте, узловатый,
Натужный, жилистый, как радужный божок,
Такой воинственный, в бою с другим помятый,
Землей присыпанный и пылью, как ожог.

Вот встал на цыпочки, вот снова в прах улегся,
Как будто вымазан в запекшейся крови.
О, есть ли кто-нибудь, кто в жизни не отрекся
Ни разу, праведный, от жизни, от любви?

Безумный, взвинченный, охрипший, безголосый,
Как сладко заново нам каждый раз с утра
Все начинать опять, как горько: помнишь слезы —
не наши, жидкие, но, может быть, Петра?

The Rooster

Rooster, you monster with a blood-red crest, a jagged,
spongy comb cocked to one side: even in your looks,
your undeniably feral, ancient face, an angered
current runs, as if your eyes might give off sparks.

Oh, how you stamp your feet in place, you weather-beaten,
sinewy, tense animal like an idol in polychrome!
You're warlike, rumpled from battle with a fellow creature,
dirt-spattered, as if you were soothing a burn with loam.

Here you strutted, here you hit the dust all over
again, apparently smeared with clotted blood.
Could there be anyone so pious that he's never
once in his life repudiated life and love?

Wild-eyed, high strung, hoarse, and out-of-tune screamer,
how sweet it is, as each new morning comes, for us
to start again. How bitter, too: don't you remember
the tears—not our weak ones, but Peter's tears perhaps?

Viktor Sosnora

Виктор Соснора

Viktor Aleksandrovich Sosnora was born in 1936 in Alup-
ka, Crimea. During World War II, Sosnora was in Lenin-
grad at the beginning of the blockade before moving to
Kuban territory, where he joined the partisans for a short
period. After completing his military service in 1958, he
worked as a locksmith in a Leningrad engineering works
while studying philology by correspondence. His poetic
mentor was Nikolai Aseyev, who wrote the foreword to
Sosnora's first book of poetry, *Ianvarsky liven'* (January
Shower), published in 1962. Sosnora has since published
six more volumes of poems, many of which continue to
develop the author's ironic, playful relationship to early
Russian history and literature: *Triptikh* (Triptych, 1965),
Vsadniki (Riders, 1969), *Aist* (The Stork, 1972), *Stikhotvore-
nia* (Poems, 1977), *Kristall* (Crystal, 1977), and *Pesn' lunnaia*
(Moon Song, 1982), as well as a book of short stories, *Le-
tuchyi gollandets* (The Flying Dutchman, 1979). Sosnora
also works as a translator, notably of American poet Allen
Ginsberg. Viktor Sosnora currently lives in St. Petersburg.

*Translations by Maia Tekses, Mark Halperin & Dinara
Georgeoliani, and F. D. Reeve*

Все было: фонарь, аптека,
улица, поцелуй,

фонтан, самозванство, Мнишек,
Евгений и ночь Невы,

лунатик и револьверы,
гений и ревность рук,

друзья с двойными глазами,
туман от ума у нас,

Сальери ошибся бокалом,
все в сердце: завтра, любовь …

Как праздно любить мертвых!
Как поздно любить живых!

There it all was: the gaslamp, drugstore,
street, a kiss,

a fountain, imposture, Mniszech,
Evgeny and the Neva night,

a madman and revolvers,
a genius and the jealousy of hands,

friends with double eyes,
wit of our will-o-the-wisp,

Salieri with the wrong goblet,
take everything to heart: tomorrow, love ...

how light it is to love the dead!
how late it is to love the living!

Письмо

О, вспомни обо мне в своем саду,
где с красными щитами муравьи,
где щедро распустили лепестки,
как лилии, большие воробьи.

О, вспомни обо мне в своей стране,
где птицы улетели в теплый мир
и где со шпиля ангел золотой
все улетал на юг и не сумел.

О, вспомни обо мне в своем саду,
где колокольные звонят плоды,
как погребальные,
         а пауки
плетут меридианы паутин.

О, вспомни обо мне в своих слезах,
где ночи белые, как кандалы,
и где дворцы в мундирах голубых
тебя ежевечерне стерегут.

A Letter

O, remember me in your garden,
where there were ants with crimson shields,
where large sparrows would spread out
their petals, like a lily's, to the full.

O, remember me in your land,
where the birds flew off to a warm world
and where the golden angel, from its spire,
kept trying to fly south, but always failed.

O, remember me in your garden
where ripened carillons are ringing out
like funeral bells
                and where the spiders
spin meridians of cobwebs.

O, remember me in your own tears
where the white nights resemble manacles,
and palaces in uniforms of blue
keep watch on you evening in and out.

Ворона

И красными молекулами глаз
грустны-грустны, взволнованы за нас

вороны в парке (в нем из белых роз
валетики из влаги и волос).

И вот ворона бросилась. И вот
я все стоял. Она схватила в рот

билетик театральный (как душа
у ног моих он был — дышал, дрожал,

использованный). И остался снег.
Спектакля нет. Вороны нет.

Crow

And with red molecular eyes
sad oh sad, they worried about us,

the crows in the park (where little jacks are
of white roses made, of dew and hair).

And here a crow rushed. And here, a patch
of ground, I stood. In its mouth it snatched

a theatre ticket (like a soul
at my feet and breathed, trembled —

expended). What remained was snow.
There's no performance, no crow.

Верховный час

Новая книга — ваянье и гибель меня, — звенящая вниз на Чаше Верховного Часа!

Как бельголландец стою на мосту, где четыре жираф-жеребца (монстры Клодта!).
Нервами нежной спины ощущаю:
ДРУЖБУ ДЕРЖАВ:
гименей гуманизма — германец
мини-минетчица — франк
с кольтами заячья мафья илотов — итал,
а пред лицом моим в линзах Ла Манша — сам
англосакс!
ходят с тростями туризма:
Єра у них ірмитажа …
Панмоголизм!
Ах с мухами смехом!
НЕ ПРОЩЕ ЛЬ ПЕЛЬМЕННОЕ ПЛЕМЯ?
Адмиралтейская Игла — светла, как перст револьвера, указующий в Ад.
Цапли-цыганки в волосьях Востока: сераль спекуляций (цены цветам у станций Метро!).
Мерзли мозги магазинов: под стеклами сепаратизма кости кастратов (х, Єстетизм!).
Там и туман … Двадцать девиц. Я, Ємиссар Ємансипаций, — двадцать, вам говорю, — с фантиками, в скафандрах, морды в цементе, ремонтницы что ли они драгоценных дворцов? (Счастье — ты с чем-то?) Кто они — я говорю, — их похвально похмелье: лицами лижут стекла у дверей, колонны зубилом клюют. Домы-дворцы забинтованы в красные медицины (нету ковров!), *ибо заветное завтра* — триумф Тамерлана.
СОСТОИТСЯ САТАНИНСТВО!
Тумбы афиш: темы билетов там были. Тембры певиц — наше нужное Єхо Єнтузиазма. Что-то чтецы? В царствах

The Supreme Hour

A new book — the making and breaking of me — ringing out from the Tower of the Supreme Hour!

Like a Dutchman in Flanders I stand on the four giraffe-stallion bridge (Klodt's monsters!).

With my soft spine's nerves I can sense:
THE GREAT POWERS' PARLEY:
The Hun humming the hymen of humanism
The Frenchie flaunting his mignonette in her mini
The Guinea a rabbity Mafia of helots with loaded six-
          shooters
and in front of my face as seen by Don Q — myself as a
          WASP!

all taking a tour with their walking-sticks:
High on the Hermitage era …
Alleverythingism!
A right tight sight!
WHAT ABOUT PICKING UP ON THE PASTA TRIBE?

The Admiralty spire shines, like a revolver's finger pointing to Hell.

The gypsy herons in the hair of the East — a seraglio of speculation (the price of flowers in the Metro stations — think!)

The stores' gray matter has stiffened — in the glass cases of separatism lie eunuchs' bones (phew, fancy stuff!)

Foggy dew, too … Babes twenty-plenty. Emancipation emissary, I'm telling you twenty — covered by forfeits, wearing their space suits, mugs cast in cement, making like they're the repairers of priceless palaces. (Happiness, what's up?) Who are they, I say, with their high-faluting hangover? pressing their pusses against the glass doors, pecking the columns with their chisels. The palaces-penates are wrapped in red bandages

концерта царит Торичелли … и тогда — и т.д. и теперь — и т.п.

Ходят машины в очках, как павлины (о как!), как малины (во шах!) Невский проспект … но — невроз, но — Провинция Императрицы Татарств.

О, над каким карнавалом луна Ленинграда — саблей балета!

ГДЕ ВЫ ХАРЧЕВНИ МОИ, ХАРЫ ЧЕРНИ?
ВЫНИМАЕМ ВИНА В МАЕ, НЕТУ ЖИЗНИ — НЕ ТУЖИ!

Даже дожди … Даже! — Душат!… Люди, как лампочки ввинчены в вечность, но — спят:

чокаются чуть-чуть головами,
целуются в лица,
листают фотоаппараты свои, как некрологи,
в каменных мисках жуют колбасу,
давят в духовках млечных младенцев, — картофель!

Что им Гертруде, да и они что - гневу Гертруды … вредят ли братством: бушуют о будущем… Не обличаю, — так, по обычаю, лишь отмечаю: вот ведь везенье!

Сердце души моей в мире — светлая сталь.
Что мне бояться - библиотек, Бабилона, бульваров?
Кого — бедуинов?
Чьей чепухой еще унижаться мне, униату?

Ходит художник в хитоне, плачет в палитру (падло, пилатствует!) жрет человечьих червей (врет — вермишель!). Стонут в постелях стихами девки искусства.

Я — собеседник о розах без детства, я — сабленосец в седле на копытах (мои стул — Козерог!), жрец трав татар, певец поцелуев (мы — узники уст!), трус и Тристан и как страус — стило под крыло (всяк человек чур не век!), — как бельголландец нервами нежной …

пальцы пинцетов пяти континентов:
иксом Инстантов
рулями Религий

(no rugs!) *for the testamentary tomorrow* is the triumph of Tamerlane.

SATANISM IS HAPPENING!

The billboards are covered: the themes of the tickets were there. The special sound of sopranos was our inevitable echo of enthusiasm. Nothing about readings? In the kingdom of concerts Toricelli is king ... and then — and so on, and now — and so forth.

Cars are going around in glasses like peacocks (and how!), like raspberries (in soup!) The Nevsky Prospekt ... nevertheless a neurosis, nevertheless the Province of the Empress of the Tatars.

O what a show under the Leningrad moon, the crescent sword of the dance!

> WHERE HAS MY BOARDING-HOUSE GONE, THE
> MUGS OF THE MOB?
> WE DRAW OUT THE WINES IN MAY; NO LIFE LEFT,
> DON'T SOB!

Even the rain ... even the rain is strangling! People are light bulbs screwed into eternity, but they're asleep:
>   hardly clink their heads together,
>   kiss cheek-to-cheek,
>   thumb through their cameras like obituaries,
>   chew their cold cuts in ironstone bowls,
>   press potatoes in the ovens of newborn babes!

What's Gertrude to them, or they to Gertrude's wrath? Whether brotherhood hurts or not, they're fighting mad for the future. I'm not spilling secrets; I'm just pointing out, like I usually do — look at that luck!

In the world, my soul's heart is shining steel.

тир терроризма
Дуст Диссидента
лимфа любви, —
НЕ ПРОЩЕ ЛЬ ПЕЛЬМЕННОЕ ПЛЕМЯ?
Ночью ничтожеств над флягами куполами стать и смеяться!

ЕЩЕ ОБЕЩАЮ ОБЩИНАМ:
Я ЗНАЮ ЗНАМЕНЬЯ:

— Я — камень-комета, звенящая вниз на Чаше Верховного Часа!

What's there for me to be afraid of — bookstores, Babylon,
                    boulevards?
Bedouins?
Whose bull would make me, independent believer, bend
                    lower?

The painter passes by in his smock, weeping into his palette (the louse,
playing Pilate), guzzling worms made of men (the liar, it's vermicelli!).
The whores of art moan in verse in their beds.

I'm the wordcarrier for roses without childhood; I'm the
swordcarrier in the saddle of hooves (my chair is Capricorn!), priest of
the Tatar prairie, the chorister of kisses (we're prisoners by mouth), a
coward and Tristan and, like an ostrich, tuck my pen in my armpit
(Coming, ready or not!) — like a Dutchman in Flanders with my soft
spine's nerves ...

        the pincer fingers of five continents
        by the x of Instants
        by the rudders of Religion
        the target-shooting of Terrorism
        the DDT of a Dissident
        the lymph of love —

WHAT ABOUT PICKING UP ON THE PASTA TRIBE?
Laugh at the cupola canteens in the night of nonentities!

AND I PROMISE THE PEOPLE:
                I'M SURE OF THE SIGNS:

I'm the stone comet ringing out from the Tower of the Supreme
Hour!

Yunna Morits

Юнна Мориц

Yunna Petrovna Morits. Poet, essayist and children's writ-
er. Born in Kiev in 1937, Morits remembers World War II,
and her family's terrifying evacuation from Kiev, as the
major event of her childhood. After the war, the family re-
turned to Kiev, where Morits finished school before enter-
ing the Gorky Literary Institute in Moscow, where she
earned a degree in philology in 1961. Her first volume of
poetry, *Razgovor o shchastie* (Conversation about Happi-
ness) appeared in 1957. During the late 1950s and 60s, how-
ever, she had difficulty publishing her own works and so
turned her attention to translations and children's works.
She won a prize for her translation of poems by the
Lithuanian poet Salomeya Neris in 1968. Her books of po-
etry include *Mys zhelania* (Cape of Desire, 1961), *Loza* (The
Vine, 1970), *Surovoi nit'iu* (With Coarse Thread, 1974), *Pri
svete zhizni* (By the Light of Life, 1977), *Tretii glaz* (The
Third Eye, 1980), *Na etom berege vysokom* (On this High
Bank, 1987), and *Muskul vody* (Muscle of Water, 1990).

Translations by Daniel Weissbort

О яблоневой родине моей,
о вербной, о кленово-тополиной,
о пламени жасмина у дверей,
о буйстве рек, беременных былиной,

о белых аистах в рассветной полумгле
над куполами сельских колоколен,
о спящих в той лиственной земле,
о крови, напоившей каждый корень,

поет осока за ночным окном —
сестра папируса, который в Сиракузах.
И пахнет дном речным и белым льном,
плывущим над землею полотном
многострадальной родины моей,
где вышивают крестики на блузах.

~

My apple-tree, my willow,
poplar, maple land,
fire of jasmine by the door,
riot of rivers, legend-large,

white storks at dusk
over the domes of churches,
sleepers in this leafy soil,
blood watering every root —

it is the sedge, at night, that sings of you.
sister of the Sicilian papyrus,
reeking of the river mud, of flax
that floats white above the earth like a canvas
of my long-suffering country,
where on their smocks are sewn small crosses.

_ _ _ _

_____

_____

Мориц

Между Сциллой и Харибдой

*Быть поэтессой в России —
труднее, чем быть поэтом:
единица женской силы в русской
поэзии — 1 ахмацвет.*

Ходим в люльке с погремушкой,
Расцветаем, увядаем
Между Арктикой и Кушкой,
Между Польшей и Китаем.

Покидаем с вечным всхлипом
Облак над лицейским прудом
Между Лиром и Эдипом,
Между Цезарем и Брутом.

Сохраняем здравый разум,
Маслим свет над фолиантом,
Стоим ясли голым фразам —
Между Пушкиным и Дантом.

Поднося фонарь к репризам,
Связь находим колоссальной —
Между Блоком и Хафизом,
Между Музой и Кассандрой.

И, дыша гипербореем,
Проплываем каравеллой
Между Женей и Андреем,
Между Беллой и Новеллой.

Но кровавою корридой
Угрожает путь старинный
Между Сциллой и Харибдой —
Между Анной и Мариной.

Between Scylla and Charybdis

*To be a woman poet in Russia is
harder than to be a male poet:
the unit of female power in
Russian poetry is one akhmatsvet.*

With a rattle we are walking
Round the cradle, flowering, fading.
Between the Arctic and Turkmenia,
Between the Polish lands and China.

With a deep sob we abandon
Clouds above the Lycée puddle —
Between Oedipus and Lear,
Between Julius and Brutus.

We keep our reason healthy,
Dim the light above the folio,
Make a crib for naked phrases,
Between Pushkin and Alighieri.

Highlighting the reprises,
We find a vast connection
Between Blok and Persian Hafiz,
Between the Muse and Cassandra.

And breathing, hyperborean,
We sail through, caravel-like,
Between Zhenya and Andrei,
Between Bella and Novella.

But like a gory bullfight,
The ancient path is threatening,
Between Scylla and Charybdis,
Between Anna and Marina.

Между Сциллой и Харибдой,
Между Анной и Мариной —
Кто проглочен был пучиной,
Тот и выплюнут пучиной.

Стало следствие причиной.
Объясняю образ странный:
Кто проглочен был Мариной,
Тот и выплюнут был Анной.

Золотою серединой
Отродясь не обладаем —
Между Анной и Мариной,
Между Польшей и Китаем.

И над бездною родимой —
Уж незнамо как! — летаем
Между Анной и Мариной,
Между Польшей и Китаем.

Between Scylla and Charybdis,
Between Anna and Marina,
He whom the gulf has swallowed
Was spat out by it likewise.

Consequence became a cause.
I'll explain this odd idea:
He whom Marina swallowed,
Was spat out then by Anna.

In all our born days, never
Did we command the Golden Mean —
Between Anna and Marina,
Between the Polish lands and China.

And above our native chasm —
Who knows how! — look, we are flying
Between Anna and Marina,
Between the Polish lands and China.

Ворона

К нам в окно зашла ворона
За подачкой пищевой.
Не рифмуется корона
С этой черной нищетой.

Этот блеск и фанфаронство,
Страшный голос и портрет —
Лишь голодное воронство,
Что живет по триста лет.

Триста лет за пищу драться,
Триста лет хватать куски —
Тут нельзя не каркнуть, братцы,
Не свихнуться от тоски!

Эта, может быть, ворона,
Что ворует со стола,
Знала, может быть, Ньютона,
Когда птенчиком была.

Но она не промышляет
Никакими интервью —
И глазищами стреляет,
Зная выгоду свою!

Crow

A crow came to our house one time,
To our window for its pittance.
Crown, alas, does not rhyme
With crow, His Sombre Indigence.

This shininess and braggadocio,
Dreadful voice and effigy,
Is nothing but a hungry crowdom,
Which survived three centuries.

To fight three hundred years for food,
Three hundred years to snatch and grab —
Without this cawing can't be done.
Fellows, ennui drives you mad!

Perhaps the very crow that sneaks
Bits and pieces from your board,
Knew Sir Isaac Newton once,
When it was a little bird.

But it does not earn its keep
By granting sundry interviews —
The crow knows what is good for it,
As it makes huge eyes at you!

Раздвинув занавес потусторонний,
Я отшатнулась!... Там стоял отец.
Там тишина стояла, меж ладоней
Держа улов созвездий и сердец.
Там вечер был. Там чмокал тихий омут,
Давясь куском тяжелым, ледяным.
Мне дали знать, что здесь горят и тонут.
А свет был черным. А отец больным.
Одной рукой держался он за стену
Из голых досок. А другой рукой
Указывал вдали на перемену,
Ее считая не ахти какой.
Откуда мог он видеть, знать заране
Глухие тайны, скрытые во тьме
Моих грядущих дней? Какое знанье
В своем загробном он держал уме?
И я вгляделась и дошла до сути.
И эта суть была любовь отца.
Он крепко спал. Но совокупней ртути
Был тайный пот вокруг его лица.
Он крепко спал и видел сновиденья
О семени своем. И ведал он,
Какая сила сочетает в звенья.
Судьбу и звезды там, где нет времен,
А есть лишь вечность в образе кристалла,
Где гаснет жизнь и вспыхивает вновь, —
Покуда нас любить не перестала
Отца огромная загробная любовь.

Parting the curtains on the other world,
I started back! Father stood there.
Silence too was there, holding
A catch of hearts, of constellations.
Evening. There the still waters
Smacked their lips, choking as on a lump of ice.
And I was given to understand
That this was where men burn or drown.
The world was dark. Father, sick,
With one hand scraped at the wall
Of bare boards. With the other,
He pointed indifferently to where
A change announced itself.
How could he see, how know ahead of time
The secrets hidden in the darkness
Of the years before me? What knowledge
Did he entertain beyond the grave?
And I looked hard, reaching into the very core,
Discovering there my father's love.
He was fast asleep. But on his face
The sweat was more sluggish than mercury.
Fast asleep. And in his dreams
He saw his family and knew
What it is chains destiny to the stars,
Where there are no seasons,
Only eternity, its crystal image,
Where life fades and flames again, —
Until the huge paternal love
Has ceased to love us from beyond the grave.

Fazil Iskander
Фазил Искандер

Fazil Abdulevich Iskander was born in Sukhumi, Abkhazia in 1929. He lived there until 1948, when he went to Moscow to study at the Gorky Literary Institute. After receiving his degree he worked as a journalist and as an editor in his native Abkhazia before returning to Moscow in 1962. Although Iskander began his career as a poet, publishing his first volume of poetry, *Gornye tropy* (Mountain Paths) in 1957, he is perhaps best known for his humorous, satirical stories. Throughout the 1970s and 80s, Iskander walked the fine line between "official" and "unofficial" Soviet culture in his works, often and deliberately overstepping the bounds of the permissible. With the relaxation of censorship during the glasnost period, Iskander was able to publish previously banned works as well as more explicitly political ones. In addition to numerous books of stories and several 'novels in stories,' such as *Sandro iz Chegma* (Sandro of Chegem, 1973/1989), Iskander has published seven more volumes of poetry: *Dobrota zemli* (The Goodness of the Earth, 1959), *Zelenyi dozhd'* (Green Rain, 1960), *Deti Chernomor'ia* (Children of the Black Sea, 1961), *Molodost' moria* (Youthfulness of the Sea, 1964), *Zori zemli* (The Earth's Dawns, 1966), *Letnii les* (Summer Forest, 1969), and *Put'* (The Way, 1987).

Translations by Avril Pyman

Гегард

С грехом и горем пополам,
Врубаясь в горную породу,
Гегард, тяжелоплечий храм,
Что дал армянскому народу?

Какою верой пламенел,
Тот, что задумал столь свирепо
Загнать под землю символ неба,
Чтоб символ неба уцелел?

Владыки Азии стократ
Мочились на твои надгробъя,
Детей кричащих, как ягнят,
Вздымали буковые копья.

В те дни, Армения, твой знак
Опорного многотерпенья
Был жив Гегард, горел очаг
Духовного сопротивленья.

Светили сквозь века из мглы
И песнопенья и лампада,
Бомбоубежищем скалы
Удержанные от распада.

Страна моя, в лавинах лжи
Твои зарыты поколенья,
Где крепость тайная, скажи,
Духовного сопротивленья?

Художник, скованный гигант,
Оставь безумную эпоху.
Уйди в скалу, в себя, в Гегард,
Из-под земли ты ближе к Богу.

Gegard

With guilt and grief by half and half
Gouged into the mountain rock,
Gegard, you hefty-shouldered church,
What have you given the Armenian folk?

What faith flamed in the man who thought
To drive, with such ferocity,
Heaven's symbol down beneath the earth
That heaven might there find sanctuary?

A hundred times the Asian Khans
Have pissed upon your sepulchers,
And children, crying like bleating lambs,
Been raised upon their beechwood spears.

Even then, Armenia, a deep-hidden sign
of your long-suffering and your strength, Gegard
Lived on and spiritual resistance burned
With steadfast flame upon your hearth.

From age to age, the hymns and lamps
Shone on amidst the encroaching dark,
Kept from disintegration by
This air-raid shelter in the rock.

But stifled under avalanches
Of lies lie buried my land's sons ...
Where is the secret stronghold where
Our spiritual resistance yet burns on?

You, artist, giant bound and gagged,
Retreat from all the fury and the sound
Of "now"... into the rock, yourself, Gegard.
You are most near to God when underground.

Однажды девушка одна
Ко мне в окошко заглянула,
смущением озарена,
Апрельской свежестью плеснула.

И после, через много дней,
Я замечал при каждой встрече,
Как что-то вспыхивало в ней
И что-то расправляло плечи.

И влажному сиянью глаз,
Улыбке быстрой, темной пряди
Я радовался каждый раз,
Как мимолетной благодати.

И вот мы встретились опять,
Она кивнула и погасла,
И стало нестерпимо ясно,
Что больше нечего терять.

Once a girl, all April-fresh,
With shy uncertainty abloom,
Paused — and looked up with a blush
Into the window of my room.

And afterwards, for many days,
I noticed, every time we met,
How something flared, a moment's blaze,
And how she set her shoulders straight.

And every time, with quick delight,
I caught the quick smile on her face,
The dark, stray lock, the moist, bright eye,
And felt them as a glancing grace.

But then we met once more, and she
Just nodded, and the spark was gone ...
And it was clear as clear to me
That all was over with — and done.

Слепой

Когда ударит свет в оконце
И вскрикнет ласточка в саду,
Слепой, проснувшийся от солнца,
Глаза откроет в темноту.

Что впереди? Давно немолод.
Давно впотьмах пустынный зрак.
Что зимний день? Там темный холод.
Что летний день? Горячий мрак.

Но есть любимый сон о детстве:
Подсолнух в золотой пыльце
И никаких грядущих бедствий…
Там свет. И мама на крыльце.

Так что ему реальность яви?
Сон, что его врачует стон,
Он предпочесть не только вправе, —
Яснее яви его сон.

Явней — над этой черной ямой
И потому над пустотой,
Помедли, свет, помедли, мама,
Гори, подсолнух золотой…

The Blind Man

When light bursts in at the window
And the swallow calls from the garden,
The blind man, woken by sunshine,
Opens his eyes to darkness.

What is there to look forward to? Youth — long gone,
The empty pupil lost, long since, in darkness.
The winter's day? — a murky coldness.
The summer's day? — a sultry dusk.

Yet the beloved memory of childhood
Remains, the golden pollen of the sunflowers,
And no foreboding of misfortune ...
Just light and, on the verandah, Mother.

What then, to him, is the real, waking world?
Not only is the world of memory dearer,
The world of sunlit dreams where pain finds solace ...
But, to him, this dream-world is more real,

More vividly perceived beyond that black pit,
And thus beyond all desolation.
So linger, linger, light, and linger, Mother,
And shine, golden sunflower.

Gennady Aygi
Геннадий Айги

Gennady Nikolaevich Aygi was born in 1934 in Shaimurzi-
no, a village in Chuvashia. He studied at the Gorky Liter-
ary Institute in Moscow and worked for ten years at the
Mayakovsky Museum in Moscow. After being dismissed
from this post in 1969, he lived principally on his meagre
earnings as a translator into Chuvash. Aygi was a member
of the "underground" generation of avant-garde writers
and artists, and his large body of poems in Russian re-
mained almost entirely unpublished in the Soviet Union
until 1987. His work was, however, widely published
abroad, both in the original and in translation, and earned
him a European-wide reputation as one of the most im-
portant poets writing in Russian. He has received major
poetry prizes in several countries, including the Prix Des-
feuilles of the French Academy, awarded for his Chuvash
anthology of French poetry. In recent years major collec-
tions of his work, including *Zdes'* (Here, 1991) and *Teper'
vsegda snega* (There is Always Snow Now, 1992), have been
published in Moscow. He continues to live principally in
Moscow but has maintained strong ties to his native Chu-
vashia, and is the compiler of *An Anthology of Chuvash
Poetry*, which has been translated into several languages.

Translations by Peter France

Роза молчания

Б. Шнайдерману

а сердце
теперь
или только отсутствие
в такой пустоте — словно это притихло
в ожидании
место молитвы
(чистое — пребывание — в чистом)
или — скачками побыть начинающая
боль (как возможно бывает
больно — ребенку)
слабая голо-живая
будто беспомощность
птичья

Rose of Silence

to B. Shnaiderman

and the heart
now
or perhaps only absence
is in such emptiness — as if hushed
in waiting
the place of prayer
(pure — abiding — in the pure)
or — pain that begins by starts
to be there (as perhaps
a child — feels pain)
weak nakedly-living
helplessness
like a bird's

Сон: полет стрекозы

а ярко — как будто в заброшенной риге
на ночь душа!

и озеро тихим во сне очагом
беспокойно: о так по лицу бы красавицы долго
белым японским цветком!
через стога будто розы белеющие
долго и тихо … так после восторга
полянами редкими
в сердце места

и розы-раскаты — стога беспокойные
месту уже своего разговора
мозгу откроют полет стрекозы —

ярче огня по распятию-желобу!
от бога текущего
к горной поляне в высокую тьму

(к смерти засинью заночью
тонко сияя ума

в голову словно из роз
любимо бросаясь)

Dream: Flight of a Dragonfly

but bright — as if the soul had come for the night
to an abandoned barn!

and the lake a hearth quiet in sleep
is troubled: oh so to stroke and stroke the face of a beauty
with a white japanese flower!
across ricks like roses whitening
long and quietly ... thus after ecstasy
through rare clearings
in the heart of the place

and roses-resounding — troubled ricks
will open the flight of the dragonfly
to the brain to the place of their talk —

brighter than fire along the crucifix-trough!
from the god flowing
to the mountain clearing into high darkness

(to death beyondblue beyondnight
delicately shining of mind

into the head as if out of roses
throwing itself lovingly)

Сон: очередь за керосином

и в ряд стоим — спиной друг к другу:

проталкиваем
передних в лавку:

вода и кровь от матерей
в одежде! —

обнявшись
прыгаем во тьме:

лишь где-то:

лес:

готов как будто
до дна — раскатом — озариться:

меня проталкивают:

"как душу именуешь?":

сквозь ветер я кричу:

"о может быть Тоска
По может быть единственному Полю?":

и останавливаемся:

эхо к нам доносится:

друг другу руки мы кладем на плечи:

и так же прыгаем во тьме:

Dream: Queue for Paraffin

and we join the line — back to back

we jostle those in front
into the shop:

water and blood from mothers
in clothes! —

hugging each other
we jump in the dark:

only somewhere:

the forest:

is ready it seems
to the depths — with a peal — to be lit:

I am jostled:

"what do you name your soul?"

through the wind I shout:

"oh perhaps Longing
for perhaps the only Field?"

and we stop:

the echo reaches us:

we lay hands on each other's shoulders:

and so we jump in the dark:

и в вихре мы
белея
открываемся:

как будто сами — место для прихода
кого-то:

словно яркая поляна:

где ветер
как виденье
носится:

нас отовсюду ослепляющее:

и слов не слышно:

ни о чем:

не думается

and in the whirlwind
whitening
we lay ourselves open:

as if ourselves were a place for someone
to come to:

like a vivid clearing:

where wind
like a vision
moves:

blinding us from all sides:

and no words are heard:

about anything:

no thought

Засыпающий в детстве

а высоко — река моя из духов:
друг в друга вы вбегающие
и так — темнея —
вдаль и вдаль

и от ушибов дела нежащего
любимые и мягкие
вы платья странны в той реке:

не детского ли духа искрами
там в черной дали голубой

а сами — прорубями в свете открывающемся
вы в свете поля далеко мелькающие
как над полянами в лесу — их лики:

вы где-то в поле на ветру
как рукопись теперь во сне — его поверхностью
белеющей:

— светлы.

Going to Sleep in Childhood

but high up — my river of spirits:
you running inward to each other
and thus — growing dark —
far off and far off

and from bruises of cherishing
beloved and soft
you dresses are strange in that river:

could it be in sparks of child-spirit
there in the black blue distance

and — like water holes in opening light
you flicker far off in the light of the field
as over forest clearings — their holy faces:

you somewhere in the field in the wind
like a manuscript now in sleep — with whitening
surface:

are bright

Evgeny Rein

Евгений Рейн

Evgeny Borisovich Rein was born in Leningrad in 1935. He attended the Leningrad Technological Institute but was expelled in 1957, after which he continued his education at the Institute of Industrial Refrigeration, from which he received his diploma in 1959. He worked as a refrigeration engineer, freelance journalist, and screenwriter, writing commissioned works on cultural and popular science subjects as well as books for children. He moved to Moscow in 1972. A close friend of both Anna Akhmatova and of Joseph Brodsky, who considered Rein his teacher and mentor, Rein went largely unpublished, both in the Soviet Union and abroad, until 1979, when several of his poems appeared in the *Metropol'* almanac. Although a slim volume of his poems, *Imena Mostov* (The Names of Bridges) was published in 1984, true recognition came only after perestroika. He published ten volumes of poetry appearing between 1989 and 1995, and his work also appears regularly in numerous Russian periodicals. Evgeny Rein is the recipient of the Arion Prize for poetry (1995) and of the State Poetry Prize of Russia (1997).

Translations by Judith Hemschemeyer

Няня Таня

... я высосал мучительное право
тебя любить и проклинать тебя.
— В. Ходасевич

Хоронят няню. Бедный храм сусальный
в поселке Вырица. Как говорится, лепость —
картинки про Христа и Магдалину —
ель фреско по фанере. Летний день.
Не то что летний — теплый. Бабье лето.
Начало сентября...
        В гробу лежит
Татьяна Саввишна Антонова — она,
моя единственная няня, няня Таня...
приехала в тридцатом из деревни,
поскольку год назад ее сословье
на чурки распилили и сожгли,
а пепел вывезли на дикий Север.
Не знаю, чем ее семья владела,
но, кажется, и лавкой, и землей,
и батраки бывали...
        Словом, это
типичное кулачество. Я сам,
введенный в классовое пониманье
в четвертом классе, понимал, что это
есть историческая неизбежность
и справедливо в Самом Высшем Смысле:
где рубят лес, там щепочки летят...
Она работала двадцать четыре года
у нас. Она четыре года
служила до меня у папы с мамой...
А я уже студентик техноложки.
Мне двадцать лет, в руках горит свеча.
Потом прощанье. Мелкий гроб наряжен.
На лбу у няни белая бумажка,
И надо мне ее поцеловать,
И я целую, ДО СВИДАНЬЯ, НЯНЯ!
И тихим-тихим полулетним днем

Nanny Tanya

> *I sucked out the agonizing right*
> *to love you and to curse you.*
> — V. Khodasevich

They are burying my nanny. A poor
gaudy church in the village of Vyritsa.
Pretty, as they say — Christ and Magdalene
al fresco on plywood. A summer day.
Not really summery — just warm. Indian summer.
The beginning of September.
    In the coffin lies
Tatyana Savishna Antonovna — she,
my only nanny, nanny Tanya ...
She came to the city in the Thirties,
a year after her estate had been
sawed down, destroyed and burnt
and the ashes sent to the northern wilds.
I don't know what her family had,
probably a little shop, some land,
a few farm hands ...
    In a word,
typical well-off peasantry. I myself,
aware of the meaning of the Classes
since fourth grade, understood that this
was historical necessity
and justice in The Highest Sense.
When they cut a forest, chips fly ...
She worked 24 years for us, four years
for Mother and Dad before I was born ...
Now I'm a technical school student,
twenty years old, a lighted candle in my hand.
The time of parting. There's a small fancy coffin.
On Nanny's forehead a slip of white paper,
which I kiss. NANNY, FAREWELL!
And on a still, still summery day

идут на кладбище четыре человека:
я, мама, нянина подруга Нюра
и нянин брат двоюродный Сергей.
У няни нет прямых ветвей и сучьев,
поскольку все обрублены. Ее
законный муж — строитель Беломора —
погиб от невнимательной работы
с зарядом динамита. Старший сын
расстрелян посреди годов двадцатых
за бандитизм. Он вышел с топором
на инкассатора, убил, забрал кошелку
с деньгами, прятался в Москве
на Красной Пресне. Пойман и расстрелян.
И даже фотокарточки его
у няни почему-то не осталось.
Другое дело младший — Тимофей, —
он был любимцем и примерным сыном.
И даже я сквозь темноту рассудка
в начале памяти могу его припомнить.
Он приезжал и спал у нас на кухне,
матросом плавал на речных судах.
Потом война …
        Война его и няню
застала летом в родовой деревне
В Смоленской области.
Подробностей не знаю.
Но Тимофей возил в леса муку,
и партизаны этим хлебом жили.
А старший нянин брат родной Иван
был старостой села.
Он выдал Тимофея, сам отвез
за двадцать километров в полевую
полицию, и Тимофея там
без лишних разговоров расстреляли …
А в сорок третьем няню увезли
куда-то под Айлу, в плен германский.

four people are going to the cemetery:
my mother, myself, Nanny's friend Nura
and Nanny's cousin Sergei. Her family tree
had no closer branches or twigs.
They had all been lopped off. Her legitimate
husband — engineer on the White Sea Canal —
died from a mishap with dynamite.
Her older son was shot in his twenties
for banditry. He killed a money changer
with an axe, put the money in a sack,
and hid himself in Moscow on Red Presnya.
He was caught and shot. And Nanny, for some reason,
didn't even have a photograph of him.
Timofei, her younger, is a different story.
He was her favorite, a mama's boy,
and one of my first dim memories.
He would come and sleep in our kitchen.
A sailor, he worked on the river boats.
Then came the war …
        It caught up with him
and Nanny in their village, in summertime,
in the region of Smolensk.
I don't know the details.
But Timofei smuggled flour into the woods
and the partisans lived on that bread.
And Nanny's older brother, Ivan,
the village elder, gave Timofei away.
He himself drove the boy to the police station
twenty kilometers away
and there they shot him dead
without any further inquiry …
And in '43 Nanny was captured
by the Germans and worked on a cattle farm
somewhere near Aila. (She would
often lament her own cows,
taken from her for the common good.)

Она работала в коровнике (она
и раньше о своих коровах,
отобранных для общей пользы,
часто вспоминала).
А дочь единственная няни Тани
и внучка Валечка лежат на Пискаревском,
поскольку оставались в Ленинграде:
зима сорок второго — вот и все…
Что помню я? Огромную квартиру
на берегу Фонтанки — три окна
зеркальные, Юсуповский дворец
(не главный, что на Мойке,
а другой), стоящий в этих окнах,
няню Таню…
А я был болен бронхиальной астмой.
Кто знает, что это такое? Только мы —
астмотки. Она есть смерть внутри,
отсутствие дыхания. Вот так-то!
О, как она меня жалела, как
металась. Начинался приступ,
я задыхался, кашлял и сипел,
слюна вожжой бежала на подушку…
Сидела няня, не смыкая глаз,
и ночь, и две, и три,
и сколько надо, меняла мне
горчичники, носила горшки
и смоченные полотенца.
Раскуривала трубку с астматолом,
и плакала, и что-то говорила.
Молилась на иконку Николая
из Мир Ликийских — чудотворец он.
. . . .
И вот она лежит внизу, в могиле, —
а я стою на краешке земли.
Что ж, няня Таня?
Няня, ДО СВИДАНЬЯ. УВИДИМСЯ.

And Nanny's only daughter
and her granddaughter Valechka
are lying in the Piskarevsky
since they remained in Leningrad
the winter of '42 — that's all ...
What do I remember? A huge apartment
on the Fontanka Canal —
three plate-glass windows, the Yusupov palace
(not the main one on the Moika, but another),
and standing at the windows, Nanny Tanya ...
And I was ill with bronchial asthma.
Who knows what that means? Only we —
the asthmatics. It is an inside death,
an absence of breath. That's what it is!
Oh, how she pitied me, how she rushed around.
At the onset of an attack,
I would suffocate, cough, become hoarse,
and saliva thick as reins ran down the pillow ...
And Nanny sat by my bedside,
sleepless, for one night, for two, for three,
for as long as it took, emptying
the chamber-pot, changing the soaked towels
and the mustard poultices for me.
She burned a tube of asthmatol
and wept, and murmured something.
She prayed to the icon of Nicholas
of Lycian Myra — the wonder worker.
....

And now she is lying underneath, in the grave —
and I am standing on the edge of the world.
Well then, nanny Tanya?
Nanny, FAREWELL. WE WILL MEET AGAIN.

Я все тебе скажу.
Что ты была права, что ты меня
всему для этой жизни обучила:
во-первых, долгой памяти,
а во-вторых,
          терпению и русскому беспутству,
что для еврея явно высший балл.
Поскольку Розанов давно заметил,
как наши крови — молоко с водой —
неразделимо могут совмещаться …
....
Лет десять будет крест стоять
как раз у самой кромки кладбища,
последний в своем ряду.
Потом уеду я в Москву и на Камчатку,
в Узбекистан, Прибалтику, Одессу.
Когда вернусь, то не найду креста.
....
Но все это потом. А в этот день
стоит сентябрьский перегар
и пахнет пылью и яблоками,
краской от оград кладбищенских.
И нам пора. У всех свои дела,
и незачем устраивать поминок.
На электричке мы спешим назад
из Вырицы в имперскую столицу,
где двести лет российская корона
пугала мир, где ныне областной
провинциальный город.
Мне пора на лекции, а прочим на работу.
ТАК, ДО СВИДАНЬЯ, НЯНЯ. Спи, пока
Луи Армстронг, архангел чернокожий,
не заиграл побудку над землею
американской, русской и еврейской …

I will tell you everything.
That you were right in your instructions
about what we need in this life:
first, a long memory,
and secondly,
    patience and Russian dissipation,
which for a Jew is obviously the highest score,
since, as Rozanov noticed long ago,
our two bloods — milk and water —
can mix inseparably.
....
The cross will stand for ten years at the edge
of the graveyard, the last one in the row.
Then I will go to Moscow and Kamchatka
and Uzbekistan, the Baltics and Odessa.
When I return, the cross will be gone.
....
But that's the future. Today
the fragrance of September fills the air.
It smells of dust and apples
and paint from the cemetery fences.
It's time to go. Everyone has things to do,
and there's no point in having a funeral meal.
We hurry back on the train from Vyritsa
to the imperial capital,
where for two hundred years the Russian crown
frightened the world and where now
stands a regional, provincial town.
Now I must go to my lectures, others, to work.
AND SO, NANNY FAREWELL. Sleep, until
Louis Armstrong, the black archangel
sounds the trumpet call over the land,
Russian and Jewish and American ...

Возвращение

Ну, чего тебе еще от меня надо?
Почему до сих пор долетает прохлада
Этих улиц сырых, прокисших каналов,
подворотен, пакгаузов, арсеналов?
Вот пойду я опять, как ходил ежедневно
поглядеть, погулять за спиной Крузенштерна…
…………………………………………………
… вернусь через мост и пойду до Маринки,
где горят фонари до утра по старинке.
За Никольский собор загляну я украдкой,
там студент прикрепляет топор за подкладкой.
Вот и Крюков канал, и дворы на Фонтанке,
где когда-то гонял я консервные банки,
что мячи заменили нам году в сорок пятом…
Как меня заманили к этим водам проклятым?
Что мне в этом пейзаже у державинской двери?
Здесь при Осе и Саше в петроградском размере,
под унылый трехсложник некрасовской музы
мы держали треножник и не знали обузы.
Мы прощались до завтра, хорохорясь, цыганя —
а простились от Автова до Мичигана.
Виден или не виден с чужедальней платформы
сей ампир грязно-желтый, европеец притворный,
Этот Дельвиг молочный и Жуковский румяный,
и кудрявый бессрочный этот росчерк буланый,
вороной и гнедой, как табун на бумаге,
и над гневной Невой адмиральские флаги?

The Return

So, what more do you want from me?
Why does the cool breeze still reach us here,
from the damp streets, the canals gone sour,
the gateways, warehouses, arsenals?
Just as I used to every day, I'll stroll once more
behind the Kruzenstern ...
....
... I'll return over the bridge and keep going
to the Mariinsky, where the streetlights burn
till morning, as in the days of old.
Behind Nikolsky Cathedral, I spy a student
fastening an axe to the lining of his coat.
Here's the Kriukov Canal and the Fontanka courtyards
where I kicked empty cans long ago.
(They were replaced by balls after the war.)
How did they lure me to these accursed waterways?
What to me is the landscape by Derzhavin's door?
Here at Osya's and Sasha's, in Petrograd's scale,
under the spell of Nekrasov's
despondent, tri-syllabic muse,
we set up a tripod lightheartedly.
Roaming, swaggering, we would part until morning —
Then from Avtov to Michigan we took our leave.
From a far-distant platform, is it seen or unseen,
this dirty-yellow, Empire-style, fake European,
this milky Delvig and rosy Zhukovsky,
and the interminable curlicues
of handwriting — dun colored, black and bay —
a wild herd of paperwork, and over
the wrathful Neva, the flags of the Admiralty?

Московский Вокзал

В своей американской черной шляпе
широкополой
стояла ты на привагонном трапе,
там, где подковой
к Московскому вокзалу вышла площадь
и Паоло
когда-то взгромоздил на лошадь
облома,
а тот уехал.
И что-то меня мучает и гложет,
и слышу эхо
приветствий, поцелуев, тепловозов,
и вот потеха —
я снова слышу твой железный отзыв
на все вопросы,
и никогда не вытащить, о Боже,
твоей занозы,
и никогда не пересилить этой
стальной дороги,
не отвести угрозы.
И нынче, нынче, подводя итоги
и глядя слезно
в то утро, что светлеет на востоке
и где морозно,
где фонари на индевелом Невском
стоят стеною,
я думаю, что жизнь прожить мне не с кем,
ведь ты со мною.

The Moscow Station

In your wide-brimmed, black
American hat,
you stood on the train steps, there,
where the horseshoe-shaped square
empties into the station
and Paolo
perched a bumpkin on a stallion,
but he rode away long ago.
And something torments me, gnaws at me
and I hear the echo
of greetings, kisses, steam engines
and — funny —
I hear once more your iron reply
to all the questions.
I will never dig out, o God,
the splinters,
never be master of this
steel road,
nor ward off the dread.
And now, now, adding things up
and looking tearfully
into the morning brightening the east,
where the frost,
where the streetlights along the icy Nevsky
stand like a wall,
I see that since you are always with me,
I have no one to live with at all.

Тайный Агент

Посреди Великой Садовой,
В самом сердце чужой Москвы,
Ни к чему еще не готовой,
Я стою.
    Облетает осень
Свежим золотом сентября,
Как ненужный агент заброшен
И засвечен почти зазря.
Для чего генерал трехзвездный
Мне о Родине лепетал?
Для чего истребитель поздний
Над зенитками пролетал?
Для чего я ампулы с ядом
Вшил в отглаженный воротник?
Для чего я жил с вами рядом?
Постарел, поглупел, обвык ...
Там, на родине, в тайных списках,
В петроградском родном дыму ...
Никогда не увижу близких,
Мать-Отчизну не обниму.
Я узнал о Москве такое,
Что не надо царя Петра,
И она погорит, что Троя,
И останется лишь дыра.
Но забыты мои шифровки,
По ночам передатчик ждет,
И бедняга связной в столовке
Диетический суп жует.
И в свой час упаду, ощерясь,
На московский чумной погост —
Только призрак прорвется через
Разведенный Дворцовый мост.

A Secret Agent

In the midst of the Great Sadovaya,
In foreign Moscow's very heart,
Unprepared for anything as yet,
My head still on straight,
I stand.
    Autumn sheds its leaves,
The bright gold of September,
Like an unnecessary agent, forsaken
And brought to light almost in vain,
Why did the three-star general
Prattle to me about the Motherland?
Why was the lagging fighter plane
Flying above the anti-aircraft guns?
Into my collar why had I sewn
ampules of poison?
Why did I live among you?
Become aged, slow-witted, adapted …
There, on secret black lists, at home,
In Petrograd's familiar smoke …
I will never see my dear ones again,
never embrace my Mother-Fatherland.
I have learned such things about Moscow,
That it doesn't need Peter the Great
To burn down like Troy
To a guttering hole.
But I've forgotten my codes;
At night my transmitter stands waiting
And a wretched courier is slurping
Thin soup at some eatery.
When my time comes I will fall, grimacing,
In the Moscow contagion cemetery —
But through the open Palace drawbridge
A shadow will burst free.

Dmitry Bobyshev
Дмитрий Бобышев

Dmitry Vasilievich Bobyshev. Poet and literary scholar. Born in Mariupol in 1936, Bobyshev grew up in Leningrad and graduated from the Leningrad Technological Institute in 1959. He worked as a chemical engineer and later in Leningrad television. In 1959 he met Anna Akhmatova, who had a strong impact on his life and work. Her poem *Piataia roza* (The Fifth Rose) is dedicated to him as a poet.

Ostracized by official Soviet culture, Bobyshev was not widely published in the Soviet Union, and in the 1970s he began publishing exclusively in the West, in émigré journals such as *Kontinent* and *Grani*. Bobyshev's work now appears in numerous Russian literary journals, including *Den' poezii, Literaturnoe obozrenie, Znamia, Smena,* and *Petropol'*. He has also published in American journals such as *TriQuarterly, Visions, The Cumberland Poetry Review,* and *Contemporary Russian Poetry*. Since emigrating to the United States in 1979, Bobyshev has published four collections of poetry: *Ziiania* (Chasms, 1979), *Zveri Sv. Antoniia* (The Beasts of St. Anthony, 1989), *Polnota vsego* (The Fullness of All, 1992), and *Russkie Tertsiny* (Russian Terza Rima, 1992).

Dmitry Bobyshev currently teaches Russian language and literature at the University of Illinois, Urbana-Champaign.

Translations by Michael van Walleghen

Троцкий в Мексике

Дворцы и хижины, свинцовый глаз начальства
и головная боль, особенно с утра, —
всё нудит революцию начаться.
 — Она и началась, но дохлая жара…

В жару, что ни растёт, от недостатка вянет;
в сосудах кровяных — ущербный чёс и сверб.
Коричнево висит в голубизне стервятник, —
эмблема адская, живосмертельный герб.

То — днём. А по ночам — поповский бред сугубый:
толпа загубленных, и всяк — в него перстом.
Сползают с потолков инкубы и суккубы
и мозг его сосут губато и гуртом.

Опять напиться вдрызг? Пойти убить индейца?
Повеситься, но как? Ведь пальмы без ветвей.
Да из дому куда? А — никуда не деться:
поместье обложил засадами злодей.

Те — тоже хороши. Боялись термидора,
а бонапартишка — изподтишка, как раз, —
(как дико голова, и нет пирамидона)…
французу — Корсика, что русскому — Кавказ.

Но каково страну, яря сословья,
блиндированным поездом ожечь;
не слаще ль этот рык, чем пение соловье —
рёв скотской головы пред тем, как с плеч!

Мятеж, кронштадтский лёд, скорлупчатое темя…
… Боль на белый свет!.. Молнийный поток.
 — Что это, что? … А — всё. Мерцающая темень.
Жизнь кончена. В затылке — альпеншток.

Trotsky in Mexico

Palaces and hovels, the leaden eye of the authorities
and a headache, first thing in the morning —
everything compels the revolution to begin.
In fact, it has begun, but the heat is murderous ...

At this latitude, things grow or wither instantly;
and there's an itching, an irritation in the blood ...
still, an hour lasts forever. Overhead, one vulture,
a hellish coat of arms, decorates the blue azure.

Nights, of course, are worse: vampiric succubi,
mobs of tortured and accusing dead, nightmare
after nightmare hatching in the room like larvae
then changing into furniture, into ordinary chairs ...

Should he get drunk again? Should he kill an Indian?
Maybe he should hang himself. But how? Palm trees
are impossible. And besides that, he's surrounded.
Assassins crouch in every bush. There's no escape.

Idiot fanatics! They were afraid of a Thermidor
but a midget Bonaparte has done for them instead.
(His head is splitting, there's no aspirin ...)
Corsica or the Caucasus, what's the difference?

Ah, but to have snapped the whip of his armored train,
to have set the classes one against the other —
isn't that roar sweeter than a nightingale's song?
The bellowing of cattle before their throats are cut!

He can see it all: Revolt. The crackling, Kronstadt ice ...
And then an ice pick, lightning, a dagger of ice
stabs him in the eye. What is it? What's happening?
he thinks. Never guessing a pickax in the occiput.

Возврат

Рахманинов играл, Шаляпин пел,
Какие титанические люди!
— За милых дам! За Мира передел!
И голова Крестителя на блюде.

Немая мысль не шевелила уст,
лишь поднимала пепельное веко:
о явной смертобойности искусств,
о Зле и о явленьи человека.

И розовели зори и дела.
Но гибель предреклась для полу-Мира.
Когда б рябиной Родина была,
то у корней лежала бы секира.

Шаляпин пел, Рахманинов играл …
Зачем их не заснял кинематограф, —
раскрытый зев певца во весь экран
и пальцы пианиста, прыть которых

враз искресала радугу из люстр,
за звуками всё зло заиллюзорив.
А бас, а Зороастра-златоуст,
то бархатно-лилов, а то лазорев,

свободно плыл по попранным полям,
где топотно и потно убивали.
Разваленную тяжко пополам,
страну спасёт ли ария? Едва ли.

И где он, горла певчего удел,
где своды, подпирающие нёбо? …
— Ираклий, шёл бы к чорту, надоел, —
несётся осязаемо из гроба.

Return

Rachmaninoff played, Chaliapin sang.
What Titans! What Herculean spirits!
"To the ladies then! The repartitioned globe!"
And the head of the Baptist on a platter.

Mute thought did not stir the lips to life,
and hardly raised a single, pallid eyelid:
neither thought of art's clear death defiance
nor any thought of evil, nor, indeed, of man himself.

Our horizons and our deeds alike looked rosy,
but ruin was foretold for half the world.
If the Motherland were a rowan tree
then at its roots the ax would lie.

Chaliapin sang, Rachmaninoff played ...
Someone should have made a movie —
replete with close-ups of the singer's throat,
the pianist's fingers, whose lightning

sparked instant rainbows from the chandeliers
while evil simply disappeared behind that sound —
and the reverberating bass, at first Zoroastrian, golden,
now velvety and lilac-tinged, now lapis lazuli,

floated freely over the shell-shocked fields
where men drowned in their own excrement.
Exploded suddenly into ragged, bloody halves,
can a country be saved by an aria? Not likely.

And where are they finally, that golden throat,
those sturdy arches propping up the palate ...?
Listen. A voice is speaking from the grave:
"Hercules, to hell with you, I've had it!"

Ах, Франция: увидев, — умереть!
Усталому сладка твоя землица:
как на перине, в ней отрадно преть,
и прах супруги рядом пепелится.

Здесь тиховейно спи наверняка,
знай, тлей себе в могильной тайне, в Бозе,
покойся, забывайся на века.
И что властей? Смертей уже не бойся.

Как бы не так! И вдруг: туда: труба!
— А ну вставай, проклятьем заклеймённый,
проклятьем славы и клеймом раба,
принадлежи отныне миллионам.

Бери свой прах, но выбрось прах жены.
Ты не воскрес, довольствуйся субботой,
зато ошибки будут прощены.
Работай, труп. А ну живей работай!

Ты — наш, и не поможет флажолет.
Мы — до скончанья времени. Ты тоже.
Французской пломбой скалится скелет,
а будущее близко и дотошно.

O, France: having seen you, one can die happy!
Your precious ground is sweet, longed-for rest:
O, to cheerfully decay in it, as in a feather bed,
with one's own feathery, decaying wife close by!

Sleep, sleep then, afloat in absolute security,
and know you rot inviolable, in secrecy, in God.
Sink down at last to eternal peace, oblivious
to earth and earthly power, vanity and death …

But no, that's far too simple. We need a trumpet!
"Well, get up then, branded as you are, cursed
with worldly glory, the world's slave still —
henceforth, again, you belong to the millions.

Take up your remains, but leave your wife's behind.
This isn't Resurrection Sunday; it's only Saturday.
But smile, your mistakes are all forgiven.
Smile! Look lively there! Work, you corpse!

You are ours, and flutes can't help you now.
We will remain till the end of time. You too."
Thus, the skeleton flashes his French, gold fillings
and the future looms up close, in living color.

Павлин белый.

Белее ледников и снега,
белее вечности,
   и — юный, а седой,
брат облака, горы другое эго
(зато и камушки в зобу его с едой).

Белей еще чего?
     — Сказать не научился:
белее мраморно-аллейных совершенств …
И хвост — пучок из бесконечных чисел.
А тело меловое — цифрой 6.

Но вот: неисчислимо-глазый веер,
   белее
тем, что глаза все спят,
что видит он под каждым белым веком?
 — Регаты парусов?
    Иль: выблески Плеяд?

Сон этот — белизна ль,
   невинность, что не рвана,
не комкана никем, невинность ли?
Или исполненная небытием
   нирвана, —
последним опытом земли?

То ль это — белизна в отеле:
   туалета,
крахмальной скатерти,
   простынных ли прохлад?
Или: в алмазах это
белосеребрянный — вокруг себя — оклад?

The White Peacock

Whiter than a mountain glacier,
    whiter than eternity,
the very mountain's alter-ego —
his youthful, silver, cloud-brother
    (who by way of brotherhood
    takes a pebble with his food)

and even whiter yet than that —
    whiter than mere words certainly
    or any marble-white pavilion …
His tail's a swatch of infinite numbers.
His chalky body forms the figure six.

And his sudden, blizzard-eyed fan
    is made still whiter by the fact
    that all the eyes are sleeping.
What do you suppose he dreams in there
    behind those lily-white lids?
Sailboat regattas? The sparkling Pleiades?

Or perhaps it's all just whiter emptiness —
    a perfect innocence
    or wonderful Nirvana
full of the nonexistence of all experience.

Or does he dream in fact the whiteness
of hotels — toilets and starchy tablecloths
linen-sheet froideurs
and the diamond-glitter of good crystal,
    porcelain and heavy silver …

Все враз… И плюс — прохладный гений,
   иней,
что негде из яйца, проклюнувшись, возрос.
Растает… Потому что —
   мнимый,
а сам — гермафродит и альбинос.

All of this and more,
since he is, after all, imaginary —
   a mere figment of snow.
   Poor hermaphrodite albino
who pecks through the world's cold shell
   and melts so quickly back again.

Тот свет …

посвящается О. С. — Б.

… куда пути непоправимы.
Где то звезда, то снова полоса.
Грядущего нарядные руины,
лириодендроны, бурундуки, раввины …
И — галактичие небеса.
И — механические херувимы.

И — ты. По вавилонам барахла,
живой, идешь, хотя отпет и пропит,
свой поминальный хлеб распопола-,
где палестинам снеди несть числа …
Делясь, ты половинишь вкус и опыт
по зарослям дерев Добра и Зла.

Да, ты — туда ж — с утопией великой,
с ужасною, как тот кровавый хлеб,
духовностью! Ты встречен будешь в пику
улыбкою тончайшей, поелику
Здесь души не давались на зацеп
десятка двух "единственных религий."

И — каждая — для них за то не та,
что к счастью стыдному отнюдь не доступ.
(Единственность — язвимая пята.)
Тоталитарна только пестрота,
и абсолютны сдобные удобства, —
в них даже грязь охранна и чиста.

The Other World

for O.S. — B.

From whence no paths return ...
Just stars and stripes forever,
the gaudy, catastrophic future —
liriodendrons, chipmunks, Hari Krishnas ...
whole new galaxies in fact
complete with mechanical cherubim

and you. Alive amid the alien trash.
Otherwise, the funeral went perfectly,
right down to the bloodstained bread
of last remembrance, yours to offer up
in Babylon — your taste and wisdom too —
where everyone is gorged on bread

And forbidden fruit alike. And you —
your winked-at "Russian" spirituality
reeking of that selfsame bloody bread —
what can you say to these utopians
who have resisted at least two dozen
"true and apostolic faiths"? And why?

Can you deduce for them a noble motive?
Unconditional happiness? Is that it?
A one and only anything is anathema here.
Only variety, change, endless multiplicity
have value; and sybaritic comfort is the law.
Even their shit is privileged and clean.

Учись на всем.
И слушай содроганья
(бутылочная сыплется гора)
и рев зеленоводного органа.
По небу письмена над Ниагарой
цветут, опять УДОБСТВА предлагая…
Горит закат огромно и угарно.
Горячих красок хладная икра.
Тот свет. И мы живые, дорогая.

Learn from everything. Listen to the shuddering
boom of Niagara Falls (a celestial organ —
a mountain of green glass shuddering down)
while over the city, lights start coming on,
signs offering us even more CONVENIENCES ...
And dusk flares up again like an Aurora Borealis,
an icy spray of dazzling, otherworldly color ...
to find us here, my darling. Still alive.

Bella Akhmadulina
Белла Ахмадулина

Bella Akhatovna Akhmadulina was born in Moscow in 1937 to a Tartar father and a Russian mother. She studied at the Gorky Literary Institute in Moscow from 1955 to 1960. She was expelled for writing "apolitical" verse but was reinstated through the efforts of the poet Pavel Antokolsky. She emerged on the literary scene as one of the "new Wave" poets of the post-Stalin thaw, publishing her first poems in 1955 and a book of poetry, *Struna* (The String), in 1962. Her work was well-received initially, but it was later criticized during the more repressive Khrushchev years as being "superfluous" and "too intimate." As a result, she was expelled from the Writer's Union, although she was later reinstated as a translator, mainly of Georgian poetry. She continued to write both poetry and prose, however, and her work appeared in most major Soviet literary journals. Akhmadulina has published 16 books of poetry, the most recent of which is *Sozertsanie stekliannogo sharika* (Contemplating the Glass Sphere, 1997). She received the State Prize for Literature in 1989. Bella Akhmadulina currently resides in Moscow with her husband, Boris Messerer.

Translations by F. D. Reeve

Кофейный чертик

Опять четвертый час. Да что это, ей-богу!
Ну, что четвертый час, о чем поговорим?
Во времени чужом люблю свою эпоху:
тебя, мой час, тебя, веселый кофеин.

Сообщник-гуща, вновь твой черный чертик ожил.
Ему пора играть, но мне-то — спать пора.
Но угодим ему. Ум на него помножим —
и то, что обретем, отпустим до утра.

Гадаешь ты другим, со мной — озорничаешь.
Попав вовнутрь судьбы, зачем извне гадать?
А если я спрошу, ты ясно означаешь
разлуку, не любовь, и ночи благодать.

Но то, что обрели, — вот парочка, однако.
Их общий бодрый пульс резвится при луне.
Стих вдумался в окно, в глушь снега и оврага.
И, видимо, забыл про чертика в уме.

Стих далеко летал, вернулся, но не вырос.
Пусть думает свое, ему всегда видней.
Ведь догадался он, как выкроить и выкрасть
Тарусу, ночь, меня из бесполезных дней.

Эй, чертик! Ты шалишь во мне, а не в таверне.
Дай помолчать стиху вблизи его луны.
Покуда он вершит свое самотворенье,
люблю на труд его смотреть со стороны.

Меня он никогда не утруждал нимало.
Он сочинит свое — я напишу пером.
Забыла — дальше как? Как дальше, тетя Маня?
Ах, да, там дровосек приходит с топором.

The Coffee Imp

"Past three again! Honest to God, what are you doing?"
"So it's after three — what'll we talk about?"
In a period that's alien I love the time that's mine:
you, special hour, and you, my cheery friend, caffeine.

Coffee grounds, accomplice, your black-faced imp has come
to life again: it's his time for playing; mine, for bed.
But let's satisfy him: we'll multiply our mind by him
and before dawn comes set free the answer in our head.

Others you tell fortunes; with me you just play tricks.
Once you know the outcome, why pretend to guess?
Yet if I ask directly, you flagrantly predict
a separation, no lovemaking, and night's amazing grace.

The answer we got — but here's a couple coming by.
Their bold and single heartbeat is quickened by the moon.
That verse composed itself from the snowscape out the window
and surely overlooked the imp that was on our mind.

It flew far off, returned but never really formed.
Let it think itself — it always knows what's best.
After all, it figured out how to scissor out and snatch
Tarusa, night and me from countless, pointless days.

Hey, imp! It's me you're scampering in, not in some bar!
And let that verse keep quiet when it gets near his moon.
While he's working on his self-creation, I love to watch
the way he sweats but always keep myself aloof.

He never causes me the slightest bit of trouble.
He makes his own things up — I write in ballpoint black.
Wait, I've forgotten — what comes next? What, Aunty Manya?
Oh yes: *Here comes the woodsman with a heavy ax.*

Пока же стих глядит, что делает природа.
Коль тайну сохранит и не предаст словам —
пускай! Я обойдусь добычею восхода,
вы спали — я его сопроводила к вам.

Всегда казалось мне, что в достиженьи рани
есть лепта и моя, есть тайный подвиг мой.
Я не ложилась спать, а на моей тетради
усталый чертик спит, поникнув головой.

Пойду, спущусь к Оке для первого поклона.
Любовь души моей, вдруг твой ослушник — здесь
и смеет говорить: нет воли, нет покоя,
а счастье — точно есть. это оно и есть.

Meanwhile, the verse turns watchful eye on nature's doings.
As long as it keeps mystery safe, not betraying it
to language, fine! I'll make do by catching the sunrise —
you lay sleeping — I was escorting it to you.

I've always thought that getting to an ungodly hour
is my own mite, my secret and mysterious feat.
Here, I haven't gone to bed, and on my notebook
a tired, droopy-headed imp is sound asleep.

I'll go down to the Oka to pay my respects.
Your disobedient servant now, the love that lies
within me makes bold to speak: *There's no free will, no peace,
but there's good luck. That's precisely what this is.*

Озноб

Хвораю, что ли, — третий день дрожу,
как лошадь, ожидающая бега.
Надменный мой сосед по этажу
и тот вскричал:
— Как вы дрожите, Белла!

Но образумьтесь! Странный ваш недуг
колеблет стены и сквозит повсюду.
Моих детей он воспаляет дух
и по ночам звонит в мою посуду.

Ему я отвечала:
— Я дрожу
все более — без умысла худого.
А впрочем, передайте этажу,
что вечером я ухожу из дома.

Но этот трепет так меня трепал,
в мои слова вставлял свои ошибки,
моей ногой приплясывал, мешал
губам соединиться для улыбки.

Сосед мой, перевесившись в пролет,
следил за мной брезгливо, но без фальши.
Его я обнадежила:
— Пролог
вы наблюдали. Что-то будет дальше?

Моей болезни не скучал сюжет!
В себе я различала, взглядом скорбным,
мельканье диких и чужих существ,
как в капельке воды под микроскопом.

Все тяжелей меня хлестала дрожь,
вбивала в кожу острые гвоздочки.

Chills

I guess I'm sick, because this is the third day
I've been shivering like a horse waiting for the start,
Even my snobbish neighbor on the floor
keeps shouting: "Bella, you're practically shaking yourself
apart!"

"Pull yourself together! Your weird disease
makes the walls tremble and blows through all the cracks.
It gives my kids inflammation of the feelings
and rattles the dishes drying in the rack."

And so I'd say to him:
          "I'm shivering
more and more — without malice prepense.
But by the way, tell everyone on the floor
that this evening I'm quitting our residence."

But the general unease rendered me so queasy
that I kept making stupid verbal slips,
one leg began to hop, and I couldn't even
get a smile to form upon my lips.

Leaning over in the stairwell, my neighbor
eyed me squeamishly and kept away.
I buoyed him up:
          "You watched the introduction.
What do you suppose will happen today?"

The plot my sickness followed wasn't boring!
With one sad glance I could see inside
me strange and savage creatures glimmering
as in a water drop on a laboratory slide.

The shivering lashed me ever more painfully,
driving its sharp tacks into my soft skin,

Так по осине ударяет дождь,
наказывая все ее листочки.

Я думала: как быстро я стою!
Прочь мускулы несутся и резвятся!
Мое же тело, свергнув власть мою,
ведет себя свободно и развязно.

Оно все дальше от меня! А вдруг
оно исчезнет вольно и опасно,
как ускользает шар из детских рук
и ниточку разматывает с пальца?

Все это мне не нравилось.
Врачу
сказала я, хоть перед ним робела:
— Я, знаете, горда и не хочу
сносить и впредь непослушанье тела.

Врач объяснил:
— Ваша болезнь проста.
Она была б и вовсе безобидна,
на ваших колебаний частота
препятствует осмотру — вас не видно.

Вот так, когда вибрирует предмет
и велика его движений малость,
он зрительно почти сведен на нет
и выглядит, как слабая туманность.

Врач подключил свой золотой прибор
к моим предметам неопределенным,
и острый электрический прибой
охолодил меня огнем зеленым.

as rain strikes hard upon an aspen, punishing
each quivering leaf again and again.

I kept thinking: how rapidly I'm standing!
My muscles are running and jumping playfully!
Having dethroned my power, my body's behaving
openly, familiarly and free.

And going farther, dangerously away from me.
Will it one day decide to leave without a sound,
the way a balloon slips from a young child's hands
and string around his finger comes unwound?

I didn't like how things were going. And so
I told the doctor, despite my reticence:
"I have some self-respect, you see, and can't
forever take my body's disobedience."

The doctor then explained: "It's very simple.
Your harmless illness might even be derisible
if the frequency of oscillations preventing
examination didn't render you invisible.

"You see, when an object's in vibration
and the smallness of its movements is very great,
to the naked eye it shrinks to almost nothing
and appears like distant, blurry haze."

The doctor connected his golden apparatus
to all my indeterminate, vague parts,
and a piercing electronic roller
swept its cold, green fire over my heart.

И ужаснулась стрелка и шкала!
Взыграла ртуть в неистовом подскоке!
Последовал предсмертный всплеск стекла,
и кровь из пальцев высекли осколки.

Встревожься, добрый доктор, оглянись!
Но он, не озадаченный нимало,
провозгласил:
— Ваш бедный организм
сейчас функционирует нормально.

Мне стало грустно. Знала я сама
свою причастность к этой высшей норме.
Не умещаясь в узости ума,
плыл надо мной ее чрезмерный номер.

И, многозначной цифрою мытарств
наученная, нервная система,
пробившись, как пружины сквозь матрац,
рвала мне кожу и вокруг свистела.

Уродующий кисть огромный пульс
всегда гудел, всегда хотел на волю.
В конце концов казалось: к черту! Пусть
им захлебнусь, как Петербург Невою!

А по ночам — мозг навострится, ждет.
Слух так открыт, так взвинчен тишиною,
Что скрипнет дверь иль книга упадет,
и — взрыв! и — все! и — кончено со мною!

Да, я не смела укротить зверей,
в меня вселенных, жрущих кровь из мяса.
При мне всегда стоял сквозняк дверей!
При мне всегда свеча, вдруг вспыхнув, гасла!

The dial was horrified! The hands leapt back!
The mercury started jumping up and down in fits!
Then came the deathbed crashing of the glass,
whose pieces sculpted blood from my fingertips.

"Watch out, good doctor; take another look!"
Unfazed, unflappable, he formally
announced: "Your pitiful, poor organism
has now begun to function normally."

That made me sad. I had been well aware
of my connection with this upper sphere.
Far too big to fit inside a mind,
its giant size floated in the air.

And schooled by my many-figured number of
ordeals, my nervous system, like a spring
breaking through a mattress, ripped my skin
and hissed and whistled at everything.

The enormous pulse that made my wrist so ugly
kept thundering, trying to get away.
Hell, let it go! As Petersburg choked on the Neva,
This is mine to swallow the wrong way.

Now at night my brain is sharp, expectant.
My ears, excited by the silence, are so keen
that the creaking of a door or a book's falling
is — bang! — explosion! — boom — the end of me!

Indeed I never dared to tame the wild
animals in me that fed on blood from meat.
I always felt a draft from under doors!
I always saw the candle flare then die!

В моих зрачках, нависнув через край,
слезы светлела вечная громада.
Я — все собою портила! Я — рай
растлила б грозным неуютом ада.

Врач выписал мне должную латынь,
и с мудростью, цветущей с человек,
как музыку по нотным запятым,
ее читала девушка в аптеке.

И вот теперь разнежен весь мой дом
целебным поцелуем валерьяны,
и медицина мятным языком
давно мои зализывает раны.

Сосед доволен, третий раз подряд
он поздравлял меня с выздоровленьем
через своих детей и, говорят,
хвалил меня пред домоуправленьем.

Я отдала визиты и долги,
ответила на письма. Я гуляю,
особо, с пользой делая круги.
Вина в шкафу держать не позволяю.

Вокруг меня — ни звука, ни души.
И стол мой умер и под пылью скрылся.
Уставили во тьму карандаши
тупые и неграмотные рыльца.

И, как у побежденного коня,
мой каждый шаг медлителен, стреножен.
Все хорошо! Но по ночам меня
опасное предчувствие тревожит.

My pupils shone with gigantic pools of tears
that welled above the rims, ready to fall.
I spoiled it all myself! I would have corrupted
heaven with the dreadful wastes of hell.

The doctor wrote me out the proper Latin,
and — as some people are innately sage —
a young girl in the pharmacy then read it
as if reading music by black marks on a page.

Valerian's kiss-to-make-it-better touched
the tender feelings of my whole apartment house,
and for weeks the minty tongue of Medicine
has been licking my old wounds.

My neighbor's pleased. Three times he's had his children
report his joy at my recovery,
and he even has, I understand, extolled
me at a meeting of the Management Committee.

Visits I've returned, and debts paid back,
and even answered letters. I go walking myself,
intentionally, making useful circles.
I don't allow wine to be kept on the kitchen shelf.

There's not a sound around me, not a soul.
My table's dead; dust covers every part.
All my pencils aim their little blunt
illiterate snouts into the ignorant dark.

As with a defeated racehorse, every step
I take is hobbled now and extra slow.
All's well, all's well! But every night I shake
with fear of things that I don't know.

Мой врач еще меня не уличил,
но зря ему я голову морочу,
ведь все, что он лелеял и лечил,
я разом обожгу иль обморожу.

Я, как улитка в костяном гробу,
спасаюсь слепотой и тишиною,
но, поболев, пощекотав во лбу,
рога антенн воспрянут надо мною.

О звездопад всех точек и тире,
зову тебя, осыпься! Пусть я сгину,
подрагивая в чистом серебре
русалочьих мурашек, жгущих спину!

Ударь в меня, как в бубен, не жалей,
озноб, я вся твоя! Не жить нам розно!
Я — балерина музыки твоей!
Щенок озябший твоего мороза!

Пока еще я не дрожу, о, нет,
сейчас о том не может быть и речи.
Но мой предусмотрительный сосед
уже со мною холоден при встрече.

My doctor hasn't yet declared me guilty,
but no point in pulling the wool over his eyes,
for everything that he had cured and cherished
I'll in an instant turn to fire or ice.

I, like a snail inside its bony coffin,
can save myself by being quiet and blind,
but falling sick, tingling in my forehead,
my antennae's horns will leap forth again.

O meteor shower of all dots and dashes,
come rain upon me! May I be lost to sight
while trembling from time to time in the pure silver
of a mermaid's gooseflesh burning up my spine!

Beat on me like a tambourine; don't spare me,
chills — I'm wholly yours! Apart, I'm lost!
I'm the ballerina of your music!
I'm the frozen puppy of your frost!

I haven't yet begun to shiver — not yet —
and even talking about it's against the rules;
but every time we meet my prudent neighbor
is already extremely cool.

Elena Ignatova

Елена Игнатова

Elena Alekseevna Ignatova. Poet and documentary screenwriter. Born in Leningrad in 1947, Ignatova graduated from the Philology Department of Leningrad State University, where she then taught as a lecturer in Russian philology until 1979. In 1990 Ignatova and her family emigrated to Israel. Her poetry was first published in 1963 in the journal *Smena*, but thereafter she published mostly in samizdat form and abroad. Her first book of poems, *Stikhi o prichastnosti* (Verses about Belonging), published in Paris in 1976, was followed by two more collections published in samizdat: *Zdes', gde zhivu* (Here where I live, 1983), and *Stikhotvorenia* (Poems, 1985). Her work has appeared in both Russian periodicals such as *Den' poezii*, *Molodoi Leningrad*, *Zvezda*, and *Neva*, and émigré journals such as *Kontinent*, *Skopus*, and *Vstrechi*. Her poetry has been translated into Serbian, German, Swedish, Polish, Hebrew and English. She has also written books and film scripts on the history of Saint Petersburg.

Translations by Sibelan Forrester

Я повстречала равнину в рваной рогоже,
я полюбила холмы, оползавшие древнею кожей,
крупную соль подморозка, мятную стужу,
голубизны родника — око наружу.

Мне говорят: "Обернитесь на жизнь и воспойте строенья!"
Глянула я — и прыщавый бетон оцарапал мне зренье,
а присмотреться — железные ребра сочатся простудой,
сетки ячеек жилых держатся чудом.

А за домами закат яркий играет
и чернокрячка-равнина бредит о рае …
Хляби лежат под землей, мерзлые трубы.
Слабых лесов городских синие губы.

Но обмороженным сердцем, робостью ока
я прилепилась к равнине, спящей глубоко
под чешуей голубою рыбьего меха,
где полуглавья холмов — форма для эха.

I have encountered a valley, in ragged bast matting,
I fell in love with the hills, slipped like skin that is ancient,
with the coarse salt of the freeze, the hard peppermint frosting,
with the blue sky of a spring — an eye on the outside.

They tell me : "Turn towards life and start singing of buildings!"
I turned to glance — pimply concrete scratched at my vision,
and looking closely — the iron ribs dribble a wintry infection,
grids of the residence cells stay up by a miracle.

But past the houses a bright sunset is playing
and the black-duckweed flat place raves about heaven ...
Pipes frozen stiff, under the earth lie abysses.
Indigo lips of the weak forests of cities.

But with a frost-bitten heart, an eye looking timid
I stuck myself to the valley sleeping so deeply
under a blue scaly armor of fur resembling fishes,
where the half-heads of the hills are the form for an echo.

из "Стихов о музыке"

Итальянец Марчелло, ты сладостным воздухом дышишь.
То бьенье воды ключевой, то посвист пастуший услышишь,
То подругу окликнешь, а голос потонет в тумане,
То припомнишь, как ветер гуляет в дырявом кармане.

Как весло на реке, как трава под косой захлебнется,
Тотчас вскрикнет гобой, а валторна ему отзовется.
"Кто полюбит мое почерневшее грубое тело?" —
Спросит полночь у сада, и голос ответит: "Марчелло!"

Кто Марчелло полюбит? Чье сердце затронешь, бедняга?
Ты у дома стоишь, но не сделаешь к двери ни шага.
То поденщик поет, то красотка крадется от мужа…
Мимо… Мимо… Как больно … И музыка кажется вчуже.

from "Verses about Music"

Italian Marcello, you breathe a much sweeter air.
First the beat of spring water, then some shepherd's whistle you hear,
First you call to your girlfriend, but fog drowns the sound
    of your voice,
Then you think how the wind strolls about in a pocket of holes.

Like an oar on the water, like grass choking under the scythe,
Right away, first the oboe cries out, then the French horn replies.
"Who will love my rude body, the blackening curve of my belly?" —
Midnight asks in the garden, and someone's voice answers —
    "Marcello!"

Who will love my Marcello? Whose heart will you touch,
    you poor fellow?
Here you stand by the house, but you won't take a step to the doorway.
First a laborer sings, then a beauty steals out from her husband ...
Past you ... Past you ... How painful ... The music seems disinterested.

Летний сад

1

Ты зачем, Летний сад, припадаешь к губам,
В полоненье души обретаешь свободу?
Кроме голоса, что я тебе передам?
Но тебя обучает жестоким стихам
Ветер, что разоряет древесные своды.

Начинается утро корявых небес,
Облака поражает припадок боязни…
Здравствуй, здравствуй, зверинец постылых чудес:
Чугуна тирания и каменный лес —
Мы готовы для праздничной казни,

Начинается утро — и сад освещен,
Он крепится к воде в исполинском замахе,
Он сверкает, как лезвие над палачом,
Но мы неуязвимы, мы тоже живем
И в Неве не полощем смертельной рубахи.

2

Дроги твоих мастеров,
Судьбы людские — все мимо.
Страшен бессмертья удел.
В зимние ночи, о сад,
Ты покинут стоишь, нелюдимый.
камень улыбчив и бел.

Или мы тени тебе,
Скользим с шелестеньем бесплотным —
Бренного мира слюда?
Трубы оркестров парадных,
Краски гуляний народных —
Не отражает вода.

The Summer Garden

1

Why do you, Summer Garden, press close to my lips,
And why do you turn freedom into the soul's durance?
Besides voice, can I pass you along any gifts?
But then you are instructed in a harsh verse's arts
By the wind that transforms the trees' vaults into ruins.

Now a morning below the gnarled skies is begun,
The clouds are attacked by a new fit of dread …
Greetings, greetings menagerie of hateful wonders:
In a cast-iron tyranny, a forest of stones —
We're already prepared for the festive beheading.

Now the morning's begun — and the garden is lit,
With a threatening gesture it clings to the water,
It gleams, like the edge of the headsman's raised blade,
But we too are invulnerable, we also live
And we don't rinse the smock of death in the Neva.

2

Hearses of your master-craftsmen,
All human fates — pass you by.
The lot of not dying is frightful.
Nighttimes in winter, oh garden,
You stand abandoned, unsocial.
Stonework is smiling and white.

Or are we shadows to you,
Sliding with some fleshless rustle —
Mica of the transient world?
The trumpets of holiday orchestras,
Pigments of the outdoor parties —
Do not reflect in the water.

Но никогда мне с тобой,
Никогда не проститься,
эта любовь без утрат:
Черные сети ветвей,
На которых не селится птица,
Неостывающий сад ...

But you and I never shall,
Never bid farewell in parting,
This is a love without loss:
Black nets of branches on which
Birds never settle to nest,
Uncooling garden ...

К Овидию

Слепой пастух и каменные овцы.
Дымят овраги, вырытые солнцем.
Праматери-земли по ним стекало млеко.
Вот наших судеб край:
Овраги да колодцы,
Мочи овечьей стойкое болотце,
Солончаки да степь …
И — до скончанья века.

Наверно, души те, что выгнаны из плоти,
Здесь коротают век в забвенье и дремоте
До новой бренности, до будущей тюрьмы.
Заквасят молоко для старика слепого,
Овечью шерсть прядут и забывают слово —
Постылой речи плен, в котором вечно мы:

"Земля, не отнимай моих любимых!
Вода, не отбирай моих любимых!…
Пойдет моя душа, растеряна и боса,
Туда, где есть подруги ей …"

Спеленут сыр травою,
Старик качает мертвой головою,
Солончаки в степи — как пыльные колеса …

To Ovid

The shepherd is blind, the sheep are made of stone.
Ravines are smoking, dug out by the sun.
They trickle with the milk of earth-foremother.
The limit of our fates:
The wells, ravines,
The steadfast little swamps of sheep's urine,
Salt-flats and steppe …
So — till the age is over.

For sure, those souls who had to flee the body
Here while away their age, oblivious and drowsy,
Till new impermanence, until the future prison.
They'll sour the milk the blind old man has poured,
They spin the sheep's wool and forget the word —
Cold speech's grip, to which our age is given:

"Oh earth, don't take away my loved ones!
Oh water, don't pick out my loved ones!
My soul shall set off, barefoot and confused,
Someplace where there are friends for her …"

The cheese is wrapped in grass,
The dead head of the old man shakes at last,
Salt flats and steppe — just like wheels in the dust …

Aleksandr Tkachenko
Александр Ткаченко

Aleksandr Petrovich Tkachenko was born in Simferopol in 1945. He holds a degree in philology and was a member of the Writers' Union of the Soviet Union. After finishing his education he played for various Moscow and Leningrad soccer teams for seven years, until an injury forced him to retire from professional sports. Tkachenko's work has appeared in many major Soviet and Russian literary journals such as *Iunost'*, *Novyi mir*, *Oktiabr'*, *Ogonek*, and *Literaturnaia gazeta*. He published his first book of poetry, *Po pervomu svetu* (By First Light) in 1972; this was followed by six more volumes, the most recent of which, *Koren' kvadratnyi iz minus ia* (The Square Root of Minus I), appeared in 1998. He has participated in numerous international poetry festivals — in Moscow, Philadelphia, Palermo, San Francisco, and Boston — and is a member of the Russian PEN club.

Aleksandr Tkachenko currently lives in Moscow, where he is director general of the Russian PEN Center.

Translations by Maia Tekses

Как Тысяча Других

А дома бросишься в постель открытую
и даже не увидишь снов плохих,
а утром ты похож на статую отрытую,
как тысяча других, как тысяча других.

Ты втиснешься в вагон, как будто в том заветный,
среди людей по крови неродных,
поедешь на работу такой же незаметный,
как тысяча других, как тысяча других.

А там доверчивый вполне
к словам поверхностей любых,
ты — камень в стенке, ветка на столбе,
как тысяча других, как тысяча других!

Не думай, человек, со всех сторон сосед,
что случаем из тысяч дорогих,
ты любишь женщину совсем не так, как все, —
как тысяча других, как тысяча других.

Нет, это не обидно. Тебя мой взгляд отыщет,
по водам жизни, какие б ни прошли круги,
ведь ты, ведь ты один из тыщи,
как тысяча других, как тысяча других!

Like Thousands of Others

Once home, you'll throw yourself on an unmade bed
And sleep undisturbed by any nightmares,
And in the morning you rise like an unearthed statue,
Just like thousands of others, thousands of others.

You squeeze onto the tram, as if embracing fate,
among people definitely not your brothers,
you go to work completely unnoticed
Like thousands of others, thousands of others.

And there, completely trusting in words
Anyone your superior utters,
you are a stone in the wall, a twig on the tree
Like thousands of others, thousands of others!

Don't think, human, a neighbor on all sides,
That by chance among a thousand lovers,
You love your woman any differently from
Thousands of others, yes, thousands of others.

Don't take offense. My eyes will find you out,
whatever ripples churn among life's eddies,
you see, you see you are one among a thousand,
Like thousands of others, thousands of others!

Гравюра

В тот день осенний, когда зима
уже стояла в окнах, как слеза,
и медленная муха
              меж стекол умирала,
когда в кварталах еще туман
бродил полночной белой лошадью,
наутро обещая марсианскую теплынь,
я жил тобой…

И было мне отпущено немало —
надежда и печаль, и сон среди бессонниц,
и понимание природы
всех неустроенных вещей…
В тот день осенний тикал дождь,
мотоциклист свербил в глубинах ночи,
и люди шли навстречу людям
с безжалостью друг к другу,
я ждал…

Но шло все, проходило,
из ничего и в ничего происходило,
все было на местах своих,
я жил тобой, я ждал излома,
мартен, засыпанный металлоломом
школьным…
И было больно мне. И вольно
так жить тобой еще
неосязаемой, духовной,
в толпе столичной растворенной
вплоть до платформы Курского вокзала
и зала ожиданья времени протяжного…

An Engraving

On that day in autumn, when winter
already stood outside the window like a teardrop,
and a slow fly
        was dying between the panes,
when fog still roamed the neighborhood
like a white horse at midnight,
with the promise of a warm Martian day in the morning
you were my life ...

And indeed I had been absolved of much —
hope and sorrow, dreams in the midst of insomnia,
and an understanding of the nature
of all disorderly things ...
On that day in autumn the rain ticked,
a motorcyclist revved up in the depth of night,
and people walked to meet people
with no pity for one another,
I was waiting ...

But everything came, went on by,
passed from nothingness into nothingness
everything in its own place,
you were my life, I waited for some break,
Like a smelting furnace sprinkled with metal scraps.
I was in pain. And still
willing to live this way
for the sake of an impalpable, spiritual you,
melted into the metropolitan crowd
right up to the plaform of the Kursky train station
and the endless time of a waiting room ...

Да, времени протяжного,
где пиво пьют, сдувая пену,
студент с подружкою
такою современной,
что до сих пор в потертых джинсах,
когда давно уже не модно это…

В тот день осенний
пыль торопилась залечь в укромные места,
чтобы в дождях не раствориться, не исчезнуть…
Я ждал тебя, я жил тобой,
а ты все это не со мной
переживала…

Yes, of time dragged out,
where, having blown the foam off his beer,
a student drinks with his girlfriend
so up-to-date,
she's still in shabby blue jeans,
when that fashion passed long ago ...

On that day in autumn
the dust hurried to settle in secluded corners,
in order not to be dissolved in the rain, not to disappear ...
I waited for you, I lived for you,
but you lived through all of this
with someone other than me ...

Стадион "Динамо," 1980 Год

И довоенный стадион и довоенная игра
опять вошли в послевоенного меня,
и хоть вовсю горят прожектора —
все в свете олимпийского огня!

Все в свете олимпийского явленья
через века на современных перегонах,
и возвращение на круги, и обновленье
слегка уставшей формы стадиона.

И в поручнях трибун — я чувствовал руками —
тысячелетия теплели. И два тайма,
казалось, продолжаются веками,
и тайна времени — уже не тайна.

Она была передо мной. На склоне дня,
раскрытого до зелени футбола —
вся в свете олимпийского огня,
вся в свете долгожданнейшего года.

Dynamo Stadium, 1980

A prewar stadium and a prewar game,
again entered into postwar me,
and although the searchlights burn their utmost —
everything seems lit by an Olympic flame.

Everything in the light of the Olympic phenomenon
shining through the centuries down the tracks
everything come round again, and renovation
of a slightly dilapidated stadium.

And on the rails of the bleachers — I felt with my hands —
Millennia burned. And the two halves,
It seemed, took centuries to play,
and the mystery of time was no longer a mystery.

She was in front of me. In the decline of the day,
Where the football field opened up green —
all in the light of the Olympic flame,
all in the light of a goal long awaited.

Битва

Рванется конь, ноздрями черен,
под всадником, под веком свирепея.
Промчится век и далее так спорен,
а всадник —
пригнуться не успеет.

Вонзится с хрустом в грудь чужую
стрела иль острие копья.
Через столетье кто-то нарисует
паденье всадника с коня.

И понесется конь с пустым седлом
по полю самых острых трав,
почуя кровь и битвы перелом…
Он конь без всадника,
                со всадником — кентавр.

У пропасти он долго будет ржать
и, череп свой к созвездиям подъемля,
сорвется вниз, не охлаждая жар,
в который раз не понимая землю.

Battle

Its nostrils black, the horse plunges
Raging under its rider, under the age.
The age flashes by just as rambunctious,
but the rider —
can not jump off or dodge.

An arrow or a sharp spearhead will pierce
crunching into a stranger's breast.
In the next century someone will paint
the rider falling from his destry,

And the empty-saddled steed will bolt
through a field of thorns and sawgrass,
scenting blood and the turning-point of battle …
With his rider, a centaur —
                without, only a horse.

He will give a long whinny at the brink
and, raising to the constellations his skull,
Plunge down the cliff, still steaming,
without ever understanding the world.

Genrikh Sapgir

Генрих Сапгир

Genrikh Veniamovich Sapgir. Poet, prose writer and scriptwriter. Sapgir was born in 1928 in Biysk, Altai, but has lived most of his life in Moscow. He was a member of the famous Lianozovo group in the 1960s and 70s, which also included such dissident poets and artists as Brodsky, Zverev, Ilya Kabakov, Oscar Rabin, and Ernst Neizvestny. He also led the avant-garde poets' group known as "Konkret" (which included such poets as Edvard Limonov and Vsevolod Nekrasov) and organized exhibitions of non-conformist art in his apartment. One of these exhibitions also featured Sapgir's own "Sonnets on shirts" (*Sonety na rubashkakh*) — literally poems written on shirts and exhibited alongside his friends' paintings. Although Sapgir's writings for children were highly successful and even earned him inclusion in the Writers' Union in 1968, his poetry was published almost exclusively in *samizdat* and abroad, mainly in France and Germany, until the late 1980s. He is now widely published and immensely popular in his own country; his works appear regularly in major literary journals such as *Novyi Mir, Znamia, Oktiabr'* and others. Genrikh Sapgir is the author of eight poetry collections.

Translations by J. Kates

Из альбома

Фото: на холме желтый дом с белой колоннадой
Фотография учеников колледжа — третий слева
Любительское: с девушкой на фоне чего-то
Он и еще кто-то в пустой комнате — угол окна

Фото на документ: выпучил глаза как рыба
Фото: не похож на себя — голый весь в мыле
Тот же вид — другой ракурс — пьян или не по себе
Фото с закрытыми глазами — убит или притворяется

Переплыв: какие-то люди поджидают у садовой ограды
Дорожка в парке — солнце — вот-вот появится
Крупно: лицо — мелькание — ладонь лезет на объектив

Где? Кто снимал? Почему во мне напечаталось?
Чья жизнь? Чья смерть? Втоптан в глину брелок с ключом
Фотография смуглой девушки с белыми волосами

From an Album

A photo: on a hill a yellow house, white portico
A picture of the classmates from some school — third from the left
An amateur job: with a girl in some kind of background
He and someone else in an empty room — the corner of a window

A passport photo: eyes wide open like a fish
A photo: doesn't look like him — all naked and wrought up
The same shot — foreshortened — drunk or not himself
A photo with closed eyes — dead or faking it

Skimming along: some people are waiting in a garden
A path in a park — sun — look what suddenly
appears: a face — just a glimpse — a hand climbs on the lens

Where? Who took them? And why this impression on me?
Whose life? Whose death? A keyring trampled in the clay
A snapshot of a swarthy young woman with white hair

Псалом 1

1. Блажен муж иже не иде на сборяища нечестивых
как-то
не посещает собраний ЖАКТа
и кооператива
не сидит за столом президиума —
просто сидит дома

2. Соседи поднимают ор —
не вылезает в коридор
(не стоит на пути грешных)

3. Три страшных
удара
в дверь
— Убил! Убил! — из коридора

4. Лампу зажги
Хочешь — можешь прилечь
о законе ЕГО
размышляй день и ночь
сосредоточь …

Psalm 1

1. Blessed is the man that walketh not in the assembly of the wicked
somehow
nor attendeth meetings of the Housing Society
nor of the co-operative
nor sitteth at the table of the presidium —
but simply stayeth home

2. The neighbors take up ar —
he crawleth not into the stairwell
(nor standeth in the way of sinners)

3. Three terrible
blows
on the door
— Murder! Murder! — from the stairwell

4. Light a lamp
you want — you may lie down
meditate day and night
in HIS law
concentrate …

5. И вот —
дерево
омываемое потоками вод:
и ствол
и лист
и цвет
и плод

6. Весь от корней волос
до звезд
ты медленно уходишь в рост ...

7. Внизу подростки — гам и свист
бьют железом по железу
один на другом
ездят верхом в пыли
— Дай эму! дай!
— ай!
— Пли! —
две пули в фотокарточку

8. — Тань! А, Тань!

9. Встань
закрой форточку

5. Behold —
a tree
washed by rivers of water:
trunk
leaf
blossom
fruit

6. From the roots of your hair
up to the stars
you slowly stretch to your full height …

7. Down below the uproar and whistling of youth
they beat iron on iron
one on another
they go galloping in the dust
— Let him have it! At him!
— Got him!
— Shoot! —
two shots into a photograph

8. — Tanya! Tanya!

9. Get up
and shut the window

Псалом 136

1. На реках Вавилонских сидели мы
            и плакали
— О нори — нора!
— О нори — нора руоло!
— Юде юде пой пой! Веселее!
смеялись пленившие нас
— Ер зангт ви ди айнеге Нахтигаль
— Вейли башар! Вейли байон!
— Юде юде пляши! Гоп — Гоп!

2. Они стояли сложив руки на автоматах
— О Яхве!
их собаки — убийцы глядели на нас
            с любопытством
— О лейви баарам боцы Цион
на земле чужой!

3. Жирная копоть наших детей
оседала на лицах
и мы уходили
в трубу крематория
дымом — в небо

4. Попомни Господи сынам Едомовым
день Ерусаима
Когда они говорили
— Цершторен! приказ № 125
— Фернихтен! Приказ № 126
— Фертельген! № 127

Psalm 137

1. By the rivers of Babylon there we sat down and wept
— O nori — nora!
— O nori — nora ruolo!
— Sing Jew sing! Make merry! —
For they that carried us away laughed
— Er singt wie die einige Nachtigall
— Veyli bashar! Veyli bayon!
— Dance Jew dance! Hop — hop!

2. They stood with their hands on their automatics
— O Yahweh!
their killer-dogs looked us over with curiosity
— O levi baaram batzi Tzion
in a strange land!

3. The greasy soot of our children
settled on our faces
and we went up
the crematory chimney
in smoke — to heaven

4. Remember o Lord the children of Edom
in the day of Jerusalem
who said
— Zerstören! Order No. 125
— Vernichten! Order No. 126
— Vertilgen! No. 127

5. Дочери Вавилона расхаживали среди нас
поскрипывая лакированными сапожками —
шестимесячные овечки
с немецкими овчарками
— О нори — нора! руоло!
Хлыст! хлыст! —
Ершиссен

6. Блажен кто возьмет и разобьет
   младенцев ваших о камень

5. The daughters of Babylon walked among us
their lacquered boots squeaking —
six-month old lambkins
with German Shepherds —
O nori — nora! ruolo!
The whip! The whip!
Erschießen

6. Happy shall he be who taketh and dasheth
   your little ones against the stones.

Дионис

Накануне праздника Сбора Картофеля
На главной улице Города
Привлекая всеобщее внимание
Появлялся смуглый юноша
В венке из виноградных листьев
Мальчишки бегут глядеть. Женщины
Становятся на цыпочки. Кто-то
Выронил верток. Резко
Тормозит голубой автобус
— Смотрите смотрите! артисты
И верно — по улице имени
Великого Основателя
Двигается процессия
Вида непристойного и дикого
Ухмыляются рогатые бородатые
Щеки и носы раскрашены свеклой
Груди и зады едва прикрыты
Беспокойно — что они изображают?
И зачем их так ужасно гримируют?
Там какие-то растерзанные бабы
На осле везут лысого пьянчужку
И выплясывают и вопят в небо
Алые от флагов и полотнищ
— Эвоэ Эвоэ!
Что-то в Городе заметно изменилось
Люди побежали в магазины
И как будто крянули с двух сторон вразнобой
Духовые оркестры

У прилавка винного отдела
Напирают — чуть не дымятся
За стеклом — две продавщицы
Тычут им серебро и бумажки

Dionysus

On the eve of the Festival of The Potato Harvest
On the main street of the City
Appeared an olive-skinned youth
Who attracted everybody's attention
By his garland of grape leaves.
Little boys run to stare. Women
Stand a-tiptoe. Somebody
Has dropped a package. Suddenly
A blue bus puts on the brakes
— Take a look take a look! Circus
In town! — along the street
Named after the Great Founder
Moves a procession
With an aspect wild, obscene
Horned and bearded faces grin
Cheeks and noses colored beet-red
Breasts and backsides barely covered at all
Nervously — who do they think they are?
And why so frightfully made-up?
Over there some harum-scarum women
Are leading a bald drunkard on a donkey
Dancing and howling to a sky
Scarlet with banners and flags
— Evoë! Evoë!
Something in the City has noticeably changed
People have run into the shops
As though from all sides suddenly burst out
Ghostly orchestras

They converge on the counter
Of the wine department — they can hardly breathe
Behind the glass — two salesgirls
They prod them with silver and papers
And these respond by shoving bottles

Без конца — серебро и бумажки
Без конца — зеленые бутылки
Что за суетливая спешка?
Что за непонятная жажда?
Будто Весь многовековый Город
С парками вокзалами домами
С памятниками в бронзе и камне
Разом в этот день решил напиться

А на площади имени Поэта
В свое время
Сочинившего Оду Государству
Уже — драка

Развернулась как на Экране
(кадр)
Кто-то гонится за кем-то через площадь
(кадр)
Двое лупят парня в кожаной куртке
(кадр)
Лицо зашедшееся в крике
(кадр)
Человек в разорванном костюме
Шарит очки на асфальте
(кадр)
Один обливается кровью
А другой его поспешно уводит
(кадр)
Башмак давит очки с хрустом …
Завывает желтая машина
И мигает синей вертушкой
Юноша с античной улыбкой

An endless stream of silver and paper
An endless stream of green bottles
What kind of hurly-burly is this?
What unheard of thirst is this?
As if the whole centuries-old City
With parks railway stations houses
With monuments of stone and bronze
As one today went on a sudden tear

And on the square named after the Poet
Who composed
In his own era an Ode to the State
Already a fistfight

Has unrolled as if on a screen
(cut to)
One guy chases someone through the square
(cut to)
Two guys strip a fellow of his leather jacket
(cut to)
A face caught in a scream
(cut to)
A man in a torn suit
Is groping for his eyeglasses on the pavement
(cut to)
One is bathed in blood
And another quickly leads him away
(cut to)
A shoe crunches eyeglasses underfoot. . .
A yellow car begins to howl
And its revolving blue light starts blinking
And watching over all of this
Is the young man with the antique smile

И повсюду где он проходит
С козлоногой и блаженной свитой
Водка льется в праздные глотки
Красное вино течет по лицам

Песни крики драки поцелуи
И творится что-то неприличное
Явно непредусмотренное
Правительственной Комиссией
По организации Праздника

Впрочем кто-то там распорядился …
Но плющем опутало машины
И в руках блюстителя порядка
Превратились дубинки в тирсы
Автоматы — в толстые бутылки
И стреляют пробками и пеной
Лопаются звезды фейерверка!

А на площади имени Поэта
В свое время
Оказавшего услугу Государству —
Синий дым прожекторов
Топчется и двигается площадь

Люди наслаждаются свободой
Инженер танцует с наядой
Плосконосый сатир — с иностранкой
А военный танцует с вакханкой
Продавщица осла обнимает
Ее в танце осел понимает
А студентка на фавне повисла
Ах как много в движениях смысла

And everywhere he passes
With his blissful, goat-horned retinue
Vodka pours down holiday throats
Red wine courses along their faces

Songs, screams scuffles kisses
And something indecent is being created
Obviously unexpected
By the Government Commission
For organizing the Festival

All the same, somebody issued the proper orders ...
Cars are entangled in ivy
And in the hands of the long arm of the law
Billyclubs have been transformed into thyrsi
Automatic weapons into jeroboams
Shooting corks and foam
The pyrotechnical stars exploding!

And on the square named after the Poet
Who displayed
In his own era his service to the State —
The blue smoke of searchlights
Whirls around and the square moves

The people revel in their freedom
An engineer is dancing with a naiad
A snubnosed satyr with a foreign lady
While a soldier dances with a Bacchante
A salesgirl embraces the donkey
In the dance the donkey understands her
A schoolgirl hung on a faun
Oh, there is so much meaning in movement

С нимфой топчется пьяный рабочий
Нимфа пьяного дядю щекочет
Ее ловит взъерошенный дядя
И хватает другую не глядя
И танцуют какие-то твари
И хохочут какие-то хари
И кричит Калибан с Магадана
Вскидывая нелепые ноги
— Свобода! Свобода! Свобода!
Девочки из ресторана
Обнимают и уводят лысого Силена

С фасада среднего дома
Памятным лицом пятиметровым
Смотрит Основатель Государства
А у памятника Поэту
Улеглась огромная кошка
Поблескивая лунными зрачками

И танцуют люди и птицы
Лилипуты крысы и мокрицы!

Но безумье и ночь на исходе
Прочь уходит длинная пантера
А за нею — фавны и менады

Опустела площадь
На дощатой эстраде
Пианист уснул за пианино
Барабанщик спит на барабане
Пьяный музыкант
Вливает в медное горло
Своей тубы

A drunken workman stamps around with a nymph
The nymph is tickling the drunken fellow
A dishevelled fellow catches her
And grabs at another without looking
And all kinds of weird creatures dance together
And all kinds of weird mugs are laughing
And Caliban screams from Magadan
Kicking up ridiculous legs
— Freedom! Freedom! Freedom!
Waitresses from a restaurant
Embrace Silenus and lead him away

On the facade of an ordinary house
The Founder of the State is watching
With his monumental five-metre face

And at the statue of the Poet
A gigantic cat with gleaming moonlike eyes
Has settled down

And the people are dancing and birds
And lilliputians rats and woodlice!

But the madness and night are coming to an end
A sleek panther slinks off
Carrying fauns and mænads

The square has emptied out
On the wooden stage
The pianist has dozed off at his piano
The drummer sleeps on his drum
A drunken musician
Can not recall which bottle it is
He empties down the brass throat

Уж не помнит которую бутылку
— Пей приятель!
Лишь один еще стоит качаясь
Дергает струну на контрабасе
И струна гудит в пустое небо
— ДИОНИС!
— ДИОНИС!

Of his tuba
— Drink up friend!
Only one is still standing, swaying back and forth
He strums a string of his double bass
And the string hums into an empty heaven
— DIONYSUS!
— DIONYSUS!

Mikhail Yeryomin

Михаил Еремин

Mikhail Fyodorovich Yeryomin was born in the Northern Caucasus in 1937 but grew up in Leningrad, where he studied at the Philology Department of Leningrad State University. Thereafter he worked as a professional dramaturg and translator of poetry. A participant in underground culture, Yeryomin saw few of his poems published in his homeland during the Soviet period, but instead turned to émigré journals such as *Kontinent* and *Ekho* to publish his works. A volume of poetry, *Stikhotvorenia* (Poems), appeared in the United States in 1986, and in 1991 a book of Yeryomin's selected works was published in Moscow. His poems almost always consist of only eight lines and often feature foreign-language words (Latin, Hindi, hieroglyphics, and so on) and mathematical and chemical formulas.

Translations by J. Kates

∼

Боковитые зёрна премудрости,
Изначальную форму пространства,
Всероссийскую святость и смутность
И болот журавлиную пряность
Отыскивать в осенней рукописи,
Где следы оставила слякоть,
Где листы, словно платья луковицы,
Слезы прячут в складках.

1957

Polyhedral kernels of wisdom,
Primordial form of space.
All-Russian holiness, hodgepodge
And the herony tang of swampland
To be searched out in autumnal writing,
Where the slush has left its traces,
Where leaves, like the skirts of an onion
Conceal tears in their creases.

1957

~

Сшивает портниха на швейной машинке,
Подобно дождю, голубое с зеленым,
Дождю, который окном изломан,
Как лодкою камышинки.
Гром за окном покашливает.
Капли дождя к стеклу прилипают,
Полузеленая каждая
И полуголубая.

1957

The seamstress stitches on a sewing machine,
Light blue with deep green, like rain,
Rain broken by the window
As reeds are broken by a little boat.
A thunderstorm coughs outside the window.
Raindrops stick to the glass,
Every one of them half green
And half light blue.

1957

По-за кряквой ходит селезень,
То прищелкнет клювом плоским,
То крылом взмахнет, как сеятель,
Глазом ласковым поблескивая,
Чтоб, живущий возле заводи,
Мальчуган нашел гнездо,
Чтоб яишенные завтраки
Подавала мать на стол.

1958

The drake pays court to the duck,
He snaps his flat beak,
He swings his wing like a man sowing seed,
His affectionate eye glitters now and again,
So that the good boy who lives
Near the creek can find the nest,
So his mother can serve up eggs
At the breakfast table.

1958

~

Y ❋ ⟨экскаватор-symbol⟩ ⟨справедливость⟩ ⟨вертолет⟩

Гелиоптер гостиницы высотной,
Как перистое небо над поблекшим
Пришкольным сквером.
Владелицы осенних ранцев
Трепещут над сетями "классов."
Уносит вдаль летучки кленов
Поток асфальта, огибая сквер.

1971

Y — антенна

❋ — лотос (др.-египтск.)

⟨символ⟩ — экскаватор

⟨символ⟩ — справедливость (др.-египтск.)

⟨символ⟩ — вертолет

Y ✿ ⚖ ⚒ 🚁

Helioptér of a skyscraper hotel,
Like a feathery sky over a faded
Public park beside a school.
The owners of autumnal knapsacks
Tremble over networks of hopscotch.
A flow of asphalt circling the park
Carries the maple wings far away.

1971

Y — antenna

✿ — lotus (ancient Egyptian)

⚖ — backhoe

⚒ — justice (ancient Egyptian)

🚁 — helicopter

~

Над сквером дом — букет вечерних окон.
Собор от мира сквером огражден.
Лист золотой намотан, словно локон,
На ту же ветвь, которой был рожден.
Осенний день, на грех и слезы падкий,
Молчанье и раскаянье поймет,
Оставив пепел от письма в лампадке
И в медальоне дьявола помет.

1972

The house over the garden is a bouquet of evening windows.
A cathedral fenced off from the world by a garden.
A golden leaf is wound like a ringlet
On the very twig that gave it birth.
An autumn day, susceptible to sin and tears,
Will understand silence and repentance,
Ashes of a letter have been left in the icon-lamp
And devil's dung in the medallion.

1972

Фонарь. Отсутствие. Аптека.
И ртутна наледь на металле
Патрульного автомобиля. В тарлатановых тюниках
Метель разучивает па сколопендреллы.
А полуптица-полутяжесть
Белее крыльев, явственных во сне.
И ни задатка, и ни предостережения
Не отразили святочные зеркала.

1986

Street lamp. Something missing. Drugstore.
And an icy crust like mercury on the metal
Of a patrol car. In tarlatan tutus
The snow storm studies the dance-step of scolopendrella.
But semibird and semiburden
Is whiter than wings distinct in a dream.
And Yuletide mirrors reflected
Neither good luck nor a warning.

1986

Sergey Stratanovsky
Сергей Стратановский

Sergey Georgievich Stratanovsky was born in Leningrad
in 1944. He received a degree in Russian language and liter-
ature from Leningrad University in 1968 and began writ-
ing poetry that same year. An active participant in Lenin-
grad unofficial culture in the 1970s and 80s, Stratanovsky
edited the samizdat journal *Obvodnyi kanal* and was a
member of the unofficial literary group "Club 81." His
work was first published in the Paris émigré journal *Apol-
lon* in 1977, but it was not until 1986, with the publication
of Club 81's anthology, *Krug* (Circle), that he was pub-
lished in his own country. Since then, however, his work
has frequently appeared in Russian literary journals. His
first collection of poems, *Stikhi* (Poems, 1993), was award-
ed the Tsarskoe Selo Prize in 1994. Sergei Stratanovsky
continues to write criticism and essays and works as a bib-
liographer at the Russian National Library in St. Peters-
burg.

Translations by J. Kates

~

Ленинградская лестница,
    щи,
    коммунальная дверь,
Провода от звонков:
    Иванов, Розенцвейг, Иванов,
В шапке снега бескровного,
    с холода,
    зябкими пальцами спичку —
В коммунальную бестолочь, выморочь,
    в джунгли обид в коридоре.
Там женщина плачет в смятенье и горе,
В норе бытия
    без любви и без света.
И ни единым словом не согрета.

A Leningrad stairwell
   cheap cabbage soup,
   a communal doorway,
Doorbell wires:
   Ivanov, Rosenzweig, Ivanov,
In a hat of anemic snow,
   from the cold,
   with chilly fingers a match —
Into the communal muddle, exhaustion,
   into that jumble of grievances the corridor.
There a woman weeps in confusion and sorrow,
In the burrow of her existence
   without love and without light.
Unwarmed by a single word.

Геростраты

А мы — Геростраты Геростратовичи
Мы — растратчики
    мирового огня
Поджигатели складов сырья
И хранилищ плодоовощей.
И вот со спичками идем
Осенней ночью, под дождем
Мы — разрушители вещей
Мы ищем страшного экстаза
А там, у жизни на краю
Живет она, овощебаза
За Черной речкой, с небом рядом,
Как Афродита с толстым задом
Овощебаба во хмелю.
О ней мы грезили в постели,
И вот она на самом деле
И роща пушкинской дуэли
Сияет рядом с ней
И Стиксов греческих черней
Здесь речка Черная течет,
Но тот, кто пел, был счастлив тот
Не умер тот и не умрет
Не для него, для нас течет
Забвений страшная вода
Осенней ночью, под дождем
Из жалкой жизни мы уйдем
Неведомо куда.
Беги от ужаса забвений,
Беги, как некогда Евгений
От бронзы скачущей по мусорной земле
Туда, где в слякоти и мгле
Лежит мочащаяся база
Пустые овощи для города храня

Herostratos and Herostratos

And we are all
Herostratos son of Herostratos,
Disseminators
    of a worldwide fire,
Arsonists of treasuries of raw material
And storehouses of the harvest.
See how we strike our matches
On a fall night, out in the rain —
We the destroyers of things,
Seeking a terrible ecstasy.
But out there, beyond the Black Stream
Up against heaven, on the very edge
Of life, the vegetable bin
Like fat-rumped Aphrodite
lies drunk on her own tomamatoes.
We lay on our beds dreaming of her
And here she is, as a matter of fact,
And the grove where Pushkin fought
Shines in her vicinity,
And here the Black Stream flows
Even blacker than any Grecian Styx —
Happy the one who drank from its current,
He did not, and will not die.
Not for him, but for us
Flows the terrible water of oblivion.
On a fall night, out in the rain,
We will abandon this wretched life
For an unknown destination.
Run from that terror of oblivion,
Run, as Evgeny once
Fled the Bronze Horseman in a trashed land.
Wherever in slush and mist
Urinous warehouses stand,
An empty harvest for the city stores,

И как любовного экстаза,
Ждет геростратова огня,
А мы — порыв, а мы — угроза
Крадемся тихие как мышь,
И словно огненная роза
Ты засияешь и сгоришь.
Ведь мы — Геростраты Геростратовичи
Расточители греческого первоогня
Поджигатели складов сырья
И овощехранилищ.

Like all-embracing ecstasy,
waits for the Herostratic brand.
We are a sudden squall, a menace,
We are quiet thieves like mice.
And like the fiery rose
You will ignite, and perish.
Well then,
        we are all
Herostratos son of Herostratos,
Wastrels of the Promethean fire,
Arsonists of treasuries of raw material
And storehouses of the harvest.

Террорист

“Смертопощечина
           ангелу сдобного рая
Сексопаркам щебечущим,
           завлекалищам дево-хрустальным
Порно-норам зияющим,
           мессам, щекочущим Бога
Их благоденствию, их неподкупному небу
их демократии, партиям, телевизорам, виллам на взморье
Смертопощечина, ненависть, ненависть … месть”

Ищут убийцу: Кто он? Араб? Итальянец?
Немец? Монгол? Выдает варианты компьютер
Кто он, губивец?
           Человек или призрак из книги
Век назад сочиненной
           в Петербурге промозглом, больном
Порожденье подполья
           фантом достоевского мозга

The Terrorist

"A death slap
  to the angel of a buttery paradise,
To twittering sex-parks,
  and a string of seductions,
To gaping porno-burrows,
  to church-services, to the tickling of God,
To their common weal, incorruptible heaven,
their democracy, parties, television sets and seaside villas
A death-slap, abomination, abomination … vengeance."

They're hunting for the killer: Who can he be? Arab? Italian?
German? Mongol? The computer spits out possibilities
Who is he, this citizen of destruction?
  A real person — or a ghost
From a work of a century ago
  in sodden, febrile Petersburg
A confection from underground
  a phantom out of the mind of Dostoevsky

Olga Sedakova
Ольга Седакова

Olga Aleksandrovna Sedakova. Poet, prose writer and literary critic. Born in Moscow in 1949, Sedakova holds degrees from Moscow State University and the Institute of Slavic and Balkan Studies, and currently teaches in the Department of Philology of Moscow University. She is considered one of the foremost Russian poets writing today and is also an outstanding literary scholar. Sedakova published her first poems at the age of eleven, in a collection entitled *Deti pishut stikhi* (Children Writing Poetry, 1960). Her next collection of poetry, *Vorota, okna, arki* (Gates, Windows, Arches), was published in Paris in 1986. Although she was primarily a samizdat poet, Sedakova's work has been published more recently in journals such as *Druzhba narodov, Novyi Mir, Volga,* and *Laterna magika.* Several of her poems are included in *Third Wave: The New Russian Poetry* and in the anthology *Contemporary Russian Poetry* (1993), translated by G. S. Smith. She has recently received the Paris Prize for a Russian Poet (1991) and a Schiller Fund Award (1993).

Translations by Catriona Kelly

Женская Фигура

Отвернувшись,
в широком большом покрывале
стоит она. Кажется, тополь
рядом с ней.
Это кажется. Тополя нет.
Да она бы сама охотно в него превратилась
по примеру преданья —
лишь бы не слушать:
— Что ты там видишь?
— Что я вижу, безумные люди?
Я вижу открытое море. Легко догадаться.
Море — и все. Или этого мало,
чтобы мне вечно скорбеть, а вам — досаждать
   любопытством?

Female Figure

In a long wide veil
she stands, turning her face
away: that looks like a poplar
beside her;
looks deceive; there is no poplar there.
But she herself would gladly become one,
as the old legends have it,
if she could only stop hearing:
"What can you see there?"
"What can I see there, you madmen?
The ocean, can you not guess?
The ocean, and nothing more. Or is this not enough,
that I should be grieving forever, and you
    pestering me with your questions?"

Кузнечик и сверчок

The poetry of Earth is never dead.
— Keats

Поэзия земли не умирает.
И здесь, на Севере, когда повалит снег,
кузнечик замолчит. А вьюга заиграет
и забренчит сверчок, ослепший человек.
Но ум его проворен, как рапира.
Всегда настроена его сухая лира,
Натянут важный волосок.
Среди невидимого пира —
он тоже гость, он Демодок.
И словно целый луг забрался на шесток.

Поэзия земли не так богата:
ребенок малый да старик худой,
кузнечик и сверчок откуда-то куда-то
бредут по лестнице одной —
и путь огромен, как заплата
на всей прорехе слуховой.
Гремя сердечками пустыми,
там ножницами завитыми
все щелкают над гривами златыми
коней нездешних, молодых —
и в пустоту стучат сравненья их.
Но хватит и того, кто в трубах завывает,
кто бледные глаза из вьюги поднимает,
кто луг обходит на заре
    и серебро свое теряет —
и всё находит в их последнем серебре.

Поэзия земли не умирает,
но если знает, что умрет, —
челнок надежный выбирает,
бросает весла и плывет —

The Grasshopper and the Cricket

The poetry of Earth is never dead.
Keats

The poetry of earth can never die.
Here in the North, when once the first snow falls,
the grasshopper is still, but blizzards start to whirl
and crickets start to strum like men gone blind.
A cricket's mind is searching as a sword;
his dry-grass lyre is kept in tune,
each vital thread so tightly strung.
A guest at feasts beyond our sight
Demodocus, the cricket sits
with a whole meadow rustling on his perch.

The poetry of earth is not so rich:
a scrawny ancient and a tiny child,
the hopper and the cricket climb together
from somewhere into somewhere on a ladder,
their journey stretching like a patch
across the gash that hearing made.
Rattling their empty hearts the while,
they clip their scissors' curving blades
above the springing gilded manes
of horses from the underworld:
analogies resound in emptiness.

Enough to wail like sounding brass,
to raise your whitened eyes from blizzards
and wander through the paling fields,
    losing your silver in the grass
yet finding it all in their, that ultimate, silver.

и что бы дальше ни случилось,
надежда рухнула вполне
и потому не разучилась
летать по слуховой волне.
Скажи мне, что под небесами
любезнее любимым небесам,
чем плыть с открытыми глазами
на дне, как раненый Тристан?…

Поэзия земли — отважнейшая скука.
На наковаленках таинственного звука
кузнечик и сверчок сковали океан.

The poetry of earth can never die,
but if it knows that it must go
it picks a hopeful-seeming boat
casts loose the oars, and starts to glide.
No matter what might happen now,
hope has vanished clean away,
which means it's not forgotten how
to skim the crest of hearing's waves.
Tell me what thing below the skies
more pleases heaven's pleasantness
than sailing with eyes fixed and wide
in the deep, like the wounded Tristan?

The poetry of earth is most heroic boredom;
and on the anvils of mysterious sound
the grasshopper, the cricket, have beaten out an ocean.

Пятые стансы

I

Большая вещь — сам себе приют.
Глубокий скит или широкий пруд,
таинственная рыба в глубине
и праведник, о невечернем дне
читающий урочные Часы.
Она сама — сосуд своей красы.

2

Как в раковине ходит океан —
сердечный клапан времени, капкан
на мягких лапах, чудище в мешке,
сокровище в снотворном порошке —
так в разум мой, в его скрипучий дом
она идет с волшебным фонарем…

3

Не правда ли, минувшая строфа
как будто перегружена? Лафа
тому, кто наяву бывал влеком
всех образов сребристым косяком,
несущим нас на острых плавниках
туда, где мы и всё, что с нами, — прах.

4

Я только в скобках замечаю: свет —
достаточно таинственный предмет,
чтоб говорить бог ведает о чем,
чтоб речь, как пыль, пронзенная лучом,
крутилась мелко, путано, едва…
Но значила — прозрачность вещества.

Fifth Stanzas. De Arte Poetica

1

A great thing is a refuge for itself,
a broad deep pond or Trappist's far-off cell,
a mythic fish that swims the hidden depths,
a righteous man, reading his Book of Hours
concerning the day that has no evening;
a vessel holding its own beauty in.

2

And as the ocean swims inside a shell —
a valve in the heart of time, a trap as well,
walking on velvet paws, a marvel in a bag,
a treasure hidden in a sleeping draught,
so in my mind, inside this creaking house,
she goes, and holds her magic lantern up ...

3

But tell me, don't you think the verse above
is crammed too full? All right, it's well enough
for one who feels the pull, outside his dreams,
of images aslant with silvery gleams,
carrying us on pointed fins to where
we and all we have known are dust, no more.

4

The light (for let me note in brackets this)
is something we might call a mystery,
speaking at will of God knows what,
whilst speech, like a sunbeam's dancing motes,
spins slowly as the eddied fragments spin,
but means — the transparency of things.

5

Большая вещь — сама себе приют.
Там скачут звери и птенцы клюют
свой музыкальный корм. Но по пятам
за днем приходит ночь. И тот, кто там,
откладывает труд: он видит рост
магнитящих и слезотворных звезд.

6

И странно: как состарились глаза!
им видно то, чего глядеть нельзя,
и прочее не видно. Так из рук,
бывает, чашка выпадет. Мой друг!
что мы, как жизнь, хранили, пропадет —
и незнакомое звездой взойдет…

7

Поэзия, мне кажется, для всех
тебя растят, как в Сербии орех
у монастырских стен, где ковш и мед,
колодец и небесный ледоход —
и хоть на миг, а видит мирянин
свой ветхий век, как шорох вешних льдин:

8

— О, это всё: и что я пропадал,
и что мой разум ныл и голодал,
как мышь в холодном погребе, болел,
что никого никто не пожалел —
все двинулось, от счастья очумев,
как «все пройдет", горациев припев…

5

A great thing is a refuge for itself,
a place where beasts can leap and the birds peck
music for food. But panting on the heels
of day comes night. And he who sees it fall
puts down his work, soon as the stars appear
with their magnetic pull, and ready tears.

6

It's odd how old one's eyes have got!
for they see only what they can't,
and nothing else. Even so from one's hands,
sometimes, a cup may fall. My friend!
what we have kept, like life, will slide away,
and the unknown will rise like a star in the sky.

7

Poems, it seems to me, are grown for all,
as Serbian nut-trees grow along the walls
of monasteries, that keep a scoop of honey,
a well, with stars floating like ice in springtime,
so for a moment someone in the world
sees fragile life, like the spring stars that whirl:

8

— O, that is all: I knew that I was doomed,
and that my reason cried for lack of food;
trapped like a mouse in chilly vaults, it pined;
I knew no one felt pity for a friend, —
all is in flight, and all is drunk on joy,
for "things must pass," as Horace used to say ...

9

Минуту, жизнь, зачем тебе спешить?
Еще успеешь ты мне рот зашить
железной ниткой. Смилуйся, позволь
раз или два испробовать пароль:
"Большая вещь — сама себе приют."
Она споет, когда нас отпоют,

10

и, говорят, прекрасней. Но теперь
полуденной красы ночная дверь
раскрыта настежь; глубоко в горах
огонь созвездий, ангел и монах,
при собственной свече из глубины
вычитывает образы вины …

11

Большая вещь — утрата из утрат.
Скажу ли? взгляд в медиоланский сад.
Приструнен слух; на опытных струнах
играет страх; одушевленный прах,
как бабочка, глядит свою свечу:
— Я не хочу быть тем, что я хочу! —

12

и будущее катится с трудом
в огромный дом, секретный водоем …

9

Why hurry, life, why chivvy on the hour?
You'll soon have time to sew my mouth right up,
stitching with iron threads. So humor me,
deign, then, to give my *sententia* a try,
"A great thing is a refuge for itself":
It will sing when singing us to rest.

10

— they say, most beautifully. Now
at noontide, beauty's night-time door
is open wide, and high up in the hills
the constellatory fire, both monk and angel,
reads by the light of its own candle-ends
the exemplary lives of guilty men.

11

A great thing is a loss to end all loss:
a Mediolanian glimpse of paradise;
its hearing is attuned; on the tuned string
fear strums away; dust is an animate thing,
and like a flame-drawn butterfly, it cries,
"I will not be the thing that I will be!"

12

The future rolls into the spacious house,
the secret cistern, forcing its way at last ...

Elena Shvarts

Елена Шварц

Elena Andreevna Shvarts was born in 1948 in Leningrad, where she still lives. Her first published poems appeared in the Tartu University newspaper in 1973, but for ten years thereafter, none of her other work was published in her own country. In 1978 her work began to appear in émigré journals. She subsequently published two volumes of poetry abroad, *Tantsuiushchii David* (Dancing David, 1980) and *Stikhi* (Poems, 1987), as well as a novel in verse, entitled *Trudy i dni Lavinii, monakhini iz ordena obrezaniia serdtsa* (The Works and Days of Lavinia, a Nun of the Order of the Circumcision of the Heart, 1987). In 1989 her first Soviet collection, *Storony sveta* (The Four Corners of the World), was published in Leningrad, bringing her immediate recognition both at home and abroad. Since then, five more collections of her poetry have been published in Russia, and a bilingual edition of her poems, *Paradise*, appeared in England in 1993.

Translations by Catriona Kelly & Michael Molnar

Свалка

Нет сил воспеть тебя, прекрасная помойка!
Как на закате, разметавшись, ты лежишь со всклоченною
    головой
И черный кот в манишке белой колко
Терзает, как пьянист, живот тяжелый твой.
Вся в зеркалах гниющих — в их протресках
Полынь высокая растет —
О, ты — Венеция (И лучше, чем Венецья),
И гондольером кот поет.
Турецкого клочок дивана
В лиловой тесноте лежит
И о Стамбуле, о кальяне
Бурьяну тихо говорит.
В гниющих зеркалах дрожит лицо июля.
Ворона медленно на свалку опустилась,
И вот она идет надменнее, чем Сулла,
И в цепкой лапе гибель или милость.
Вот персик в слизи, вспухи ягод, лупа,
Медали часть, от книги корешок.
Ты вся в проказе или ты — ожог,
Ребенок, облитый кипящим супом.
Ты — Дионис, разодранный на части
Иль мира зеркальце ручное.
Я говорю тебе — О Свалка,
Зашевелись и встань. Потом,
О монстр, о чудовище ночное,
Заговори охрипло рваным ртом.
Зашевелись и встань, прекрасная помойка!
Воспой — как ты лежишь под солнцем долго,
Гиганта мозгом пламенея, зрея,
Все в разложенье съединяя, грея.
Большою мыслью поцвети, и гной
Как водку пей, и ешь курины ноги.
Зашевелись, прекрасная, и спой!
О rosa mystica, тебя услышат боги.

The Dump

O glorious dump, how shall I sing your praise!
You lie in the flickering sunset, sprawling, disheveled;
A black cat, immaculate in evening dress,
Tweaks at your swelling paunch, deft as a pianist.
The rotting and shattered glass of mirrors
Enclose a wormwood's straggling roots;
You are as grand as Venice! (No, far grander!)
The cat is your gondolier, and sings a serenade.
The ruined wreck of an ottoman
Lies cramped in a pool of lilac shade,
Whispering tales of hookahs by the Golden Horn
To lionizing clumps of willowherb.
July bobs to admire its face in shards of glass.
A crow dives slowly, then plumps down,
And struts upon you, stately as Sulla,
Holding doom, or mercy, gripped in each claw.
You're peaches' slimy shreds, and berries' slippery bubbles,
Lost lenses, torn book-covers, broken medals;
Your skin is leprous; you're pink and blistered
As a child inundated in scalding soup.
You're Dionysus ritually dismembered,
You're a microcosm in a make-up mirror.
But I say this to you: shake your sleepy limbs,
Get up on your feet, and walk. And then,
You monster, incubus of night,
Open your tattered mouth and speak.
O glorious dump, shake out your limbs and walk!
Sing of the days spent lying in the sun,
Your body warm, your giant's brain crackling, burning,
Yet unifying all that you survey.
May great thoughts bloom and rot in you
As you feast on vodka droplets, chicken bones.
O glorious dump, get to your feet and sing!
O Rosa mystica, the gods must hear your voice.

Элегия на рентгеновский снимок моего черепа

Флейтист хвастлив, а Бог неистов —
Он с Марсия живого кожу снял, —
И такова судьба земных флейтистов,
И каждому, ревнуя, скажет в срок:
"Ты меду музыки лизнул, но весь ты в тине,
Все тот же грязи ты комок,
И смерти косточка в тебе посередине."
Был богом света Аполлон,
Но помрачился —
Когда ты, Марсий, вкруг руки
Его от боли вился.
И вот теперь он бог мерцанья,
Но вечны и твои стенанья.

И мой Бог, помрачась,
Мне подсунул тот снимок,
Где мой череп, светясь,
Выбыв из невидимок,
Плыл, затмив вечер ранний,
Обнажившийся сад,
Был он — плотно-туманный —
Жидкой тьмою объят,
В нем сплеталися тени и облака —
И моя задрожала рука.
этот череп был мой,
Но меня он не знал,
Он подробной отделкой
Похож на турецкий кинжал —
Он хорошей работы,
И чист он и тверд,
Но оскаленный этот
Живой еще рот...

Elegy on an X-ray Photo of My Skull

The flautist boasts but God's enraged —
He stripped the living skin from Marsyas —
Such is the destiny of earthly flautists:
Grown jealous, He will say to each in turn:
"You've licked the honey of music but you're just muck,
You're still a lump of that same dirt
And lodged inside you is the stone of death."
Apollo was the god of light
But he grew dark
When round his hands, you Marsyas,
Twisted in pain.
And now he is a god of glimmer,
But eternal also are your groans.

And my God, growing dark,
Slipped me this photograph
In which my glowing skull,
Etched from the invisible,
Swam, blocking out the dusk
And the stripped naked park —
It was a mass of fog
Embraced in liquid dark.
In it shadow and cloud were blended
And my hand began to tremble.
This skull was my own
But it didn't know me,
Its intricate pattern
Like a damascene dagger
Is skillfully crafted,
How pure and how strong.
But the mouth is bared,
Still alive in its grin.

Кость! ты долго желтела,
Тяжелела, как грех,
Ты старела и зрела, как грецкий орех, —
Для смерти подарок.
Обнаглела во мне эта желтая кость,
Запахнула кожу, как полсть,
Понеслася и правит мной,
Тормозя у глазны арок.
Вот стою перед Богом в тоске
И свой череп держу я в дрожащей руке —
Боже, что мне с ним делать?
В глазницы ли плюнуть?
Вино ли налить?
Или снова на шею надеть и носить?
И кидаю его — это легкое с виду ядро,
Он летит, грохоча, среди звезд, как ведро.
Но вернулся он снова и, на шею взлетев, напомнил мне для
        утешенья:
Давно, в гостях — на столике стоял его собрат, для украшенья,
И смертожизнь он вел засохшего растенья,
Подобьем храма иль фиала.
Там было много выпито, но не хватало.
И некто тот череп взял и обносить гостей им стал,
Чтобы собрать на белую бутылку,
Монеты сыпались, звеня, по темному затылку,
А я его тотчас же отняла,
Поставила на место — успокойся,
И он котенком о ладонь мою потерся.
За это мне наградой будет то,
Что череп мой не осквернит никто —
Ни червь туда не влезет, ни новый Гамлет в руки не возьмет.
Когда наступит мой конец — с огнем пойду я под венец.
Но странно мне другое — это
Что я в себе не чувствую скелета,
Ни черепа, ни мяса, ни костей,

Bone, you yellowed a long time,
Grew heavy as sin,
Like a walnut you aged and you ripened,
A present for death.
Grown brazen inside me, this yellow bone
Has lapped itself in a sleigh-rug of skin
And taking my reins sped off headlong
But come to a halt at my brow.
In anguish here before my God I stand
Holding my skull in a trembling hand —
O Lord, what shall I do with it?
Spit in its eyesockets?
Fill it up with wine?
Or put it on my neck and wear it once again?
So I hurl it aside — this light-looking shell
And it flies off thundering among the stars like a pail.
But it returned and landing on my neck, reminded me
          in consolation:
Way back at someone's house, its fellow stood as table decoration
And led the deathlife of a dehydrated plant
As if it were a temple or a chalice.
There was a lot to drink but not enough —
And someone took this skull and began to pass it round
To collect the money for a vodka bottle.
Small change was scattered clinking on the dark occiput
But straightway I confiscated it,
Put it back where it belonged — calm down —
And like a kitten it rubbed against my palm.
For this I shall be granted as reward
That nobody will desecrate my skull —
No worm will crawl inside, no new Hamlet take it in his hands.
When my end comes — I shall walk up the aisle in flames.
But something else strikes me as weird,
That I can't sense my skeleton inside —
Neither skull nor flesh nor bones —

Скорее же — воронкой после взрыва,
Иль памятью потерянных вестей,
Туманностью или туманом,
Иль духом, новой жизнью пьяным.

Но ты мне будешь помещенье,
Когда засвищут Воскресенье.
Ты — духа моего пупок,
Лети скорее на Восток.
Вокруг тебя я пыльным облаком
Взметнусь, кружась, твердея в Слово,
Но жаль — что старым нежным творогом
Тебя уж не наполнят снова.

More like a crater after the explosion
or a memory of missing news,
Mistiness or mist
Or a spirit drunk on its new life.

But you will be my lodgings when
They start to pipe the Resurrection.
You, my spirit's navel, fly
Sooner to the East. And I
All around you as a dusty cloud
Erupting, swirling, hardening as the Word.
But what a shame you won't be filled again
With all that soft old curd.

Попугай в море

Вот после кораблекрушенья
Остался в клетке попугай.
Он на доске плывет — покуда
Не заиграет океан.

Перебирает он слова,
Как свои шелковые перья,
Упустит — и опять поймает,
Укусит и опять подбросит.

Поет он песню о мулатке
Иль крикнет вдруг изо всей мочи
На самом валу, на гребне,
Что бедный попка водки хочет.

И он глядит так горделиво
На эту зыбкую равнину.
Как сердце трогает надменность
Существ беспомощных и слабых.

Бормочет он, кивая:
Согласен, но, однако…
А, впрочем, вряд ли, разве,
Сугубо и к тому же…

На скользкой он доске
Сидит и припевает,
Бразилия, любовь
Зажаты в желтых лапах,

Косит он сонным глазом,
Чтоб море обмануть:
Год дэм!… В какой-то мере
И строго говоря…

A Parrot at Sea

After a ship had been wrecked
A parrot was left in a cage.
He floats on a plank — for as long
As the ocean pleases.

He picks away at words
Like his own silky plumage,
Lets them go — and seizes them again,
Pecks them and again throws them aside.

He sings a song of a mulatto woman
Or suddenly shrieks at the top of his voice
On the very crest of a roller,
Poor little polly wants a vodka.

And he casts such proud glances
Across that watery plateau.
How the arrogance of weak and helpless
Creatures touches the heart.

Nodding his head he murmurs:
I agree, but even so ...
On the other hand, hardly, surely,
Essentially and moreover ...

On his slippery plank
He sits and sings along,
Brazil and love are clutched
In his yellow claws,

He squints a sleepy eye
In order to trick the sea:
God damn! ...To some extent
And strictly speaking ...

А волны все темней и выше,
И к ночи океан суровей,
он голову упрячет в перья
И спит с доверчивостью детской.

И растворяет тьма глухая
И серый океан косматый
Комочек красно-золотистый,
Зеленый и голубоватый.

But the waves grow darker and steeper
And at nightfall the ocean rages.
He tucks his head in his feathers
and sleeps, as trustful as a child.

And the blind darkness and the gray
Dishevelled ocean dissolve
The tiny reddish-golden,
Green and light blue bundle.

Воспоминание о странном угощении

Я отведала однажды
Молока своей подруги,
Молока моей сестры —
Не для утоленья жажды,
А для вольности души.
Она выжала из груди
Левой в чашку молоко,
И оно в простой посуде
Пело, пенилось легко.
Оно пахло чем-то птичьим,
Чем-то волчьим и овечьим,
Больше вечным, чем путь Млечный,
было теплым и густым.
Так когда-то дочь в пустыне
Старика-отца поила,
Став и матерью ему.
Силой этой благостыни
В колыбель гроб превратила,
Белизной прогнала тьму.
Из протока возле сердца
Напоила ты меня —
Не вампир я — ой ли — ужас —
Оно понилось, звеня,
Сладким, теплым, вечным, мягким
Время в угол, вспять тесня.

Remembrance of Strange Hospitality

Once I had a taste
Of a girlfriend's milk,
My sister's milk —
Not to quench my thirst
But to satisfy my soul.
Into a cup she squeezed
Milk from her left breast
And in that simple vessel
It gently frothed, rejoiced.
There was something birdlike in its odour,
Whiffs of sheep and wolf, and something older
Than the Milky Way, it was
Somehow warm and dense.
A daughter in the wilderness,
Once let her aged father drink
From her breasts and thus became
His mother. By this act of grace
Her whiteness drove away the dark,
A cradle substituted for a tomb.
From the duct next to your heart
You offered me a drink —
I'm not a vampire, am I? — Horror.
It frothed and tinkled, warm
And sweet, soft, everlasting,
Crowding time back into a corner.

Viktor Krivulin
Виктор Кривулин

Viktor Borisovich Krivulin was born in Krasnodon, Ukraine in 1944. He moved to Leningrad at an early age and completed his degree in Russian literature there in 1967. An important participant in alternative or "unofficial" culture of the 1970s and 80s, Krivulin co-edited the samizdat journals *37* (1975-81) and *Severnaia pochta* (1979-80). He also participated in the semi-official group "Club 81" and published his first work in the Soviet Union in the Club's anthology, *Krug* (Circle, 1985). In recent years his poetry, journalism and cultural commentary have appeared regularly in Russian newspapers and journals, and he has also written regularly for the Frankfurter Allgemeine Zeitung. Several volumes of his poetry have been published in Russia in the 1990s: *Kontsert po zaviazkam* (Concert by Demand, 1993), *Predgranich'e* (Borderland, 1994), and *Posledniaia kniga* (The Last Book, 1996). He was on the editorial committee of the journal *Vestnik novoi literatury* and is vice-president of the St. Petersburg PEN club.

Translations by Michael Molnar

~

"Китайский дворец в Ораниенбауме"

Цветное художественное фото размер 1,5м x 2м², автор Б.
Смелов

Бухгалтерия ф-ки народных музыкальных инструментов им.
А. В. Луначарского

пройдясь по клавишам дворца
по складу пьяных клавесинов
где апельсинная пыльца
горючим облачком висит
горя на сквозняке зеркал
на правильном огне студеном
не понимаешь, как попал
сюда? и по каким законам
здесь вещи прежние растут
а время — время усыхает
оно в седых пучках минут
какими щели затыкают
оно в соломенных очах
то вожделеет, разгорясь
то стало стайкой арапчат
то, как фарфоровый китаец,
покачивает головой
с неудовольствием: ты, братец,
нездешний вроде бы, не свой —
и так не вовремя, некстати!
ну ладно, хоть глаза прикрой

~

The Chinese Palace at Oranienbaum [1]
Color artphoto (dim. 1.5 x 2m). Photographer B. Smelov

Accounts dept. of the A. V. Lunacharskii factory[2]
of folk instruments

crossing the keyboards of the palace
past a stock of tipsy harpsichords
where an inflammable and tangerine
cloud of pollen hangs suspended
burning on a mirrored draft
in a frozen formal blaze
you can't understand how come
you landed here? and by what right
antiques flourish in this place
but as for time — time's drying up
it's in gray tufts made of minutes
that are used to stuff up cracks
it's in the eyes the color of straw
now flaring up aflush with lust
now changing to a swarm of blackamoors
now like a porcelain chinaman
rhythmically nodding his head
in dissatisfaction: you, my friend,
look like a foreigner, not at home —
and so ill timed, so out of place!
well, all right then, just shade your eyes

*the rococo Chinese palace—an imagined
photo by a real photographer. Silent
instruments, static time. Voluted
rococo palace, mutely voluble, tumbling
continually further from identity or
center. And Smelov's implied cityscapes
of icywhite streets, canals, courtyards
timelessly poised in an infintely
allusive anticipation. Behind these
images and imaginings, a dark negative
anti-image. (No one knew Smelov had
really photographed the Chinese palace.
he had never printed the negatives.
Only the voice of the poem brought them
to light.) The stark glare of silence
streams through these surfaces freezing
its object in contorted poses. Adopt a
style. Your exotic servant-master, the
chinaman, has estranged you from your
homeland in sound and change. Your
voice is not your own.*

---

[1] "The Chinese Palace at Oranienbaum" — a masterpiece of rococo architecture built by Rinaldi in 1768 for Catherine the Great. Oranienbaum, now Lomonosov, is famous for its porcelain.

[2] "A. V. Lunacharskii factory" — Produces imitation folk instruments for which there is no demand - balalaikas, low-quality guitars, etc.

Lunacharskii was First Commisar for Culture during the early years of Soviet rule, and died in 1933 while ambassador in Spain.

~

Худ. Феодотов. Картон с эскизом к неосущевленному
жанровому полотну *"Утро петербургской барыни, или
Благовещение 1848 года"*

Копия, выполненная неизвестным автором в 20-е годы
нашего века, оригинал утрачен — вероятно, в период
эвакуации

Фонды Пермской государственной галереи

слава кесарю! слава и Господу в горних!
барабанное утро. к заутрене колокол. мышка в углу
печь остыла. пришел истопник. выгребает золу
возле каждых ворот возвышается дворник
стоя спит опершись на метлу

власть устойчиво-крепкая, в позе Паллады
ей опорой копье, на груди ее знак номерной
но в полярных Афинах под великопостной весной
ломит кости. глядит из кивота Распятый
занимается в топке обдерыш берестяной

"Богородице-Дево" начнет и запнется и девку сенную
кличет (ах ты, какая досада, не идет на язык
Божье слово): Палашка! — потоками пяток босых
затопляет людскую, переднюю ... — (так я тоскую
по утрам, ты бы знала — пока не затих

гул таинственный в сердце, остаток ночного озноба)
человек состоит из предчувствий и смертных глубин —
то ли гоголь об этом писал то ли сказывал старец один
возвратясь на покой от Господнего Гроба
голубиный свой век ореолом венчая златым

Art. Fedotov.[1] Pasteboard with a sketch for an unrealized genre
canvas: *"Morning of a Petersburg Lady or*
Annunciation 1848"

Copy executed by an unknown artist during the 20s of this century,
the original lost in the course of the evacuation
Collection of the Perm State Gallery

the immaculate
concept

its archetype
disappeared

glory word
slava slovo
a protolanguage
founded
in glorification

glory to caesar! and glory to God in the highest!
kettledrum morning. a bell calls to matins. a mouse in the corner
the stove has gone cold. the stoker arrived. digs out the cinders
by each entrance gate a janitor rises
resting on a broom and standing slumbers

iconic images
funnels
of
concentric rings
excluding any
human presence

power strong and stable, posed like Pallas
resting on a spear, her chest bearing a numbered badge[2]
but in polar Athens during its lenten springtime
bones are racked. the Crucified stares from his icon-case
splinters of birchbark in the furnace burst into flame

that stammers—
inglorious
interference
between word
and utterance

"Maiden-Mother of God" starts up then falters, a voice calls
the chambermaid (oh bother, my tongue's in a knot, it won't utter
God's word): Palashka! a torrent of bare heels scuttles
drowning the servants' quarters, the hall ... — (how downcast I feel
in the mornings, if only you knew — until the mysterious murmur

murmur
gul
indistinct
oceanic noise
that utterance
dies into
and rises from

in the heart falls silent, a night chill's final trace)
humankind is composed of forebodings and mortal abysses —
that was either written by a gogol or said by a certain elder
returned from our Savior's tomb to repose in peace
crowning his columbine years with a halo of gold

annunciation
as vision
penetrating
ear and eye
leaving
no trace
or access to its
triangulated
closed circle

dress me, palashka! church must already have started
the Annunciation service, icefloes shuffle outside the shutters
I dreamed, a triangular dream: an arcade, the garden of my parents
but deep down as if in a pit and yearning for daylight —
how could it be reached? how could it be placed back on earth?

одеваться, палашка! в соборе поди уже служат
Благовещенье нынче, за шторами льдины шуршат
сон я видела, сон треугольный: аркада, родительский сад
но глубоко внизу, будто в яме, а рвется наружу —
как достать бы его? как на землю поставить назад?

я, бессильная, в белом стою на коленях
наклоняюсь над ямой и слышу: из глубины
"Марья! Марья!" зовут — и деревья уже не видны
то ли мокрая глина внизу то ли вроде сапожного клея
что-то вязкое, дышит … я в ужасе, погружены

руки словно бы в тесто — и тесто вспухает
в утесненьи душевном проснулась: лежу-то я где?
на булыжнике уличном! голая, в холоде и срамоте —
надо мной наклоняется дворник, железной метой помавает
"Мусор, барыня…" — плачет — и слезы в его бороде

"мусор … мусор" — бормочет, меня, как бумажку, сметая.
шелестя просыпаюсь — неужто я смята в комок?
и зачем это снится? и холод, бегущий от ног,
отчего-то врывается в сердце ордою мамая
морем валенок, бурок, сапог

как там душно — внутри меня — как надышали!
Пелагея, смотрю на тебя, и темно:
ты по-русски "морская" — что имя? звучанье одно —
а смотрю на тебя — в океанские страшные дали
погружаюсь, тону, опускаюсь на дно

a name
from the depths

estranging
identity
and engulfing

I am powerless, dressed in white, I am kneeling
leaning over the pit, I can hear: from the abyss
"Maria! Maria!" they call — and the trees are no longer in sight
either wet clay below me or else it's like shoemaker's glue
something sticky, that breathes ... I am seized with terror, my hands

snare

they that are
not
with their self
are against

orders

immersed as in dough — and the dough is swelling up
in anguish of spirit I woke: where am I lying? on the street
cobblestones! naked and in the cold and the disgrace —
a janitor is leaning over me waving his iron broom
"Rubbish, lady ..." — he weeps — and there are tears in his beard

through the
grid
of a social
present
they fall into
mythical
history

"rubbish ... rubbish" — he mutters, and sweeps me like paper aside
rustling I wake — am I really crushed up in a lump?
and why should I dream this? the cold streaming up from my feet
for some reason bursts in my heart like the horde of mamai[3]
in a sea of feltboots, kneeboots, jackboots

scene
of archaic
sense
lost
in translation
seen but not
heard
"the sea"

how close it is — there inside me — a fog of warm breath!
Pelageia, I look at you, and it's dark all around:
translated you are 'of the sea' — what's a name? just a sound
but I look at you — in awful oceanic expanses
immersed, I sink down to the seabed, I drown

[1] Fedotov — Famous Russian artist of the time of Nicholas I. Ex-officer. Worked in the genre of
scenes from everyday life. Painter of socially critical pictures. Died not having completed many
projects, having gone mad. In 1848 he was already mentally ill. He is considered a victim of the
stifling cultural climate of Nicholas I's time.

[2] "a numbered badge" — Caretakers or janitors in old Petersburg were mainly Kasimov Tatars.
They wore white aprons with a big badge on the breast on which was indicated the number of the
house they served. Often they combined their duties with the functions of secret police informers.

[3] Mamai — Tatar khan whose enormous army was defeated on the field of Kulikovo in 1380 by the
forces of Dmitrii Donskoi.

Dmitry Prigov
Дмитрий Пригов

Dmitry Aleksandrovich Prigov. Poet, visual artist and crit-
ic. Born in Moscow in 1940, Dmitri Prigov received his de-
gree from the Sculpture Department of the Moscow Art
Institute in 1967. Prigov was and continues to be one of
Russia's leading postmodernist poets and a major figure
on the contemporary art scene. Although he has written
an astonishing number of poems (over 21,000), arranged
in more than 150 "books" or cycles, his work remained un-
published in the Soviet Union until 1990. It did, however,
circulate in samizdat tape recordings and manuscript,
winning him great popularity in both Russia and the West.
The first book of Prigov's selected poems, *Slezy geraldi-
cheskoi dushi* (Tears of a Heraldic Soul), was published in
1990, and several more have appeared since then. Since the
early 90s his work has frequently appeared on the pages of
major Russan periodicals such as *Den' poezii*, *Zerkaka*,
Almanakh poezii, *Ogonek*, and *Novyi Mir*. Prigov's visual art
has been exhibited in the United States, Great Britain, Ger-
many, Italy, Switzerland, Finland, Poland, Sweden and
Spain. He has also been the subject of a film, *Dmitri Prigov:
Poet and Rebel*, which was shown extensively on Soviet
television. His theoretical and critical writings have
appeared in journals such as *Flash Art*, *Novostroika*, and
Iskusstvo. As a free-lance artist and writer, Prigov divides
his time between Russia, Germany and England, giving
numerous poetry readings and performances in both
Europe and the United States.

Translations by Robert Reid

~

Представьте: спит огромный великан
То вдруг на Севере там у него нога проснется —
Все с Севера тогда на Юг бежать!
Или на Юге там рука проснется —
Все снова с Юга к Северу бежать!
А если вдруг проснутся разом
Ум, совесть, скажем, честь и разум —
Что будет здесь! Куда ж тогда бежать?!

Imagine this: a mighty giant asleep
And suddenly his foot stirs in the North
Then everybody in the North will run to the South
Or maybe in the South he stirs a hand
Then everyone will run back North again!
But say there suddenly awake at once
Reason, honor, wit and conscience
What will happen here! And which way will we run?!

Уж лучше и совсем не жить в Москве
Но просто знать, что где-то существует
Окружена высокими стенами
Высокими и дальними мечтами
И взглядами на весь окрестный мир
Которые летят и подтверждают
Наличие свое и утверждают
Наличие свое и порождают
Наличие свое в готовом сердце —
Вот это вот и значит — жить в Москве

It's better not to live in Moscow
Enough to know that it exists
Surrounded by its lofty walls
And by dreams remote and tall
And perspectives on the world around
Which soaring up affirm
Its presence and confirm
Its presence and can form
Its presence in the waiting heart
And this is what it means to live in Moscow

В пустыне

Большие пустые чужие каменья безводной пустыни
Пустые чужие каменья безводной пустыни
Чужие каменья безводной пустыни
Каменья безводной пустыни
Безводной пустыни
Пустыни

In the Desert

Mighty empty alien stones of the waterless desert
Empty alien stones of the waterless desert
Alien stones of the waterless desert
Stones of the waterless desert
Waterless desert
Desert

Въезд в Иерусалим

Осел шел, как осел
Толпа бежала, как толпа
Осанна звучала, как Осанна
Он въехал, как Он ехал
Ехал, ехал
Осанна звучала, как Осанна звучала
Толпа бежала, как толпа бежала
Осел шел, как осел шел
Как осел шел
Как осел шел
Шел, шел, шел

Entry into Jerusalem

The ass passed like an ass
The crowd ran like a crowd
Hosanna rang out like Hosanna
He entered as He went
Went, went
Hosanna rang out like Hosanna rang out
The crowd ran like a crowd ran
The ass passed like an ass passed
Like an ass passed
Like an ass passed
Passed, passed, passed

Диалог № 5

Сталин	На свете счастья нет!
Пригов	Счастья нет!
Сталин	А что есть?
Пригов	Что есть?
Сталин	Сталин есть!
Пригов	Сталин есть!
Сталин	А что есть Сталин?
Пригов	Что есть?
Сталин	Сталин наша слава боевая!
Пригов	Слава боевая!
Сталин	Сталин нашей юности полет!
Пригов	Юности полет!
Сталин	С песнями борясь и побеждая
Пригов	Побеждая!
Сталин	Наш народ за Сталиным идет!
Пригов	За Сталиным идет!
Сталин	А что еще есть Сталин?
Пригов	Что еще?
Сталин	Три великих принципа!
Пригов	Три великих принципа!
Сталин	А что еще есть Сталин?
Пригов	Что еще?
Сталин	Пять великих смыслов!
Пригов	Пять великих смыслов!
Сталин	Шесть великих букв!
Пригов	А что будет, если отнять одну букву?
Сталин	Что будет?
Пригов	Булет Талин!
Талин	Талин!
Пригов	А если отнять еще одну?
Талин	Еще одну?
Пригов	Будет Алин

Dialogue No. 5

Stalin   There is no happiness on earth!

Prigov   No happiness!

Stalin   What is there then?

Prigov   What is there?

Stalin   There is Stalin!

Prigov   There is Stalin!

Stalin   And what is Stalin?

Prigov   What is he?

Stalin   Stalin is our military glory!

Prigov   Military glory!

Stalin   Stalin is our youth's high aspiration!

Prigov   Youth's high aspiration!

Stalin   Singing in battle and victory!

Prigov   Victory!

Stalin   Our people follow Stalin!

Prigov   Follow Stalin!

Stalin   What else is Stalin?

Prigov   What else?

Stalin   The three mighty principles!

Prigov   The three mighty principles!

Stalin   What else is Stalin?

Prigov   What else?

Stalin   The five great ideas!

Prigov   The five great ideas!

Stalin   The six great letters!

Prigov   And how would it be if we left one letter off?

Stalin   How would it be?

Prigov   It would be Talin!

Talin   Talin!

Prigov   And if we left another off?

Talin   Another?

Prigov   It would be Alin.

Алин	Будет Алин!
Пригов	А если отнять еще одну?
Алин	Еще одну?
Пригов	Будет Лин
Лин	Будет Лин!
Пригов	А еще одну?
Лин	Еще одну?
Пригов	Будет Ин
Ин	Ин!
Пригов	А еще одну?
Ин	Еще одну?
Пригов	Будет Н!
Н	Будет Н!
Пригов	А еще одну?

Alin	It would be Alin!
Prigov	And if we left another off?
Alin	Another?
Prigov	It would be Lin
Lin	It would be Lin!
Prigov	And another?
Lin	Another?
Prigov	It would be In
In	In?
Prigov	And another?
In	Another?
Prigov	It would be N!
N	It would be N!
Prigov	And another?

Arkadii Dragomoschenko

Аркадий Драгомощенко

Arkadii Trofimovich Dragomoschenko was born in Pots-
dam, Germany in 1946. He studied Russian literature and
language at the Pedagogical Institute in Vinnitsa, Ukraine,
and the history and theory of theatre at the Leningrad
Theatre Institute. Dragomoschenko was active in Lenin-
grad literary counter-culture in the 1970s and early 80s and
a member of "Club 81," an independent association of
Leningrad writers and artists founded in 1981. Although
his work was distributed in samizdat journals such as
Chasy in the 1970s, his contribution to *Krug* (1985), the an-
thology of "Club 81," was his first Soviet publication.
Since then his work has appeared in numerous periodicals
both in Russia and abroad. He has also published six vol-
umes of poetry and prose: *Dvoinaia raduga* (The Double
Rainbow, 1988), *Nebo sootvetstvii*, (Sky of Conformity,
1990), *Description* (1990), *Xenia* (1993), *Phosphor* (1994) and
Pod Podozreniem (Under Suspicion, 1994). Arkadii Drago-
moschenko currently resides in St. Petersburg.

Translations by Lyn Hejinian & Elena Balashova

Мартовская Элегия

… розы
… морозы
Из поэтического

Пораскисло, слиняло тырло чумовое мороза,
Розы солнечный куколь парным гипсом белеет,

Рыщет волк-брат по чащобам, икая утробой,
По оврагам да по худым перелескам,

На себя неотступного скалясь в тумане,
Прижав к черепу уши, облезлая мечется шкура
         и тужит,
Рыскает,
Глазом кося на луну в промоинах черных,
Что глядит в очи прямо гипсовой в золоте кукле…
Никого.

Хоть бы поганый татарин!
Ох, стерня на юру да так тонко и жалостно ноет,
Хоть бы старец какой на пути повстречался —
Не обидел бы помощью, так бы горло и вырвал.
Ничего.

Шерсть клоками роняет, давится корками пены,
Скучен желтым клыкам в переливах дивного дыма,

Не луна в пасть то брызжет морозной водицей,
Не звезда моровая скребется по сердцу сестрицей,

Разрывая лапы до кости о наст адамантов,
Ночь и день,
День и ночь в одну дугу сгибая,
Брат меньшой, Царевича-Ваню поминая, несется
Прямо к белому солнышку —

Ишь, что вздумала шкура!

March Elegy

... rose
... snows
(from the poetic)

The ridiculous shack of frost is slush, faded,
The solar hood of the rose is white as damp plaster.

Brother wolf with his ravenous belly is foraging through thickets
along the ravines and in sparse brush

Relentlessly baring his teeth at himself in the fog,
Ears laid back against his scalp, rushing about
        in his mangy skin,
He grieves,
Forages,
Squinting an eye at the moon in the black gullies,
Staring straight at a plaster doll in the gold ...
Nobody.

If only a stinking Tatar!
Oh, how thin and mournful the whining of the stubble
        on the hillside —
If only a venerable old man would cross his path,
He wouldn't insult him with aid, he'd just rip open his throat.
        Nothing.
He sheds clumps of fur, chokes on crusts of foam,
Wretched with his yellow fangs
        in the tints of wonderful smoke —
It's not the moon that splashes icy water into his jaws,
It's not a pestilential star that scratches his heart like a sister —

Ripping his paws to the bone on the crust of diamondlike snow,
Night and day,
        day and night bending into one bow,
The younger brother, recalling little Prince Ivan, gallops
Straight into the white sun —

Look, what he got into his head, the cur!

Примечания

I

Был избран вкус пыли.
Почему молоко? Привыкание…
Вкус пыли познанный навсегда ни к чему не обязывает,
Пыли укус не заметен вначале —
Меня больше там, где я о себе забываю,
эти легкие светлые ниши, впадины, чаши пустые,
      ключицы были чисты, как будто пожара истоки
поили их, цвета лишая. Привыкшие?
Вкус молока это вкус истинной пыли,
"Я волосы знал твои в зной, каждый волос звал поименно,"
Часы так лились меж камней, как они откликались
Пылью над крышей,
Когда ладонь обжигает железо и вишни,
Я знал тебя всю в одном слове — забыто…
словно за солнечной кожей, что стала изнанкой
прикосновения,
бесполым зерном, из которого вычтено время.
Белые глины — пластами, и глубже,
Меж ними кости хранились корней и монет серебряных,
      черных, как улицы, разбирающие седину полдня —
Мать в изножьи над нами стоит,
Мы в постели нагие как законы грамматики,
И гримаса блуждает окисью тонкой — в совершенстве
            познавшие пыль перед нею.
Снова прохожий, доски забора,
Жар негатива,
Виснут в зеркале угрюмые яблоки,
Осы покидают гнезд серые раковины.
Ум осторожней. Как стал он похож на осу,
И рожденье.
Три дня осталось быть снегом — потом снова пылью.

Footnotes

I

You chose the taste of dust.
Why milk? It's a question of habit …
The taste of dust, forever familiar, doesn't obligate you to anything
The sting of dust isn't noticeable at first —
There is more of me where I forget about myself
These bright shallow niches, hollows, empty bowls,
    collar bones pristine as if sources of fire
had let them drink, leaching out the color. A habit?
The taste of milk is the taste of real dust
"I knew your hair in the heat, I called each hair by name"
Time flowed between the stones as hours echoed
Dust over the roofs
In the hand iron and cherries burn equally
I knew you in a single word completely — forgotten …
as if behind a skin of sun that turned into the reverse side of touch
the sexless seed from which time has been subtracted.
White clay — in layers and deeper
Root's bones and silver coins are buried between them
    black as the streets which sort through the gray streaks of noon —
Mother stands over us at the foot of the bed
We are naked as rules of grammar
And a grimace strays like thick tarnish — we know to perfection
                    the dust in front of her.
Again a passerby, the boards of a fence
The negative's fever
Gloomy apples hang in the mirror
Wasps abandon the gray shells of their nests.
The mind is more cautious. It has come to resemble a wasp
And birth.
There will be three more days of snow — then dust again.

2

Из-за ивы, занявшейся внезапно
Сотое солнце в глаза метнулось,
На траве ворон. Ворон в траве —
       не говори в изумрудной,
Ибо никто теперь так не напишет,
Кожа вещей в пестрых узорах,
Облака сентября, небесные учителя зеленого
И белый бомбардировщик, вростающий
          в ткани дня,
разрежения. Не говори о траве.
Как и вино птицы легки на помине —
Так жилось нам в год сотого солнца и ивы.

2

From behind a willow which suddenly caught fire
The hundredth sun rushed into view
In the grass a raven. A raven in the grass —
                    don't say in emerald grass
Nobody writes that way any more
The skin of things has colorful patterns
September clouds, heavenly teachers of green
And a white jet fighter entwined
                    in the texture of the day
evaporating. Don't talk about the grass.
If you simply mention birds, like wine they're sure to appear —
That's how we live in the year of the hundredth sun
                    and willow.

Обучение чистоте в смешанном.

I

Как черное в провалы белизны
летит очнуться гибельным цветеньем, дым разостлав
по мятежу снегов подземной мелью промедлений

(какая сила недостатка гонит?
и клонит к узкогубой мгле, подобно записи, что
          впитана веками —
кипит опять в несносном толкованьи,
И кроме букв бестенных в жерновах порядка — ни городов
          в знобящих ветра каплях,
ни басен о природе;

нет
в помине и драгоценного как эхо вещества,
          любовниками бывшего когда-то,
когда
"поэты были всем" однако…
но чаще смертью (смехом?), чтобы не делить мозг
          с лабиринтом корневой системы,
всплеск
разночтений — тысячи! —
в единственном сцепленьи с прелестной перстью временных
          сращений,
под стать материи
возлюбленных —
          телам, плывущим тьмою в реках, низведенных
к колодцам тлеющим ума …

2

Жизнь шелушится речью. Странствует кора, юродствуя
          вдоль тока смол,

Instructing Clarity in a Confusion

1

As black in the hollows of white
rushes to wake with fatal blooming, smoke is spread out
by procrastination's underground shoals over the mutiny of snows
(what force within failure drives one on?
and leans over the narrow-lipped gloom like an inscription
          saturated with centuries —
it seethes again in unbearable commentary
And letters appear, furthermore, without shadows
    in the grindstones of order — they're not cities
        in feverish drops of wind
nor fables about nature;

and there is no trace
of matter that's as precious as an echo,
      lovers of some past time and thing,
when
"poets were everything" although ...
death (laughter?) occurs more often, so as not to divide the mind
    into a labyrinthian root system,

a splash
of readings — thousands! —
in a singular link with beautiful fingers of temporary
          unions,
material appropriate
to lovers —
    bodies, swimming in darkness in rivers, going
down to the rotting shafts of the mind ...

2

Life flakes off with speech. The husk goes off, playing the fool
      along a flowing path of sap,

идут холмами зимы
и дерево стареет по часам,
как состраданья кольца в неусыпном шуме), как черное —
росою белизны,

ночь претворяет в плазму
соты звезд и осы
заколосятся пламенем богов. Кружит туманом строй равнин и
гор,
чьи камни венами опутывают месяц, и золото где: сирин на суку.

Но перемен развитие — незримей дыма,
витающего радугой венца над кроной сизого не инея,
            но льда,
подобно смерти, протекающей к началу
но и концу
сквозь мысль (… о гребни промедлений!), однако мысль и есть
            в окрестности сомненья, где
вечно ждет
что б узнанною быть,

стерев себя как запись в обновленьи,
как
борозду весной сотрет распад зерна, волокон обращая тесноту
      в суть сердцевины — в немоту,
в безбрежность острия
(о промедленье лезвий …)

Ель тяжела глазами.

Стволов и хвои травленная чернь.
Тропой прямится бирюзовой берез сверкающая траурная тень

winters pass over the hills
and a tree ages hour by hour
with rings of compassion in an endless din) like the black —
with white dew

night transforms honeycombs of stars
into plasma
    and wasps
begin to ripen with the gods' fires
        The line of plains and mountains
           whirls like a fog
whose stones envelop the moon in veins and the Siren is gold
              on the bough.

But the evolution of changes is less visible than smoke
hovering like a rainbow of achievement over a steel-gray crown
           not hoarfrost but ice
resembling death, flowing back to the beginning
but also out to the end
through thought (… o billows of procrastination!)
    but thought lies in the neighborhood of doubt, where
it waits eternally
to be recognized

erasing itself renewed like a written record
as
in spring the sown seeds level the furrow, turning the density
       of the fibers into the heart of matter — mute
a boundless knife point
(o procrastinating blades …)

The fir is heavy with eyes.

Needles and trunks etched black.
A sparkling funereal shadow lies straight as a pathway

и, желтизною женственной затянутый, огонь изломы веток
        обнажает нежно.
И здесь стоять водою о себе? Без берегов. Под настом
трав

настоя терпко нетерпенье, горячечное, будто муравьиный рот
кого-то,
искривленный на стакане, когда в лекарственном, хмельном чаду
пол с потолком меняется местами
и холодок кривой   игрой у губ — брат бестелесый лба,
        сухого созерцанья
в семян неведеньи неслышном, точно невод,
способном ум обрушить косностью значенья
в истлевший, пресный час зари. Но даже память здесь — не боле,
        чем изъян,
впивающийся центром круга. Не уходить.

Склонись.
И слушай гул — бурьян. Он гол. Безвиден.
Слух — это ждать, когда в ответ не ждать,
Такой удел струне завиден …

Нас разделяет пестрый искры миг
золою мотылька, расправленного в копоть свободной радугой
        ресниц,
Нас разлучив, венчает вспышка век — гарь десяти секунд глаз
        в совпаденьи,
отсекшем на хрусталик как побег, так и безлюдья
        тростниковый стебель
и крыш асбестовый лежалый цвет,
забитый падалью размокшей голубиной.

                    under the turquoise birches
and fire wrapped in womanly yellow tenderly bares
                    the jutting twigs.
To stand here alone as water. Without shores. Within a rind
of grasses

the impatience of the brew is bitter, delirious,
                    as if someone's ant-like mouth
were distorted on the glass, in medicinal drunkenness
when the floor changes places with the ceiling
and the crooked cold
            toying with the mouth — that disembodied
                    brother of the forehead,
                    of dry reflection
in seeds of inaudible ignorance like a net
set to destroy the mind caught in stagnant meaning
in the dull, dying hour of dawn. But even here a memory is no more
                    than a flaw
sucked in by the center of the circle. Don't leave.

Bend down.
Listen to the hum — tall weeds. Bare. Unseen.
Sound — this is waiting, when there's nothing to hear in response,
The string envies such a fate …

A spark's colorful moment separates us
with a moth's ash spread in the soot
            by the free rainbow of eyelashes
Having separated us it crowns the eyelids' flash — cinders
            of the ten seconds when the eyes meet,
cut off like a shoot in a crystal lens, such is the bamboo stem
            of the uninhabited
and the stale asbestos color of the roofs
covered with the sodden pigeon carrion.

3

Но плавное восстание руки,
вторгаясь в остов геометрии предвечной (не дерево заката,
    что прожжен дырою кружев маслянистых,
а несколько расправленных прямых, готовых слиться
вымышленной вещью
в единственном из вымысла числе) — руки восстание проводит
    уже вторжение туда, где "в" и "вне"
пульсируют смиренно
в купели накопления "ни-что."
            Светает.
Оттепель.
Лицо.
    Фонарь, как тварь морская высыхает, скребя лучом
            по слякоти камней.
Прилив рассвета
равен всем прорехам.
        Снег не меняет направленья ветра,

и первый лязгает трамвай.

3

But the graceful raising of a hand
encroaching on the framework of geometry
    before eternity (not sunset's tree
    which is burnt through with holes of oily lace
but a few extended lines ready to be joined
by an imaginary thing
out of all imaginary numbers into one)
        — the lifting of the hand will
    carry out the encroachment already there
        where "in" and "out"
pulsate peacefully
in the font of accumulated "nothing."
        It's getting light.
A thaw.
A face.
    A streetlight like a sea creature dries, scraping its beam
        on the slushy stones.
The tide of dawn
equals all rifts.
    The snow doesn't change the direction of the wind
The first streetcar clanks.

Nina Iskrenko
Нина Искренко

Nina Iurievna Iskrenko was born in Moscow in 1951, where she lived until her death in 1995. She earned a degree in physics from Moscow State University and worked as a translator of scientific literature until 1989. Thereafter she devoted herself fully to her writing, performances, and art work. She was a member of the unofficial Moscow Club Poetry from its inception in 1986. Her work has appeared in many periodicals, including *Iunost'*, *Literaturnaia gazeta*, and *Moskovsky komsomolets*, and English translations of her verse have been published in American literary journals such as *Talisman*, *Five Fingers Review*, and *Agni*. Iskrenko has published three books of poems, all of which appeared in 1991: *ILI* (OR), *Referendum*, and *Neskol'ko slov* (A Few Words). Her poetry and prose have also been included in the anthologies *Third Wave: The New Russian Poetry* (1992) and *20th Century Russian Poetry: Silver and Steel* (1993) and a volume of her selected poems in English translation, *The Right to Err*, appeared in 1995.

Translations by John High,
with Patrick Henry & Katya Olmsted

Как пережить эту ночь
(сон)

Она набрала номер и сказала
"Я люблю тебя"
Дура   ответил он   Кому звонишь?
Зажмурившись она перезвонила и повторила то же самое
залпом еще раз После паузы и короткого вздоха донеслось
Вы ошиблись
Она снова дернула рычаг и диск телефона связь барахлила
обрывалась Боясь что ее не услышат она орала в трубку
уже после третьей цифры но все варианты ответов были в
общем-то неудовлетворительны

К утру о ее любви знала вся Москва что странным образом
сказалось на поведении отдельных блоков жилищного
строительства. Отдельные блоки попросту развалились, а старая
мостовая на Красной площади выперла из-под мнимого, более
духовного, как тогда казалось, покрытия, причем каждый
камень побелел, набух и напрягся, имитируя женскую грудь.
Двое гэбэшников, постоянно торчащих в святых местах и
кажущихся особенно одинокими в это пустынное время суток,
внезапно почувствовали, что теряют почву под ногами. Грудь
поехала, волнуясь и накатываясь отдельными ячейками на
другие, создавая узлы и пучности. Что-то ойкало и повизгивало в
воздухе, и не ожиданно в ночное небо ударили фонтаны молока.
"Красиво живем," — подумал один, не зная, за что хвататься и
чувствуя, что засасывает.

Между тем она все звонила
От резонанса повылетали донышки консервных банок в
дипломатическом гастрономе на Большой Грузинской.
Небезызвестная шишка под носом у алжирского бея достигла
угрожающих размеров минарета, а у высокопоставленных
гриппозников из ушей выпал чеснок и мелкой дрожью
задрожали на подзеркальниках малахитовые запонки и

How To Live Through This Night
(A Dream)

She dialed a number and said
"I love you"
Fool   he answered   Who are you calling?
Squinting   again she rang and repeated the same thing in a single
breath Following another pause and a brief sigh the words finally
came out
Wrong number
Once more she pulled the switch-hook and dialed   the connection
crackled and broke off
Fearing she wouldn't be heard she yelled into the receiver after the
third digit but all of the various responses were in general
unsatisfactory

By morning her love was famous throughout Moscow
evident in the behavior of the construction site's individual
apartment blocks. Some blocks had collapsed, and the old paving on
Red Square protruded from beneath an imaginary, more spiritual (as
it then seemed) surface, and every stone whitened, swelled and
strained, imitating the movement of female breasts. A couple of KGB
agents, who hung around in holy places, and who seemed peculiarly
solitary at this deserted hour, suddenly sensed they were standing on
shaky ground. Propelled by discrete cells, the breasts took off,
agitating now and rolling into still more breasts, creating nodes and
loops along the way. Something exclaimed Oh and screeched in the
air, and fountains of milk unexpectedly struck the night sky. One
agent thought to himself, "Life is sweet," not knowing what to take
hold of, and feeling that the whole of his existence was being
swallowed up.

Meanwhile she kept on calling
As a result of the resonance the lids of the canned goods in the
diplomatic grocery store on Great Georgia Street flew off. A not
unknown boil beneath the nose of an Algerian bey attained the

серебряные вилочки для лимона. эскалация чувств приобретала необратимый характер.

Я люблю тебя
неслось по номерам 01, 02, 03 и по всем знакомым и незнакомым телефонам аэропортов и моргов и разных всеобъемлющих служб не ограниченного доверия, республиканских, гражданских, военных, приемных, родных и частных лиц, и она сколупывала рождественские узоры со стекла автоматной будки и ударяла носком сапога со скрюченными от холода пальцами в металлическую стенку. Бум. Бум. Потом через восьмерку — 8, 10, 12 и дальше международные коды — 212, 415, 422 — но Европа спала, а Америка делала вид, что не понимает по-русски. Затаилась, сука, и ничто не шевельнулось в ее зажравшихся просторах в ответ на отчаянный любовный призыв. Лишь на главной фондовой бирже Нью-Йорка слегка приподнялся индекс Доу Джонса. И то ненадолго.

Длинные тени от фонарей и редкие огни пролетающих мимо машин шелковое шуршание ветра в трех соснах ощупью бредущих в темноте навстречу несуществующей опасности и пес с ним с этим случайно подвернувшимся под руку пейзажем лунной московской ночи бестрепетно глотающей самые изысканые мерцающие и недоступные усталому человеческому уху звуки и дуновения

Она звонила подставляя то правую то левую щеку Несколько странных фигур бежало по подземному переходу, таща за собой странную поклажу. Увидев ее у очередного автомата, один из странников ненадежно улыбнулся и зачем-то попросил закурить. Она успела набрать еще один номер и произнести по крайней мере два из трех, входящих в идиому слов, прежде, чем переход наполнился едким, возбуждающим в первые секунды запахом нитрокраски, и видимость резко ухудшилась.

menacing dimensions of a minaret, and the garlic fell from the ears of
high-ranking flu-sufferers, and cuff-links of malachite and silver lemon
forks began to tremble slightly on looking-glass tables. The escalation
of sensations acquired an irreversible character.

I love you
went out to emergency numbers 01, 02, 03, and to all the known and
unknown numbers of airports and mortuaries and all-embracing crisis
hotlines, republic, civil, military, offices of relatives and private
persons, and she scratched the Christmas designs off the glass of the
phone booth. Her toes throbbing from the cold, she kicked the metal
wall with the toe of her boot. Boom. Boom. Then she started in on
the listings beginning with the number 8, then 10, and 12, and then the
international codes, 212, 415, 422, but Europe was sleeping, and
America pretended that it did not understand Russian. America was
hiding, the bitch, and nothing stirred in her gorged expanses in
response to the desperate appeal of love. Only the Dow Jones index
at the New York Stock Exchange rose slightly, and that not for long.

The long shadows of streetlamps and occasional headlights flying by
the silky rustle of wind in the woods dragging blindly in the dark
toward an imaginary danger and to hell with it with this landscape
accidentally thrust beneath an arm of a moonlit Moscow night
swallowing without trembling the most refined shimmering sounds
and breaths of wind beyond the tired ear of man

She called, the phone pressed now to her right cheek now the left
Several strange figures ran through the underground passage,
dragging a strange load behind them. Having spotted her in the next
phone booth, one of the strangers flashed an insecure smile, and for
some reason asked for a smoke. She had time to dial one more
number and to pronounce at least two of the three words in the
phrase before the passage filled with the caustic, rousing smell of
nitric acid based paint, and visibility abruptly diminished.

Большая Медведица медленно поползла в свою берлогу, комкая и волоча за собой тяжелую влажную простыню ночного неба. Заиграла скрипка.

Официант принес мороженое. Она откинулась в кресле, положив ногу на ногу и теребя в кармане зажигалку. Сотрапезники обменивались расслабленными шутками. Она взглянула на их руки, лежащие на столе, на коленях, подпирающие щеки, свободно свешиваю —щиеся с подлокотников, разные, непохожие одна на другую руки по-разному дорогих и близких ей людей. Ее неожиданно удивила подлинность деталей.

Ursa Major, the Big Bear slowly crawled into her den, dragging behind her a heavy humid stretch of night sky. A violin began to play.

The waiter brought ice cream. She crossed her legs and leaned back in her chair, fiddling with the lighter in her pocket. Her table-companions exchanged feeble jokes. She looked at their hands lying on the table, at their knees propping up their cheeks or hanging freely over the arms of their chairs, at the various dissimilar hands of these people who were near and dear to her for various reasons. The authenticity of details unexpectedly amazed her.

Волосы

разматывающиеся в бегущую строку
наклоняющуюся к подлиннику
как луна с расстегнутой кобурой и катетером на боку
наклоняется к памятнику непоколебимому мудаку
волосы заколебавшие несчастный маятник Фуко
и камуфлирующие бестактность нервного напряжения
под бесконтактное обожание в стиле кон фу

волосы в томатном соусе в саквояже на пляже

на только что взятом и тут же оставленном рубеже
бархатного корсажа
волосы в каше в меду и в поту
доказывающие свою правоту
извиваясь на свежеокрашенном пахучем паучьем полу

волосы отирающиеся в подземном переходе
отирающие кафельное подножие мастурбирующей тверди
за элементарным неимением
того что не подвержено серьезным изменениям
волосы виснущие клубками на подножке вяло агонизирую —
щего велосипеда
хронологически ожиревшего уже в марте
уже в третьей его декаде
равнодушного к собственной
            а также общекультурной смерти
перепутавшиеся волосы Марии и Марфы
волосы которые еще в состоянии дать по морде
но и то лишь под влиянием морфия
или хотя бы инцеста

волосы которым еще не время и не место
неродившиеся
глубоко забившиеся
под кожу

HAIR

unreeling itself across the electric billboard
bowing to the original
like a moon wearing an open holster and a catheter on one side
it bows to the monument to an unwavering prick
the hair that's shaking off Foucault's unfortunate pendulum
camouflaging the nervous tension's tactlessness
with kung-fu style adoration   without physical contact

hair on the chest and in the groin

hair in the tomato sauce   in a duffel   on the beach
on the velvet bodice's border just over-run
and immediately abandoned
hair in the porridge in the honey   and in the sweat
proving its case
writhing across the freshly painted stinking spider-speckled floor

hair wiping itself dry along the underground walkway
wiping the tiled pedestal of the masturbating firmament
due to an elementary want
not susceptible to serious changes
hair hanging in tangles over the agonizing bicycle's footboard
grown chronologically fat though it's only March
lingering in its own death agony
hair already in its third week and
indifferent to its own death
      as well as the death of all culture
entangled hair of Mary and Martha
hair still capable of applying a shot in the chops
though only under the influence of morphine
or perhaps incest

hair still lacking a proper time or place
unborn
deeply penetrated

голубой виссон облепивший висок
и богатый эритроцитами пурпур
с прожилками грубой деревенской пряжи
уже и не волосы даже
а дождь
длящийся
льющийся
изнутри наружу
орошающий бледные измученные бессонницей рожи
не дождь а родник
в котором плещется и булькает и кончает от удовольствия его
собственный двойник
как богатый цитатами кипятильник

волосы благородных мужей и рептилий
сплетающиеся в подвижную влажную матрицу
завораживающую птиц охранников и коров
образующую низколетящий щадящий покров
над всем
чтимым

beneath the skin
blue byssus swarming around the temples
and the luxuriant purple from red corpuscles
with veins of crude homespun thread

already not even the hair really
but the rain
lasting
pouring
from inside to outside
watering the pale faces tortured by insomnia
not the rain but a spring
where its own double is splashing and gurgling and
        coming with pleasure
like a kettle rich with quotations
the hair of noble men and reptiles
weaving itself into a mobile humid matrix
bewitching the birds   the guards the cows
forming a low flying protective cloak
over those
revered

Секс — пятиминутка

Он взял ее через пожарный кран
И через рот   посыпался гербарий
Аквариум нутра   мерцал и падал в крен
Его рвало   обеими ногами
Мело-мело   весь уик-энд в Иране
Он взял ее
на весь вагон

Он ел ее органику   и нефть
забила бронхи узкие от гона
Он мякоть лопал   и хлестал из лона
И в горле у него кипела медь
    Мело-мело   весь месяц   из тумана
Он закурил
решив передохнуть

Потом он взял ее через стекло
через систему линз   и конденсатор
как поплавок зашелся дрожью сытой
Когда он вынимал ~~свое гребло~~   свое сверло
    Мело-мело
Мело

Потом отполз   и хрипло крикнул ФАС
И стал смотреть   что делают другие
Потом он вспомнил кадр из "Ностальгии"
и снова взял ее   уже через дефис
    Мело-мело   с отвертки на карниз
на брудершафт   Как пьяного раба
завертывают на ночь в волчью шкуру
Он долго ковырялся с арматурой
    Мело-мело
Он взял ее в гробу
И как простой   искусствоиспытатель

Sex — A Five-Minute Briefing

He took her through a fire hydrant
And through her mouth   an herbarium began to fall
An aquarium of innards   shimmered & banked
He threw up   with both legs
It snowed & snowed   the whole weekend in Iran
He took her
from one end of the train to the other

He ate her organics   while the gas fumes
choked his bronchial tubes   exhausted from his chase
the way he ate away at her tissues   swilled from her loins
and copper seethed in his throat
    It snowed & snowed   all month   from the fog
He lit a smoke
took a break

Later he took her through a plate of glass
through a system of lenses   & a condenser
like a bobber began to shake with a gorged tremor
when he took out ~~his paddle~~   his drill
    It snowed & snowed
& snowed

Then he even crawled away & yelled   SIC HER
began to observe   how the others proceeded with her too
Then he remembered a close-up shot from the film *Nostalgia*
& he took her again   through a hyphen this time
    It snowed & snowed   from the screwdriver to the fine
trim
Drink to brotherhood!   Like a drunken slave
wrapped for a night in wolf's clothing
He rummaged among the fixtures
    It snowed & snowed
He took her in a coffin

он прижимал к желудку костный мозг
превозмогая пафос   и кишечный смог

он взял ее   уже почти без роз
почти без гордости   без позы   в полный рост
через анабиоз
и выпрямитель

И скрючившись ~~от мерзости~~   от нежности   и мата
он вынул душу   взяв ее   как мог
через Урал   Потом закрыл ворота
и трясся до утра   от холода и пота
не попадая в дедовский замок
    Мело-мело   от пасхи до салюта

Шел мокрый снег   Стонали бурлаки
И был невыносимо ~~гениталeн~~   гениален
его   кадык
            переходящий
                    в голень
как пеликан   с реакцией Пирке
не уместившийся в футляры готовален
    Мело-мело   Он вышел из пике

Шел мокрый снег   Колдобило   Смеркалось
Поднялся ветер   Харкнули пруды
В печной трубе раскручивался дым
насвистывая оперу Дон Фаллос
    Мело-мело   Он вышел из воды
Сухим   Как Щорс
И взял ее еще раз

And like a simple   art investigator
he pressed her bone marrow to her stomach
overcoming the sensation of pathos   & intestinal smog
he took her without roses
& almost without pride   not posing at full height
through anabiosis and converter

And having hunched over her ~~out of vileness~~   out of tenderness
& abuse
                    he pulled out her soul   having taken her   the best he
could
across the Urals   Then he closed the gate
trembled until morning   in the cold & sweat
prick open the door
but no he never picked grandaddy's lock
        It snowed & snowed   from Easter to May Day

A wet snow fell   The barge-haulers groaned
And it was unbearably ~~genitalia~~   genius
his Adam's apple
                    dropping to his shin
like a pelican   with the Pirquet reaction
that doesn't fit the law of a draftsman's tools
        It snowed & snowed   he pulled out of the nose dive

A wet snow fell   the sky   it grew dark
the wind picked up   the pond hawked
smoke in the stove pipe   untwirled
whistling the opera Don Phallus
        It snowed & snowed   He came out of the water
Dry   Like Shchors
And then he took her once more.

Tatiana Shcherbina
Татьяна Щербина

Tatiana Georgievna Shcherbina. Poet, prose writer and essayist. Born in Moscow in 1954, Shcherbina emerged in the early 1980s as the spokesperson for the new, independent Moscow culture. Her work was first published in the official press of the Soviet Union in 1986, in the journal *Druzhba narodov*. Five volumes of her poetry were published in samizdat prior to 1990: *Lebedinaia pesnia* (Swan Song, 1981), *Tsvetnye reshetki* (Colored Grillwork, 1981), *Novyi panteon* (New Pantheon, 1983), *Natiurmort s prevrashcheniami* (Still-life with Transformations, 1985), and *Nol' Nol'* (Nothing-Nothing, 1987). Her novel, *Ispoved' shpiona* (A Spy's Confession), was published in samizdat in 1988. After 1991 some of these works were published openly, and a selected edition of her poetry entitled *Shcherbina* appeared in Moscow in 1991. Her poetry is now widely published in both established and experimental journals at home and abroad, and has been translated into Dutch, German, French, and English. Shcherbina has been a featured reader at the 1989 International Poetry Festival in Rotterdam and at the 1992 Trois-Rivières festival in Canada. From 1991 to 1994 she worked as a cultural commentator for Radio Liberty. In 1994 she was awarded a Bourse de Création from the French Ministry of Culture. After living abroad for several years in the early 1990s, Tatiana Shcherbina returned to Moscow, where she has served as editor-in-chief of the cultural journal *Estet* (Aesthete) since 1995.

Translations by J. Kates

Натюрморт

Дзынь — Бум — Хрясть:
тут упасть или там упасть,
семя чувствует почву как жадную пасть.
То ли падать не надо, а надо стоять
как последняя проросшая в воздухе белая травка,
и безумный гравер, с золотыми чернилами кафка,
пишет: "семя сие удалось непорочно зачать."

А семя Дзынь — Хрясть — Бум:
отправиться наобум
то ли к этакой матери, то ли к эдакой матери,
то ли плыть сиротой на подветренном катере:
оазис — ура! оазис — ура!
Все какая-то мура.

Хрясть — Бум — Дзынь:
мать моя — солнце родом из желтых дынь,
отец — бумеранг месяц лунный олень,
между ними — евклидова параллель:
il — отражение il, elle — отражение elle.

Семя, которое как мотылек, как форель
бьется бьется о свет фонаря,
запертый за стеклянную дверь …
Натюрморт: тьма египетская в базарный день.

Still-life

Zing — Boom — Snap:
drop here and there drop
the seed senses the ground like a greedy trap.
Whether it needs to fall, it needs to stay put
as the last white grasslet rising into the air
and kafka, with golden ink a crazy engraver
writes: "The seed succeeded, conceived immaculate."

The seed Zing — Snap — Boom:
sets out at random
either toward this mother or that mother
or swimming orphaned toward a leeside cutter:
hurrah, an oasis! hurrah, an oasis!
And all of it a mess!

Snap — Boom — Zing:
my mother's a sun descended from yellow melons,
father a boomerang full moon lunar elk,
between them a euclidean parallel:
il mirroring *il, elle* mirroring *elle* .

The seed, mothlike, like trout
knocks knocks against the lantern's light
locked behind a glass door ...
Still-life: pitch-dark on a market day.

Мачеха

Володе Сорокину

Борщи компоты и рассольники
варила Золушка в кастрюле,
которая на подоконнике
в шумерской солнечной культуре
видала за окном пейзажики
помоек строек демонстраций,
а в спальню к непорочной Машеньке
Иосиф приходил…
В кастрюле же из чиста золота
мутнел бульон из синей птицы,
и только перец черный молотый
(как подновляет тушь ресницы)
спасал птенца зазеленевшего.
В окне зазеленевший полис
встречал прохладой утро, лезшее
будильником, чтоб жнец, торговец,
кузнец микенско-критской хартии
узрел, что рядом не пантера,
а знатный хлебороб, член партии,
и коль родит, то пионера.
За что же Золушке по харе-то?
За то что жизнь у ней кастрюльная,
кастрюля кровью хоть не залита,
сравнима — с погребальной урною,
на ней гравюры процарапаны
костьми нежнейших птеродактилей,
слезами липкими закапаны
блядей и золотоискателей.
А Мариванна мужа потчует
и Золушку бранит, не зная,
что потому что непорочная,
поэтому и неродная.

The Stepmother

for Volodya Sorokin

Cinderella boiled up borscht,
pickled fish soups and jellies in a pot,
and over the windowsill
of a Sumerian, sun-drenched culture
saw her bit of landscape —
sites rites demonstrations —
while Joseph stepped into the bedroom
to his immaculate Mary ...
In the clean golden pot
bluebird bouillon stewed,
and only ground black pepper
(like kohl enlivening an eyelash)
saved the little bird from turning green
Outside the window a policy of turning green
encountered the cool morning, used an alarm clock
to climb in, so that the reaper, the merchant,
the smith of the creto-mycenean charter
saw not a panther at her side
but a known wheat-farmer, a party member,
and if he breeds: it'll be a Pioneer.
But what's that smeared on Cinderella's mug?
what about her potted life,
the saucepan unflooded not even with blood,
resembling a funerary urn,
with engravings scratched up
by the bones of the tenderest of pterodactyls,
already dripping with the adhesive tears
of hookers and gold-diggers.
Meanwhile, Mary Jane will entertain her husband
and rail against Cinderella, not knowing
that because she is immaculate
she is wholly unnatural.

Эрос Поэзис

Дурь семейства конопляного,
запах роз и *J'ai osé*,
вкус кумыса полупьяного,
нежных мусса и бизе —
в мире нет такой инъекции,
нет такого и шприца, —
так сказала б я на лекции
с идиомою лица.
А сама лежу и думаю совсем напротив, в пятистопном ямбе,
что башмачком хрустальным, крупной суммою, я не владею,
чтоб остаться в тампле "Июль в Москве."
Нет горя мчаться в Сочи!
Индийский чай подкрасит одурь ночи
в цвет фернамбука, в самый злой загар,
с которым не живут ни дольше утра,
ни дальше мест, где чтится Камасутра.
Шипит р а г у там, где затих у г а р,
(ось палигдрома: "ха" на "ах" — насмешка)
и уайт стал блэк — гарь, копоть, сажа, Пешка
взамен противуцветных королевств.
Постоем женихов-невест
становится всё та же Плешка.
Теперь мне впору зарыдать
и солью слез Эйякулировать:
любовь — есть только повод дать,
поэзия — артикулировать.

Eros Poesis

Idiocy of the hemp family,
scent of roses and *J'ai osé*,
a taste of tipsy koumiss,
tender mousse and custard —
no jolt like it in the world
and no such syringe —
so said I after a good lecture
in the idiom of the visage.
But by myself I lie thinking
just the opposite in my own special iambic pentameter —
that with a glass slipper, a stupendous sum I don't possess,
I can remain in the sanctuary of Moscow-in-July
no need yet to head for the southern shore!
Indian tea underscores the night's stupor
in the color of brazilwood, in the worst kind of sunburn,
that will kill you before noon
nor farther than Kama Sutra is exalted:
where a raga is stewed, as sober as an agar of passion,
the palindrome's axle (ha, ah) is a mockery,
and blanc turned noir — char, blacking, soot.
Sacrifice a pawn for the other-colored kingdom.
Where the bride and her jolly good fellow
might as well lie in a bordello.
Now is just the time for me
to let it all out
in sobbing or ejaculactivity:
Love is laying yourself open,
poetry is saying it aloud.

Весь город озарен влеченьем,
все улицы — мои следы,
дома как теплые печенья
вбирают запахи среды.
К зеленым нервным окончаньям
кустов добавились цвета,
средь них бордовый — цвет печали
и всякая белиберда.
Вдруг город гаснет, вдруг, воочью
он, только что еще живой,
стоит, обуглившийся, ночью,
днем как покойник — восковой.
Смотрю в чужие окна, лица,
и со знакомого пути
сбиваюсь — может, в Альпах скрыться
иль как Суворов — перейти.

The whole city seductively lit up
all the streets are my footsteps,
the homes like warm baked goods
absorb the odors of their surroundings.
Shrubbery flowers are added in
among the nervous green endings —
claret the color of sorrow
and every white heap of nonsense.
Suddenly the city is extinguished,
suddenly, in my own eyes,
only just this minute alive,
it stands charred in the night,
and in the daylight corpse-like, waxen.
I look into alien windows, faces,
slip away from the familiar
route — maybe to hide out in the Alps
or, like Suvorov, to cross them.

Vsevolod Nekrasov

Всеволод Некрасов

Vsevolod Nikolaevich Nekrasov was born in Moscow in 1934. He studied philology at the now defunct Institut imeni Potemkina in Moscow. Although he is the author of over 700 poems, distinguished by their minimalist and visual qualities, very little of Nekrasov's work was published in the former Soviet Union, where he was best known for his children's poems, and until recently, only a handful of his poetry has been published in the West. His work has been translated into English, German, and Czech and is featured in the anthology *Russian Poetry: The Modern Period*. A volume of poems, *100 Stikhotvorenii* (100 Poems) appeared in 1987. In addition to his poetry, Nekrasov has also published several critical articles and co-authored a book on A. N. Ostrovsky.

Translations by Gerald Janecek

~

Какой я Пушкин

я кто
Некрасов

не тот Некрасов
и еще раз не тот

не хвастаюсь я
а хочу только сказать

с вас

и такого хватит

What kind of Pushkin am I

I'm who
Nekrasov

not that Nekrasov
and also not the other one

I'm not bragging
but I only want to say

from you

even that is enough

~

а кто у нас
самый самый
культурный

как   кто   вон
   он
самый культурный

что   как   вот
   он
сам намекнул

~

so who of us
is the most most
cultured

what   who   there
 he's
the most cultured

that   what   look
 he's
pointing to himself

~

Это

не должно повториться

повторяю

Это

не должно повториться

Это

не должно повториться

Это

не должно повториться

повторяю

I repeat

    this
    must not
    be repeated

I repeat

    this
    must not
    be repeated

I repeat

    this
    must not
    be repeated

    this
    must not
    be repeated

    this
    must not
    be repeated

I repeat

~

Что-то я так хочу
В Ленинград

Так хочу в Ленинград

Только я так хочу

В Ленинград

И обратно

~

Somehow I really want to go
To Leningrad

I really want to go to Leningrad

Only I really want to go

To Leningrad

And back

Mikhail Aizenberg
Михаил Айзенберг

Mikhail Natanovich Aizenberg. Architect, poet and essay-
ist. Born in Moscow in 1948, Aizenberg graduated from
the Moscow Architectural Institute in 1972. He began
writing poetry in the mid-1960s but worked as a restora-
tion architect until 1989. In 1990 he became a literary con-
tributor to the newspaper *Moskovskii Nabliudatel'* and the
following year began to work as a literary consultant for
the publishing house Russlit and the magazine *Glas*. In
addition to writing articles for journals such as *Teatr, De-
korativnoe iskusstvo, Oktiabr'*, and *Literaturnaia gazeta*, Ai-
zenberg has published his poems in *Kontinent, Vremia i my,
Teatr, Glas, Zvezda, Znamia, Ogonek, Vestnik Novoi Literatu-
ry*, and others. He has published two volumes of poetry,
Ukazatel' Imen (Name Index, 1993), and *Punktuatsiia mest-
nosti* (Local Punctuation, 1995) as well as a book of essays,
Vzgliad na svobodnogo khudozhnika (1997). In English trans-
lation his poems have been published in Russia (*Glas* and
Hungry Russian Winter), England (*Novostroika*), New
Zealand (*Takahe*), the United States (*Green Mountains
Review, Harvard Review, Kenyon Review, Onthebus, Plum
Review, Poetry International, River Styx, Mr. Cogito, Sala-
mander*) and are featured in *Third Wave: The New Russian
Poetry* (1992). A special issue of *Russian Studies in Litera-
ture* (Spring 1996) was devoted completely to a collection
of Aizenberg's essays on contemporary Russian poetry.

Mikhail Aizenberg was a visiting poet at the Universi-
ty of Michigan in spring 1994.

Translations by J. Kates

Кто из тех, кто вошел в поток,
вытянет коготок?
Ни один. Ни один не выйдет.
Ни один не вырвется невредим.

Или выйдет за всех один?

Вставшая тьмой в очах,
кто же она? —
если гибнет в тысячах,
если платит тысячей за одного сполна —

Жизнь? Повтори на слух.
Звук-то какой.
Слово само с дырой.
Или трясина сила ее порук?
Ксива — ее пароль?

Не забывай: ксива.
Не забывай, что она едва
едва выносима,
если не мертва.

И скажи спасибо

И скажи спасибо

Who of those who step into the stream
wriggles out of its talons?
Not one. No one gets out.
Not one gets away unharmed.

Or does one only escape alone?

Having risen as darkness in the eyes,
who exactly is it?
If it perishes by the thousands
if it pays in full, thousands for one —

Life? Say it again out loud.
What a sound.
The word itself has a hole in it.
Did a quagmire go its bail?
Is some paperwork its countersign?

Don't forget: paperwork.
Don't forget, that it's barely,
barely endurable,
if it's not already dead.

And say thank you.

Say thank you.

Вот и открылось.
Все двери открылись, все дыры.
Сильно задуло.

Нечто, имевшее вид квартиры.
Нечто, имевшее ножки стула.
Спинку кровати. Силу привычки.
Знак спасительного отпора,
говорящего (если ввести кавычки):

"Не сегодня. Еще и не очень скоро."

Или жизнь от какой-то неведомой скрытой тяги
облетела. Остался один скелет.

Оглянулся вокруг,
а вокруг ничего уже нет.
Просто чистое поле,
по которому носятся то ли бабочки,
                    то ли обрывки бумаги.

Look what's come to light.
All the doors cracked open, all the holes.
Blown out.

Something with the look of a flat.
Something with chair-legs.
The back of a bed. The strength of habit.
The mark of a salutary rebuff,
saying (let's put it in quotes):

"Not today. Not very soon, either."

Or life scattered by some kind
of unknown secret force
leaving only the bones.

Took a look around
and there's nothing left to see.
Only an open field
fluttering with what might be butterflies
        or scraps of paper.

~

Не в печной трубе, а в газовой,
верно с первого этажа,
тихо шепчут или подсказывают,
или голосом сторожат.

Ходит гул по железной флейте —
сторожиха твердит свое,
или мысленный слабый ветер
там гуляет и так поет.

Не пугает и не забавит
голосок неизвестно чей, —
перепевы кухонных баек
и позвякиванье ключей.

Но каким-то последним звоном
все приманивает к себе,
неуверенным угомоном,
просочившимся по резьбе.

Not in the chimney, but in the gas-pipes,
probably from the first floor,
they are whispering quietly, suggestively,
like voices on guard.

A rumble runs through the iron flute —
the concierge mumbling to herself,
or a weak wind in the mind down there
floats around singing like that

whose unknown little voice wasn't
meant to frighten or to please —
the reiterations of kitchen gossip
and the jingling of keys.

But somehow with its last resonance
it lures everything to itself.
with an uncertain peace and quiet
percolating through the pipe-threads.

А где тот человек, что нам оставил ворох
изрезанных газет и дес'тилетний сор?
в дырявом пиджаке, в опорках за семь-сорок
уехал под забор.

Что, каково ему на итальянской даче,
на римском пикнике,
пока он дорожит единственной удачей —
исчезнуть налегке.

Что б вывезти на вес в разорванном пакете
с запасом сигарет?
Где б погулять ему, пока на этом свете
не выключили свет?

So where is that guy who left us piles
of torn-up newspapers and ten years' litter?
in a ratty jacket and second-hand shoes
he hit the skids.

He's got no use for Italian villas
or for a Roman picnic,
there's only one kind of success he prizes,
get out easy and quick.

What weight would he carry among his stuff
with a supply of cigarettes?
And where would he go, until in this life
they put out the lights?

Sergey Gandlevsky
Сергей Гандлевский

Sergei Mikhailovich Gandlevsky was born in Moscow in 1952. He studied at the Philological Faculty of Moscow State University, where he met and became friends with young poets such as Aleksandr Soprovsky , Aleksandr Kazintsev and Bakhyt Kenjeev. It was at this time that he began to write poetry himself and became an active participant in underground literary culture. Although not published in his own country, Gandlevsky's work appeared in émigré journals such as *Kontinent, Russkaia Mysl'*, and *Strelets*. With the advent of glasnost in the later 1980s, however, Gandlevsky's work also began to appear in Russian publications such as *Novyi Mir, Iunost', Znamia*, and *Oktiabr*. Winner of both the "Little Booker Prize" and the "Anti-Booker Prize" in 1996 for his poetry and prose, Sergei Gandlevsky has published two books of poetry, *Rasskaz* (A Story, 1989), and *Prazdnik* (Celebration, 1995), as well as a memoir, *Trepanatsia Cherepa* (Trepanation of the Skull, 1996). His work has been included in the English translation anthologies *Third Wave* (1992) and *20th Century Russian Poetry: Silver and Steel* (1993).

Translations by Philip Metres

~

Вот наша улица, допустим,
Орджоникидзержинского.
Родня советским захолустьям,
Но это все-таки Москва.
Вдали топорщатся массивы
Промышленности некрасивой —
Каркасы, трубы, корпуса
Настырно лезут в небеса.
Как видишь, нет примет особых:
Аптека, очередь, фонарь
Под глазом бабы. Всюду гарь.
Рабочие в пунцовых робах
Дорогу много лет подряд
Мостят, ломают, матерят.
Вот автор данного шедевра,
Вдыхая липы и бензин,
Четырнадцать порожних евра-
бутылок тащит в магазин.
Вот женщина немолодая,
Хорошая, почти святая,
Из детской лейки на цветы
Побрызгала и с высоты
Балкона смотрит на дорогу.
На кухне булькает обед,
В квартирах вспыхивает свет.
Ее обманывали много
Родня, любовники, мужья —
Сегодня очередь моя.

There's our street, let's say —
Ordzhonikidzerzhinsky.
Just like the Soviet provinces
But still Moscow anyway.
In the distance the blocks bristle
With the ugliness of heavy industry —
Carcasses, pipes, complexes
Stubbornly crawl to the heavens.
As you see, there's nothing special here —
Drugstore, a line of folks, a shiner under
A girl's eye. Everywhere, a burning smell.
The workers in orange overalls
Pave, break apart, and curse
The road year after year.

This is the author of some masterpiece
Inhaling linden and gasoline.
And the fourteen empty Euro-
Bottles he hauls to the store.
This is the good, no longer young
Near saintly woman who splashes water
From a child's watercan on flowers
And looks out on the road
From the balcony's height.
In the kitchen, dinner simmers.
In apartments, light blazes up.
They have let her down often
These kin, these lovers, men.
Today it's my turn.

Мы здесь росли и превратились
В угрюмых дядь и глупых теть.
Скучали, малость развратились —
Вот наша улица, Господь.
Здесь с окуджававской пластинкой,
Староарбатскою грустинкой
Годами прячут шиш в карман,
Испепеляют, как древлян,
Свои дурацкие надежды.
С детьми играют в города —
Чита, Сучан, Караганда.
Ветшают лица и одежды.
Бездельничают рыбаки
У мертвой Яузы-реки.

Такая вот Йокнапатофа
Доигрывает в спортлото
Последний тур (а до потопа
Рукой подать), гадает, кто
Всему виною — Пушкин, что ли?
Мы сдали на пять в этой школэ
Науку страха и стыда.
Жизнь кончится — и навсегда
Умолкнут брань и пересуды
Под небом старого двора.
Но знала чертова дыра
Родство сиротства — мы отсюда.
Так по родимому пятну
Детей искали в старину.

We grew up here, and now we've changed
Into gloomy uncles and foolish aunts.
We pined away, became a little perverted.
This is our street, dear Lord.
Here with an Okudjava record,
And Old Arbat sentiment,
Year after year, we pocket our contempt.
And burn down our foolish hopes
Like Drevlan reduced to ashes.
With children they play Geography:
Chita, Suchan, Karaganda.
Faces and clothes decay.
The fishermen loiter
At the dead Yauza River.

Such is this Yoknapatawpha
The last round of Sportlotto
Is finishing up (the flood is so near
You could almost touch it). And who's
to blame for all this, Pushkin, or what?
We passed with A's in this school
For the science of fear and shame.
Life will end, and forever
The swearing and the gossip will grow silent
Under the sky of the old yard.
But this godforsaken place knew
A kinship of orphanhood. We're from here.
So, by the hereditary birthmark
They searched for children in the old days.

Дай Бог памяти вспомнить работы мои,
Дать отчет обстоятельный в очерке сжатом.
Перво-наперво следует лагерь МЭИ,
Я работал тогда пионерским вожатым.
Там стояли два Ленина: бодрый старик
И угрюмый бутуз серебристого цвета.
По утрам раздавался воинственный крик
"Будь готов," отражаясь от стен сельсовета.
Было много других серебристых химер —
Знаменосцы, горнисты, скульптура лосихи.
У забора трудился живой пионер,
Утоляя вручную любовь к поварихе.

Жизнерадостный труд мой расцвел колесом
Обозрения с видом от Омска до Оша.
Хватишь лишку и Симонову в унисон
Знай бубнишь помаленьку: "Ты помнишь, Алеша?"
Гадом буду, в столичный театр загляну,
Где примерно полгода за скромную плату
Мы кадили актрисам, роняя слюну,
И катали на фурке тяжелого Плятта.
Верный лозунгу молодости "Будь готов,"
Я готовился к зрелости неутомимо.
Вот и стал я в неполные тридцать годов
Очарованным странником с пачки "Памира."

На реке Иртыше говорила резня.
На реке Сырдарье говорили о чуде.
Подвозили, кормили, поили меня
Окаянные ожесточенные люди.

Dear God, allow me to recall my works,
To give a detailed account in a concise sketch.
In the beginning there was M.E.I.,
Where I worked as a leader of the pioneers.
Two Lenins stood there: a cheerful old man
And a sullen chubby old gut of a silver color.
In the mornings the warlike cry "Be Prepared,"
Reverberating in the walls of the village soviet.
There were many other silvery chimeras —
Standard bearers, buglers, a sculpture of an elk.
At the fence a live pioneer toiled hard,
Satisfying by hand his love for the cook.

My cheerful work blossomed in a merry-
Go-round circling from Omsk to Osh.
If you drink one too many with Simonov
You'll mutter to yourself: "Remember, Alyosha ..."
And I'll damn well drop into the big-city theater,
Where for half a year and meager pay
We served actresses, slobbering saliva,
And wheeled heavy Plyatt across the stage.
True to the slogan of my youth — "Be prepared!"
I was tirelessly preparing for maturity
So I became in my unfull thirty years
The enchanted traveler on the pack of Pamir.

On the Irtysh River, daggers spoke.
On the Syr Darya, they spoke of wonders.
God-damned, life-toughened people
Gave me lifts, gave me food and drink

Научился я древней науке вранья,
Разучился спросить о погоде без мата.
Мельтешит предо мной одиссея моя
Кинолентою шосткинского комбината.
Ничего, ничего, ничего не боюсь,
Разве только ленивых убийц в полумасках.
Отшучусь как-нибудь, как-нибудь отсижусь
С Божьей помощью в придурковатых подпасках.

В настоящее время я числюсь при СУ-
206 под началом Н. В. Соткилава.
Раз в три дня караульную службу несу,
Шельмоватый кавказец содержит ораву
Очарованных странников. Форменный зо-
омузей посетителям на удивленье:
Величанский, Сопровский, Гандлевский, Шаззо —
Часовые строительного управленья.
Разговоры опасные, дождь проливной,
Запрещенные книжки, окурки в жестянке.
Стало быть, продолжается диспут ночной
Чернокнижников Кракова и Саламанки.

Здесь бы мне и осесть, да шалят тормоза.
Ближе к лету уйду, и в минуту ухода
Жизнь моя улыбнется, закроет глаза
И откроет их медленно снова — свобода.
Как впервые, когда рассчитался в МЭИ,
Сдал казенное кладовщику дяде Васе,
Уложил в чемодан причиндалы свои,

And I learned the ancient science of bullshit.
And always to cuss when asking about the weather.
My odyssey is passing fast before me
Like a film from the Shostkino factory.
Nothing, nothing, I'm afraid of nothing
Except perhaps lazy killers in half masks.
Laughing it off with a joke, with God's help
Ducking off among the foolish shepherd boys.

At present I'm signed up with the Builder's Corps
Two hundred and six led by Sotkilava.
Once in three days I take the night shift.
The cunning Caucasian keeps a whole bunch
Of enchanted travelers. Really an authentic zo-
Ological museum comprising all the visitors —
Velichansky, Soprovsky, Gandlevsky, Shazzo,
The watchguards of the building corporation.
Dangerous conversations, the flooding rain,
Forbidden books, cigarette butts in an empty tin.
Which means the nightly dispute of black-bookers
From Cracow and Salamanca continues.

It would be good to stay, but my brakes fail.
Near summer, I'll depart, and in the moment of leaving
This life of mine will smile, and close its eyes
And open them slowly again — on freedom.
Like the first time, when, leaving M.E.I.,
I returned the camp rentals to Vasya's storeroom.
I put all my own belongings into a trunk,

Встал ни свет ни заря и пошел восвояси.
Дети спали. Физорг починял силомер.
Повариха дремала в объятьях завхоза.
До свидания, лагерь. Прощай, пионер,
Торопливо глотающий крупные слезы.

Rose before dawn and went into the world.
The children were asleep. Phys. Ed. mended the handgrip.
The cook was dozing in the embraces of the Admin.
Goodbye, dear camp. Farewell, Pioneer,
Hurriedly swallowing tears.

~

Не сменить ли пластинку? Но родина снится опять.
Отираясь от нечего делать в вокзальном народе,
Жду своей электрички, поскольку намерен сажать
То ли яблоню, то ли крыжовник. Сентябрь на исходе.
Снится мне, что мне снится, как еду по длинной стране
Приспособить какую-то важную доску к сараю.
Перспектива из снов — сон во сне, сон во сне, сон во сне.
И курю в огороде на корточках, время теряю.
И по скверной дороге иду восвояси с шести
Узаконенных соток на жалобный крик элекрички.
Вот ведь спички забыл, а вернешься — не будет пути,
И стучусь наобум, чтобы вынесли — как его — спички.
И чужая старуха выходит на низкий порог
И моргает и шамкает, будто она виновата,
Что в округе ненастье и нету проезжих дорог,
А в субботу в Покровском у клуба сцепились ребята,
В том, что я ошиваюсь на свете дурак дураком
На осеннем ветру с незажженной своей сигаретой,
Будто только она виновата и в том и в другом,
И во всем остальном, и в несчастиях Родины этой.

Is it time to change the record? But I'm dreaming again
Of the motherland. At the station, shouldering past
People, bored, I wait for my train, since I intend to grow
Some apples or gooseberries. September's leaving.
I dream that I dream of crossing a wide country
To nail some important scrap of board to a shed.
Perspective of dreams is a dream within a dream.
So I smoke, squat down in potatoes, burn off time.
And over the muddy road I go home, from six
Legally owned ten-by-ten plots to the train's plaintive cry.
But damn, no matches, and there's no return home if I go back.
So I knock randomly, wherever, along the way. Matches,
And a strange old woman leans through a low frame
And blinks and mumbles as if she were to blame
That the weather's bad and there are no smooth roads,
That on Saturday in town the guys came to blows
That I wander the halls of the world like a fool,
An unlit cigarette in this hard autumn gale —
As if she were to blame for this and that, and
For the rest, for the troubles of this motherland.

Ай да сирень в этом мае! Выпукло-крупные гроздья
Валят плетни в деревнях, а на Бульварном кольце
Тронут лицо в темноте — душемутительный запах.
Сердце рукою сдави, восвояси иди, как слепой.
Здесь на бульварах впервой повстречался мне голый дошкольник,
Лучник с лукавым лицом; изрядно стреляет малец!
Много воды утекло. Старая только заноза
В мякоти чудом цела. Думаю, это пройдет.
Поутру здесь я сидел нога на ногу гордо у входа
В мрачную пропасть метро с ветвью сирени в руках.
Кольца пускал из ноздрей, пил в час пик газировку,
Улыбнулся и рек согражданам в сердце своем:
"Дурни, куда вы толпой? Олухи, мне девятнадцать.
Сроду нигде не служил, не собираюсь и впредь.
Знаете тайну мою? Моей вы не знаете тайны:
Ночь я провел у Лаисы. Виктор Зоилыч рогат."

Oh, how the lilacs are this May! Bulging-large bunches fell
Fences in the villages, and on the Boulevard Ring's turning
They touch your face in the darkness — a smell to stir the soul.
Squeeze your heart in your hand, go home like a blind man. I first
Met a naked kindergartener here on the Boulevard —
An archer with a sly look. And, may I say, that kid can shoot!
Much water has flowed under the bridge. Only an old splinter
In the flesh miraculously intact. I think it'll pass.
That morning, I sat here cross-legged and proud at the entrance
To a gloomy cave of the Metro, lilac branch in hand.
I sent a smoke-ring from my nostril, drank soda at rush hour,
Smiled and spoke my heart to my fellow citizens:
"Fools, where are you headed, all in a crowd? Dolts, I'm nineteen.
I've never held down a job, not planning to anytime soon.
But do you know my secret? Can't you guess my secret?
I spent last night at Laisa's — Victor Zoilich is now a cuckold …

Tatiana Bek

Татьяна Бэк

Tatiana Aleksandrovna Bek, born in Moscow in 1949, is the daughter of the writer Aleksandr Bek. She graduated from the Journalism Department of Moscow State University and was a member of the Writers' Union of the USSR. She has published three collections of verse: *Skvoreshniki* (Startlings, 1974), *Snegir'* (The Bullfinch, 1980), and *Zamysel'* (Scheme, 1987), and her work now appears regularly in various literary journals.

Translations by Richard McKane

~

Протяжная, как сказанье,
Короткая, как баллада,
Желанная, как касанье,
Соленая, как баланда, —

О жизнь, — не хочу, не надо,
Не буду с тобой судиться, —
И не упаду с каната,
Пока испытанье длится …

Мне силу даруют знаки:
Во-первых в дали пустынной
По склонам алеют маки
С чернильною сердцевиной.

И свет, во-вторых, не гаснет
В огромных проемах детства,
Где мир меня мучит,
                дразнит
И вводит в свое наследство.

И — в ландышах, в ливнях, в нетях —
Зовет к себе непреклонно
Родное кладбище, в-третьих,
У Водного стадиона.

И — сильный, как кровь в аортах,
Но легкий, как скарб скитальцев —
Я ветер люблю, в-четвертых
(Уже не хватает пальцев!), —

И не одинока, в-пятых,
Покуда на белом свете —
В царапинах и заплатах —
Живут старики и дети.

Oh life, long as an epic,
short as a ballad,
wished for as a caress,
salty as prison soup.

Oh life, I don't want to, don't need to
and will not go to court with you.
I will not fall off the tightrope,
while the trial is in progress.

Certain signs give me strength:
first, the poppies turning red
with their black-ink hearts
on the slopes of the distant wasteland;

second, the light that will not go out
in the huge doorways of childhood,
whose world torments and
                    teases me
and makes me come in to its inheritance;

third, the family cemetery
by Vodnoy Stadium,
that inexorably calls me to itself
with lilies-of-the-valley, cloudbursts and missing people.

fourth, the wind that I love,
powerful as blood in the aorta,
but light as the belongings of pilgrims —
now I'm running out of fingers;

fifth, that I will never be alone
while there are still in the world,
with their scratches and patched clothes:
the old and the children.

Я надышалась — и за меня выдох.
А до сих пор, беспечна и смела,
Я плакала на ваших панихидах,
Но смерть во мне без просыпу спала.

Всё переменилось. На простые вещи,
По узкому ступая рубежу,
Не то чтобы угрюмо и зловеще,
Но с ясною прощальностью гляжу.

Я не пойду дорогою окольной,
Не стану прятать знание в стогу …
Я мысль о смерти сделаю настольной,
Как лампа,
        без которой не могу.

~

I breathed my fill — and then breathed out.
And to this day, carefree and bold
I cried at your requiems,
but death slept within me and never woke.

Everything has changed. Walking the narrow borderline,
I look at simple things not so much
in malevolent depression,
but with the clear eyes of one saying farewell.

I shall not go by a roundabout way,
or hide my knowledge in a haystack ...
I shall make thinking about death so homely
that it shall be necessary as a lamp.

~

Долетает ли песня из сада,
Наклоняюсь ли низко над гробом, —
Я во всем, я во всем виновата,
И меня сотрясает ознобом

Не подхваченная малярия,
А наследственной памяти бездна
(эту бабушку звали Мария,
А про ту ничего не известно…)

И вобрав изведенные души,
Как бы ясно моя ни лучилась,
Я и нынче проснусь — не заснувши:
— Сколько боли кругом приключилось!

(это в муках ушедшая мама,
это темного времени вектор,
это над стадионом "Динамо"
Одиноко горящий прожектор…)

О, как быстро сменяются годы:
И метели, и талые воды,
И — позднее — крапивы и мята…
— Ты во всем, ты во всем виновата.

If a song flies to me from the garden,
or if I bend low over a grave —
I am guilty of everything, of everything,
and the malaria I haven't caught

makes me tremble with a fever,
and the abyss of inherited memory
(One grandmother was called Maria,
but no one knows anything about the other ...)

I absorb the souls I have come to know,
but however clearly my own shines
I shall wake up now without having slept:
"How much pain there is all around!"

(... This is my suffering mother going off,
this is the vector of dark times,
this is a solitary searchlight
burning over the Dynamo Stadium.)

Oh, how quickly years go by:
snowstorms, then the thaws,
and, later, nettles and mint ...
"You are guilty of everything, of everything."

Olesia Nikolaeva

Олесия Николаева

Olesia Nikolaeva. Poet and prose writer. Born in Moscow in 1955, Olesia Nikolaeva is one of the most widely published poets of the younger generation. She studied at the Gorky Literary Institute in Moscow, and has read widely in philosophy, religion and literature. Nikolaeva turned to religion in her twenties, becoming a church activist and learning ancient Greek, and her work is informed by a markedly religious sensibility as well as numerous allusions to the Bible. She was first published in 1972 in the journal *Smena*, and has since published three volumes of poetry: *Sad chudes* (Garden of Miracles, 1980), *Na korable zimy* (On the Ship of Winter, 1986), and *Smokovnitsa* (The Fig Tree, 1990). More recently, Nikolaeva has turned to prose, publishing a novella, *Invalid detstva* (Childhood Invalid, 1990) and a collection of shorter prose works, *Kliuchi ot mira* (The Keys to Peace / the World, 1990).

Translations by Paul Graves & Carol Ueland

Здесь всё съедят — и жир, и маринад,
и гуталин. Здесь принято гордиться
рудою в шахтах и пространством — над,
где сотня Франций может уместиться.

Не дорожат здесь небом дармовым,
что до земли — должно предназначаться
покойникам два метра, а живым
кому по шесть, кому и по двенадцать.

Здесь ритуальны подпись и печать
и диктор — для ума глухонемого.
Здесь может так в дороге укачать,
что не проснешься аж до дня восьмого.

И здесь когда-то в предрассветной мгле
кому ни есть — всем задали задачу:
построить Царство Божье на земле
с дворцам хрустальным до небес — в придачу!…

Here, everything gets eaten: drippings, marinade,
even shoe polish. Here, it's our custom to be proud
of the ore from the mines and the space up above,
where there's room enough to fit hundreds of Frances.

The sky isn't prized here for costing nothing;
as, as for earth, we have to allot the dead
their two meters, while some of the living
are given six, and some of them twelve.

Here, the signature, the seal, and the spokesman
are parts of a ritual for deaf and dumb minds.
The roads here can rock you so well
that you don't wake up until the eighth day.

And time was that here, in the dark before dawn,
whoever wanted to eat was set this task:
to build the Kingdom of God on earth
and a crystal heaven-scraping palace to boot.

Дочь

Девочка-приемыш — в порядочную семью
взята в семидневном возрасте из роддома.
Догадывается об этом. Ищет матерь свою.
Ищет отца своего. Ей кажется, что знакома
вот эта американочка с журнальных страниц
вот этот блондин из проехавшего лимузина.
Она смотрится в зеркало. Находит сходство.
⠀⠀⠀⠀Между ресниц
запечатлевается трагическая картина:
страшная буря обрушивается на корабль, —
каждый спасется на обломках.
В пасмурном небе заблудившийся дирижабль
опрокидывается от ветра. Все тонет в потемках.
Они терпят крушение у берегов Филиппин,
над Атлантическим океаном,
⠀⠀⠀⠀⠀над лесами Сибири …
Провидение их спасет из когтей, клыков и глубин,
но разбрасывает всех врозь и теряет в мире.
… Приемные родители посылают в школу,
⠀⠀⠀⠀⠀везут в метро.
Но какие-то в небе торжественные поют трубы!
Девочка поглядывает вокруг таинственно и хитро:
брови ее приподняты, поджаты губы.
Что-то ей нашептывает: вон та — волос курчав,
тонкий профиль, неизвестный мастер,
⠀⠀⠀⠀⠀английская миниатюра.
Что-то ей подсказывает: вон тот — величав,
орлиный нос, эполеты, царственная фигура!
… Перед ней выстраивается род человеческий
⠀⠀⠀⠀⠀во всей красе:
колышутся шляпы, клобуки, перья на шлеме.
На этот семейный праздник собираются все —
вплоть до Адама, который еще в эдеме …

Daughter

The little girl that a good family adopted, taken
from the maternity ward when she was seven days old,
is now full of guesses. She's looking for her real
mother and father. She sees something familiar
about that American woman who's in the magazines,
or the fair-haired man in the limo that just went by.
She studies herself in the mirror. Finds some resemblance.
Presses her eyelashes together for a tragic picture
of terrifying storms descending on a ship:
the passengers survive by hanging onto the wreckage;
or, in overcast weather a zeppelin is lost and the wind
keels it over: everything's plunged in darkness.
They've crashed on the shores of the Philippines,
or over the Atlantic, or in Siberian forests …
Providence saves them from the deep, from claws and teeth,
but scatters them through the world and forgets them.
— Though her adoptive parents send her to school and escort her
on the subway, what glorious trumpets sound for her in the sky!
The little girl casts sly, furtive glances around her;
she raises her eyebrows and purses her lips.
Something whispers, "That's her the slender woman
with curly hair!" — an English miniature by an unknown painter.
Something suggests, "That's him, that grand-looking man
with the eagle nose and epaulets; what a princely figure!"
In all its beauty the whole human tribe is gathered before her:
a fluttering of hats and mitres and plumes on helmets.
Every one of them has come to this family observance,
right back to Adam, who's still living in Eden.

Девичник

Катя гордится тем, что у нее муж престижный,
у которого есть возможность;
Лена гордится тем, что она в одиночку растит ребенка,
не требуя ничего от мира;
Света гордится тем, что у нее профессия
и высокооплачиваемая должность;
Таня гордится тем, что у нее собственная,
обставленная со вкусом квартира.

К другой женщине ушел престижный муж Кати.
Годы идут, а некому оценить мужественную душу Лены,
окрепшую средь испытаний.
Света, не сойдясь характером, ушла с работы —
ходит весь день в халате.
И как-то уныло и одиноко в доме у Тани.

Каждый год они устраивают девичник Восьмого марта.
Катя привозит торт и пирожные,
Лена — сыр с сервелатом,
Света — хорошие сигареты, кагор для азарта,
а Таня ставит современную музыку,
украшая стол жареной курицей и салатом.

— А вот, говорят, в Древней Греции, —
начинает кто-то, —
был такой остров, где одни женщины-амазонки жили,
так они мужиков к себе и на пушечный выстрел
не подпускали,
а тех, кого случайно приносила к ним буря,
убивали на месте!

A Party on Women's Day

Katya's proud she has a much-admired husband
 who's got what it takes;
Lena's proud she's raising a child by herself,
 asking nothing of the world;
Sveta's proud she's a professional in a well-paid position;
Tanya's proud she's got her own
 tastefully decorated apartment.

That much-admired husband of Katya's
 left her for another woman.
Years go by and no one prizes the brave spirit
 of Lena, toughened by experience.
Sveta, who never fit in, quit her job
 and walks around in her bathrobe all day.
And somehow it's depressing and lonely in Tanya's apartment.

Every year they throw a party on the eighth of March.
Katya brings cake and pastries,
 Lena brings cheese and salami;
Sveta, to warm things up, brings
 decent cigarettes and red wine;
Tanya puts on the latest music and arrays the table
 with fried chicken and salad.

"I've heard it said that in ancient Greece,"
 one of them begins,
"there was this island inhabited
 only by women, by Amazons,
and they didn't allow men to get within cannon-range;
any man brought there accidentally by storms
 was put to death on the spot."

эта история вызвала оживление, подняла настроение:
поговорили о греческой мудрости,
          послушали концерт мастеров эстрады
и даже сами потанцевали и обсудили
          следующее поколение,
и о пирожные с бутерброды
          вытерли праздничные помады.

До свиданья, Катя, —
выглядишь чудно при домашнем свете неярком!
До свиданья, Лена, —
тебе еще на троллейбусе, а там — через пустырь
          испуганными шажками!
До свиданья, Света, —
тебе направо, потом налево и —
          черным замерзшим парком!
До свиданья, Таня —
тебе еще мыть тарелки с недоеденными пирожками!…

And so, stirred by this tale, their mood grew lighter:
they talked about the Greeks' wisdom,
    listened to a concert of pop stars,
and even danced a little themselves; they fretted
    about the next generation
and left on their pastries and sandwiches
    the stain of festive lipsticks.

So long, Katya — you still look great in the dim apartment light.
So long, Lena — for you it's a trolley, and then
    a vacant lot to cross with frightened steps.
So long, Sveta — for you it's right, then left,
    and straight on through a black and frozen park.
So long, Tanya — for you it's time to wash up
    the plates with their half-eaten pastries.

Семь начал

I

Выходя из города,
где хозяйничают новостройки, новоселы и нувориши,
желание выбиться в люди, быть счастливым,
   убедить себя, что не страшен ад,
о дерзновеннейшая из женщин, душа моя,
      не поднимай горделивую голову еще выше,
не оглядывайся назад!

II

Выходя из города,
где кто-то любил кого-то,
где кто-то играл кому-то лучшую из Моцартовых сонат,
и рояль был совсем расстроен, и у Эрота облупился нос,
      и с Орфея осыпалась позолота,
о, не оглядывайся назад!

III

Выходя из города,
где праздновали дни рождений, дорожили мнением моды,
где, на панихиде встретившись, говорили:
      "Ба, давненько не виделись!" —
      пили вино и отщипывали виноград,
где болели хандрой и раком, убивали детей во чреве
      и принимали роды,
о, не оглядывайся назад!

IV

Выходя из города,
где тщеславились обильным столом, нарядом и башмаками,

Seven Beginnings

I

On leaving the city
where new buildings, newcomers and the nouveau riches are lords,
the desire to make it, to be happy,
    to be convinced that hell holds no terrors,
O most darling of women, my soul,
    don't lift your proud head any higher,
don't look back!

II

On leaving the city
where someone loved someone,
where someone played for someone the best of Mozart's sonatas,
and the piano was out of tune, and Eros' nose was chipped,
    and the gilding on Orpheus was flaking,
O, don't look back!

III

On leaving the city
where people had birthday parties
    and prized the dictates of fashion,
where, at a funeral, they would meet and say:
    "Well, long time no see!"
    and drink wine and pluck grapes,
where they fell ill with melancholia and cancer, killed children
    in the womb and midwifed at births,
O, don't look back!

IV

On leaving the city
where they gloried in their plentiful board, apparel and shoes,

задавали себе вопросы: "Зачем это все мне надо?" и
"Что это мне дает?" —
доказывали, что добро обязано быть с кулаками,
о, не оглядывайся, душа моя, но смотри вперед!

V

Выходя из города,
на который и жена праведника оглянулась,
ибо не всякая любовь остыла,
       и воспоминания разрывают грудь,
и не всякая стрела пропала,
       и не всякая струна прогнулась,
но ты, о душа моя, о душа моя, об этом забудь!

VI

Выходя из города,
в котором хоть один купол еще золотится
и хоть один колокол на высокой башне уверяет в том,
что не каждое слово — погибло
       и не каждая слеза в прах возвратится,
но ты, о душа моя, не оглядывайся,
       замрешь соляным столпом!

VII

Выходя из города —
уже поверженного, уже лежащего в пепле,
где даже оплакать некому своего мертвеца,
о, не оглядывайся, душа моя,
       забудь, оглохни, ослепни,
когда Господь выводит тебя из города твоего отца!

kept asking themselves, "What do I need it all for?"
    and "What will it get me?"
arguing that good was indebted to their fists,
O, don't look back, my soul, look ahead!

V

On leaving the city
at which even the righteous man's wife looked back,
because not every love has gone cold,
    because memories tear at the heart,
because not every arrow has missed,
    nor has every bowstring gone slack,
but you, O my soul, let this all be forgotten!

VI

On leaving the city
in which even one cupola still glistens
and even one bell from its high tower affirms
that not every word has perished
    and not every tear will be turned back to dust,
but you, O my soul, don't look back, you'll die
    and become a pillar of salt!

VII

On leaving the city
already overthrown, lying already in ashes,
where there isn't even anyone to mourn over the dead,
O, don't look back, my soul,
    but forget, and be deaf, and be blind
when the Lord brings you forth from the city of your father!

Olga Popova

Ольга Попова

Olga Popova was born in Leningrad in 1960. She studied Russian philology at Leningrad State University and then worked at the Museum of the History of Leningrad and as a guide at the Peter and Paul Fortress. With her husband, theologian and poet Grigory Benevich, she has published a very successful dictionary and calendar of Russian Orthodox Saints as well as one book of poems, entitled *Proshchanie* (Valediction, 1995).

Her work is included in several anthologies of contemporary poetry, including *V Peterburge my soidemsia snova* (In Petersburg We Shall Meet Again). English translations of her work have appeared in the anthology *Bread for this Hunger*, as well as in the *Crab Creek Review*, *The Moscow Guardian*, *Painted Bride Quarterly*, *Plum Review*, and *Poetry International*.

She lives in St. Petersburg with her husband and their three children.

Translations by J. Kates

Среди чёрных деревьев,
        на чёрном льду
Кружится, вьётся летит позёмка,
Соскальзываю в пропасть — упаду,
А ты так искусен — невлюблённый.
А тебе так легко играть со мной,
В геометрии ни одного просчёта,
И летает льдинка меж мной и тобой —
Надоест — отбросишь её в два счёта.
Фехтовальщик искусный —
        исчерчен лёд
На этой узкой чёрной дорожке,
Последнее дерево встаёт,
Как стрелка. Скучаете…
Пасть вам в ножки?

Among black trees,
    on black ice
A ground wind spins and writhes,
I am slipping off a precipice — done in,
While you keep on — an expert at unloving.
How easily you play rough with me
In this complex geometry:
A shard of ice careening between us
Gets in the way — instantly parried
By the artful fencer you are —
    bauchy ice
On the narrow black roadway
One final tree stands up
Like a cautionary finger. Reader,
Something is missing ...
Shall I drop to my knees?

~

Что скажу ещё я? Боже,
Боже правый!
Затекает в сердце синева
Из окна.
Какой-то бес лукавый
Напоил сполна.
Буквы собирает воронёнок;
Учит собирать слова;
Из меня по капле мой ребёнок
Истекает — его синева.
Не приедет. Хватит. Не приедет;
И чего ещё я жду?
Только слушать подголоски эти —
Как автобусы гудят в аду.
Окись сини; ломота в суставах;
Жилы намотали на их гриф;
И как страшно мне; как больно стало;
Что рука коснётся их.

What's left for me to say? God,
Almighty God!
The sky flows through the window
Into my heart.
Some cunning demon
Has filled me to the brim.
A little crow assembles letters,
Teaches me to assemble words,
My child seeps out of me
Drop by drop — It is this sky.
He won't come. Enough. He won't come.
What else am I waiting for?
Only to listen to these back-up voices —
Like buses rumbling in hell.
Blue oxide, an ache in all my joints,
They have strung my veins
Along the frets of a fingerboard,
And how terrible for me, how painful now
For my hand to touch them.

Изгиб твоих губ
Летящий гранит —
Спуск к воде
Взмах оставляющих чаек

Голова — как вербные шарики
Я облизываю твоё тело — веточку
Вкус почки во рту
О клейкая нежность мая!
А в городе горько мне
              горько мне

Дым и гарь
Жестяные заборы
Известковая пыль
Ржавчина позднего солнца
Драпированный камень предместья
Львиный мостик
Повисшая лампа луны
На длинных крюках
Опускаются звёзды
Молчанье и млечность —
Дёрг —
И болтается тело моё
Подвешенное за гортань
И горько мне горько мне
              горько мне.
Твой поцелуй на устах
Остался —
Украден мной был у другой
По—це—луй

Змеёныш
Твой яд, обжигая,
Идёт прямо в кровь

The curve of your lips
Lying granite
Down to the water
The swoop of settling seagulls

Your head is like willow pods
I lick your body —
A twiglet
The taste of buds in my mouth,
That sticky, warm touch of May!
But here in town I find it bitter
                        bitter
Smoke and soot
Sheet-metal fences
Plaster dust
The rust of a tardy sun
Suburban drapery of stone
The Lion Bridge
The hanging lamp of a full moon
Stars dangle
On long hooks
Silence and milkiness —
A pull —
And my body trembles
hung up by the neck
And I find it bitter
                        bitter

Your kiss (I stole it
From someone else)
Stayed on my lips
K i s s

Little viper in my bosom
Your burning venom

Озноб
    безъязыких ступеней оттяжка.

Мокрица ползущая вверх
По тёплой колонне ноги
Одиннадцать дней —
Ты вовремя руки успел развести —
Бесстыдная сырость реки
Окутает стены
Разбухнут плевки
И будут по стенам расти
Цветенье придётся на полночь
Трясти
Головками будут они.

Спи с блядями — они красивей
Их не рвёт от твоей нелюбви
Не выламывает костей
Склонённых в горсти на постель
Лазареты переполнены нищими
Улицы — пьяными
Налей мне ещё чтоб я до постели
Добраться смогла
Воскресенье пройдёт на дому
И порывшись в бачке
Извлечём хризантему
Дрожащую
    в росе ледяной
Меня тошнит от твоих упражнений
Безлюбый предательски нежен со мной
Сгнив развалился цветок
Как бумажный
Шапка долой
Одни только кости и святцы
Я разлагаюсь весной

Goes straight to the blood
A chill, the drawing out
By mute degrees

A wood-louse climbing up
Along the warm column of a leg
For eleven days —
Just at the right time you pulled away from an embrace —
The shameless moisture of a river
Will shroud the walls
Engorge the small membranes
And swell.
The flowering occurs at midnight.
They will emerge
As little glandular heads.

Sleep with whores. Those beauties.
Your lack of love won't turn their stomachs,
Won't break bones
Bent in the palm of a hand onto the bed.
Hospitals are overcrowded with beggars,
The streets with drunkards.
Replenish me once again, so I can get to the bed.
Resurrection occurs at home,
And having poked through the little tank
We'll pull out a chrysanthemum
Shivering
      in the frozen dew.
Your athletics make me sick,
My loveless, tenderhearted traitor.
Rotten the flower fell apart
Like paper
Hats off,
Nothing but loose bones and a calendar of saints.
Come spring, I decompose,

Набухшая кожа
Трещит синевой
Нет это не просто сирена
Машины шальной
Чавкая землю сосут за моей спиной
Изо рта у них запах дурной
А с небес осаждается мята
Знаешь как я молюсь за тебя неродной
На последней ступени разврат?

Мой дом стал похож на вертеп
В нём спермой запачкан хлеб
Он стал похож на тюрьму
Скажи мне мою вину
Открой скрипучую дверь
Апостол дверей
Ключарь охраняющий свет
Утыкана болью ведь я не стону
и не отвращаю смерть.

My swelling skin
Crackling in the livid sky.
No, it's just the horn
Of a stray car.
Smacking their lips, they suck the earth
Behind my back.
A stink drops out of their ugly mouth
But the skies are raining mint.
Do you know how I pray for you, alien
In the last stages of sin?

My home has been turned into a den of whores
Bread spotted with sperm.
It has been turned into a prison.
Tell me my crime,
Open the creaking door,
Apostle of Doors,
Keeper of the Keys, Warder of the Light.
Stuck in my own pain, you see, I don't even bother
to groan
or stave off death.

Положи мне голову на колени —
Тебе будет спокойно — и я удержу,
Ты увидишь небо и земные растенья
И прекрасное поле — всё в цвету
И не бойся, что ты опрокинут навзничь
Слабее всех, вровень травой.
Здесь не будет удара в спину, разве
Ты не видишь — твоя и слита с тобой.
Преклони ко мне лицо — не побрезгуй.
Ты стоишь так гордо, один как перст,
С головы до пят ты весь железный,
И враг не найдёт уязвимых мест,
Но я — земля и твои босые
Ступни — мне острей ножа,
Ведь он железный — они живые,
Какой ты нежный!
    О, как жаль
Этих дивных рук и дивных ног мне
Мог ваятель гордиться твоей красой,
Как две капли похож на юного бога,
Но запомни — на мне ты стоишь босой.
Положи мне голову на колени,
Я сняла одежду, забыв запрет,
Убивай теперь, говорят растенья,
Если ты боишься оставить след.

Lay your head in my lap —
you'll find peace there, and I'll hold you.
You'll see the sky and the plants of the earth
and the marvelous field — all in flower.
Don't be afraid of falling back
frailer than the grass underneath you.
There's no treachery here,
can't you see — I'm one with what you are.
Put your face down to mine. Let yourself go.
You stand there arrogant, absolutely alone,
head to toe all iron,
You leave no opening for a foe to bring you down.
But I, I am the earth and your bare soles
cut into me like knives,
and you see, even as iron, they're alive:
how delicate you are!
    Oh, such a pity —
what a sculptor could do with the beauty
of these legs and arms — my miracle.
You are the image of a young god,
but remember — you stand barefoot on me.
Lay your head in my lap,
I have shed my clothes, forgotten the taboos.
Kill me now, say the growing things,
If you're afraid to leave a trace.

Svetlana Kekova
Светлана Кекова

Svetlana Kekova was born in 1951 in Aleksandrovsk, in the southern part of the island of Sakhalin. Because her father was a soldier, she spent her early years frequently on the move, but from 1957 until 1968 lived in Tambov, where she attended school and began to write verse. In 1968 she entered the university in Saratov in the department of Russian philology and graduated in 1973. She continued as a graduate student in Slavonic-Russian language studies and defended her dissertation — on the poetic language of Nikolai Zabolotsky — in 1987. She wrote poetry throughout these years but was not published in the official Soviet press. She had a few publications in the small literary magazines *Literaturnaia Gruziia* (Literary Georgia) and *Tallin,* and in the samizdat St. Petersburg publications *Chasy* (Clock or Hours) and *Obvodnoi Kanal* (Obvodnoy Canal). Since 1989, she has been published widely in the magazines *Znamia, Soglasno, Zvezda, Iunost, Kontinent, Volga, Ogonek* and others. Three collections of poems have appeared, *Pesochnnye chasy* (Hourglass) in 1995, *Stikhi o prostranstve i vremeni* (Poems about Space and Time) in 1995, and *Po obe storony imeni* (On both Sides of the Name) in 1996. She continues to live in Saratov, where she works at the Saratov Pedagogic Institute. She has two daughters, Masha and Lena.

Translations by Judith Hemschemeyer

～

Небо в звездах, как тело в коросте,
как листва в беловатой пыли.
Проступают берцовые кости
На поверхности теплой земли.

Рвется саван заштопанный, ибо
он на нитку живую зашит.
Ангел слово, как снулую рыбу,
чистит, режет, потом потрошит.

И мелькают горбатые спины,
словно веер, дрожат плавники,
и орехов рогатые мины
на поверхность всплывают реки.

The sky is covered with stars, like a body with sores,
like leaves with whitish dust.
Shinbones poke through
the warm surface of the earth.

The stitched-up shroud tears,
for it is sewn with living thread.
An angel washes, cuts, then guts
the word like a dead fish.

And the humped backs flash,
the fins tremble like fans,
and the horned faces of nuts
rise to the river's surface.

~

Все сбылось. По заслугам и кара.
Страшный сон превращается в явь.
Не лишай меня Этого дара,
ты его, как младенца, оставь,

в сердце плачущем, в жаждущем чреве
или в кончиках пальцев. Прости —
не Лилит, а Сюзанне и Еве
жизнь иную дано обрести

и, листвою сухой и нарядной
прикрывая свою наготу,
упиваться лозой виноградной,
перекатывать слово во рту.

Ты, числа или имени зритель,
примешь Божьего слова удар.
Покидающим эту обитель
только время предложено в дар.

Только звук — колебанье эфира,
только влага замедленных вод,
в тесный воздух загробного мира
неизбежный, как жизнь, переход.

Жжет сапфир, охлаждающий страсти,
льется сладкого неба струя.
Ты — Господь. Но в твоей ли мы власти?
И любая ли воля — Твоя?

Everything has come true. The punishment fits the crime.
The nightmare has become reality.
Do not deprive me of this gift,
but leave it, like a newborn baby,

in my weeping heart, in my craving belly,
in my fingertips. Forgive —
not to Lilith, but to Susannah and Eve
another life was given

and, covering their nakedness
with elegant dried leaves,
they reveled in the vineyard,
rolling words on their tongues.

You, witness to the numbers and the names,
will receive the blow of the word of God.
To those who abandon this abode,
the only gift given is time.

Only a sound — vibrations of the ether,
only the moisture of slow-moving water,
the transition to the thin air of the world
beyond death is inevitable, like life.

The sapphire that cools passion is burning hot,
a sweet stream of sky pours down. You are God.
But are we in your power?
Is anyone's will inevitably yours?

Муравьи

I

Среди жалких растений двудольных
ангел крылья расправит свои,
увидав, как в домах треугольных
деловито снуют муравьи.

Нет для тела льняного покрова,
мелок дождь, как рассыпанный мак,
а иссохшую мумию слова
положили в пустой саркофаг.

Жизнь похожа на вечное бегство,
и себя вопрошает язык:
"Кто в воде, сохраняющей девство,
отражает измученный лик?

Кто безумное прошлое судит,
второпях не поняв одного:
если времени больше не будет,
будет слово на месте его?"

Жало плоти впивается в душу,
изнутри разрушается дух,
муравьи выползают на сушу
совершенствовать зренье и слух.

Ангел времени ранен навылет.
Всех, кто память об этом хранит,
ждет повальное бегство в Египет
к треугольным домам пирамид.

Нет у смертного опыта смерти.
Этот опыт имея в виду,
копошатся, как мелкие черти,
муравьи в муравьином аду.

The Ants

I

Among the pitiful dicotyledons,
an angel spreads its wings,
watching the ants scurrying
to their triangular houses.

They have no linen to cover their bodies,
there's a sparse rain, like strewn poppy seed,
but into an empty sarcophagus, they have laid
the dried mummy of the word.

Their life seems like an eternal flight,
and language asks itself:
"Who, in the water that protects virginity
is reflecting her suffering face?

Who will judge her senseless past,
having, in her haste, failed to understand:
if there is to be no more time,
will there be word in its place?"

A needle of flesh sticks into the soul,
the spirit collapses from within,
the ants crawl out onto dry land
to perfect their sight and hearing.

The angel of time was shot through.
Those who preserve this in memory
must wait for the mass exodus to Egypt,
to the triangular houses, the pyramids.

The mortal has no experience of death.
Bearing this experience in mind,
the ants swarm like tiny devils
in ants' hell.

2

Человек, бредущий на работу
с муравьем в косматой бороде,
платит по невидимому счету
ветру, людям, листьям и воде.

Рот его зажат монетой медной,
вьется овод около виска,
распластавшись над водою бледной,
ветер вьет веревки из песка.

Ничего-то я не слышу, кроме
звука Эль, терзающего слух,
а в долине Бен-Хинном на троне
восседает повелитель мух.

Насекомых маленькие лица
спрятаны меж крыльев от меня,
век проходит, и работа длится
мух, червей и вечного огня.

Ангел, светом осиянный горним,
прячет слезы в жестких складках век.
Наши страсти вырывает с корнем
в Бен-Хинном бредущий человек.

На костях его висит рубаха,
он никто уже и он нигде,
но сидит, зажмурившись от страха,
муравей в косматой бороде.

2

A man dragging himself to work
with an ant caught in his shaggy beard,
pays an invisible amount
to the wind, to people, to leaves and to water.

His mouth is plugged with a copper coin,
at his temple a deerfly is circling,
and spreading over the pale water,
the wind twists the sand into strings.

I can hear nothing at all,
except for the ear-splitting sound of the El,
and enthroned in the valley Ben-Hinnom
is the lord of the flies.

The tiny faces of the insects
are hidden from me by their wings,
a century goes by and the work of the flies,
the worms and the eternal fire goes on.

An angel, shining with light from the mountain,
hides tears in the rigid folds of his eyelids.
And the man dragging along in Ben Hinnom
tears out our passions by the roots.

His shirt is hanging on his bones,
he is no longer anyone or anywhere,
but the ant, squinting with fear,
is caught in the shaggy beard.

Сдав прошение на выезд,
ждешь от ангелов вестей.
Сладкий пламень тела выест
и обгложет до костей.

Долго вести ждать придется —
не утоптан неба наст.
Смерть твоя в земле найдется,
руку тонкую подаст.

А нужна такая малость —
жизнь с горчичное зерно,
только бедность, только жалость,
только времени вино.

Но несется, как в угаре,
в обнаженных небесах
заключенный в тесном шаре
с черной розой в волосах.

Having submitted your petition for dismissal,
you await news from the angels.
A sweet flame will consume your body,
will gnaw it to the bones.

The news will be a long time coming —
the sky's icy snow is not trampled yet.
But one day your death
will stretch its thin hand from the earth.

And yet all you need
is a life the size of a mustard seed,
only poverty, only compassion,
only the wine of time.

But through the naked heavens skims
someone imprisoned in a little sphere;
he looks wild, impassioned,
and there's a black rose in his hair.

Bella Dizhur
Белла Дижур

Bella Dizhur was born in Sverdlovsk, and studied bio-
chemistry at the Herzen Institute in St. Petersburg. In
addition to working in a laboratory, Dizhur began pub-
lishing science books for children. These books were very
well received in the Soviet Union and translated into
numerous languages. Her poetry, however, was another
matter. After being labelled a "writer-cosmopolitan,"
Dizhur was expelled from the Writers' Union of the USSR
in 1949. The official attitude toward her work softened
somewhat, however, after she was awarded the Korczak
prize by the West German Korczak Committee. Follow-
ing the emigration of her son to the West, Bella Dizhur
and her family received permission to leave the Soviet
Union in 1987 and settled in New York, where they cur-
rently reside. Her collection of poetry, *Shadow of the Soul*,
with English translations by Sarah Bliumis, was published
in 1990.

Translations by Sarah Bliumis

Тишина

Это было в первый день войны.
Ты стоял спокойно у стены.

Ты курил, и синеватый дым
Поднимался облаком густым.

Вот и всё. А после — ты ушел.
Солнце освещало желтый пол,
Сероватый пепел на полу
И окурок, брошенный в углу.

Так пришла ко мне в тот день война.
И была такая тишина,
Будто в мире ничего и нет,
Только твой задумчивый портрет
В солнечных квадратах. А над ним
Горьковатый папиросный дым.

Вот и всё. А после по утрам
Выметала чисто по углам.
Всё казалось, что не на виду
Где-нибудь окурок твой найду.

Silence

It was the first day of the war.
You stood calmly next to the wall.

You were smoking and the bluish smoke
Rose in a thick cloud.

That was it. Afterwards, you left.
The sun shone on the yellow floor,
The grayish ashes on the floor,
And the butt tossed in the corner.

That is how war approached me that day.
There was a silence,
As if nothing remained in the world,
Except for your pensive portrait
In little sunny squares,
And above it, bitter tobacco smoke.

That was it. And afterwards, in the mornings,
I would sweep the corners clean.
I kept thinking I would find that butt somewhere,
Though not within plain view.

Вот остров. Вот дом на сваях.
Черный бревенчатый дом.
С раскрытым настежь окном.
Зеленые волны его омывают,
Но в нем никто не живет,
Вот уж который год.
Лишь я одна здесь живу,
Сушу морскую траву,
Варю из нее обед.
И мне уже тысячи лет.
А там, где я раньше жила,
Где раньше меня любили,
Считают, что я умерла,
Оплакали и позабыли.
А я всё живу и живу...
Под грохот волны зеленой,
Друзей на обед зову
По оглохшему телефону.

Here is an island. Here is a house on stilts.
A black log house,
With a window open wide.
Green waves wash up to it,
But no one lives inside,
Not for many years.
Only I live here,
Drying seaweed
To cook for meals,
And I have lived for thousands of years.
But where I used to live,
Where they used to love me
They think that I have died,
They mourned and then forgot me.
But I live on and on …
Under the thundering green,
I call my friends to meals
On a voiceless telephone.

Монолог Евы

Чахлый кустик с ягодой волчьей
Называли древом познанья.
Хитрый улыбался молча,
Обрекая меня заранее
Быть рабыней страстей позорных,
Быть наложницею в неволе,
Под чадрою чугунно-черной
Увядать от стыда и боли.
Но была я мудрее змея
И хитрее хитрого бога,
Ни спины, ни рук не жалея,
Не щадя свои белы ноги,
Гнулась я лозой винограда
И стелилась травой пушистой,
Стала ведьмой, стала наядой,
Оставаясь мадонной пречистой.
В раскаленных песках пустыни,
На опушках ночного леса
Я рожала за сыном сына —
Одиссеев и Геркулесов.
Из моей вырастали плоти,
Как колосья из чернозема.
Я была их крылом попутным...
Теплым хлебом и крышей дома.
В море ветром была попутным...
И, бессмертие утверждая,
В праздник пела легкою лютней,
Вся иссохшая и седая.

Eve's Monologue

A sickly wolfberry shrub
Was called the tree of knowledge.
The cunning one smiled silently,
Condemning me in advance
To be a slave of disgraceful passions,
A concubine in captivity,
To wither from shame and pain
Beneath a veil, black as coal.
But I was wiser than the serpent
And more cunning than the cunning god.
Neither sparing my back, nor my arms,
Without a care for my white legs,
I bent over like a grapevine
And spread like downy grass;
I became a witch, I became a naiad,
I remained the purest madonna.
In the scorching sands of the desert,
On the edge of a forest by night,
I gave birth to son after son,
To Odysseuses and Herculeses.
They grew from my flesh
Like ears of corn from rich soil.
I was their wing in flight,
Their warm bread, the roof over their home.
I was their favorable wind at sea,
And upholding immortality,
All dried up and gray,
I sang like a soft lute on holiday.

Irina Ratushinskaya
Ирина Ратушинская

Irina Borisovna Ratushinskaya. Poet, prose writer and memoirist. Born in Odessa in 1954, Ratushinskaya is known as much for her role as a dissident as for her poetry. She studied physics at Odessa University and subsequently taught at the Odessa Pedagogical Institute. In 1980, after being forced to leave her job because of her refusal to cooperate with the authorities, she and her husband, Igor Gerasenko, became actively involved in the human rights movement. After repeated arrests and harassment by the KGB, Ratushinskaya was tried and sentenced in 1982 to seven years of hard labor for "preparing and distributing anti-Soviet materials." She spent three years in a labor camp, where she continued to write poetry — the collection *Vne limita* (Beyond the Limit), completed in 1984 — before being released in 1986 as part of the new policy of glasnost. The same year, Ratushinskaya and her husband were forced to emigrate to the West and now reside in England. In addition to several volumes of poetry — *Stikhi, Poems, Poèmes* (1984), *Ia dozhivu* (I Shall Live, 1986) — Ratushinskaya has also published her memoirs in two volumes, *Seryi tsvet nadezhdy* (Gray is the Color of Hope, 1989), and *In the Beginning* (1991).

Translations by David McDuff

~

Мандельштамовской ласточкой
Падает к сердцу разлука,
Пастернак посылает дожди,
А Цветаева — ветер.
Чтоб вершилось вращенье вселенной
Без ложного звука,
Нужно слово — и только поэты
За это в ответе.
И раскаты весны пролетают
По тютчевским водам,
И сбывается классика осени
Снова и снова.
Но ничей еще голос
Крылом не достал до свободы,
Не исполнил свободу,
Хоть это и русское слово.

Like Mandelstam's swallow
Parting falls towards the heart,
Pasternak sends the rain,
And Tsvetaeva — the wind.
So that the world's turning may be achieved
Without a false note,
The word is needed — and poets alone
Are answerable for this.
And the peals of spring whirl by
Over Tyutchevian waters,
And autumn's classicism is manifested
Time and time again.
But no one's voice has yet
Touched freedom with a wing,
Nor brought about freedom, *svoboda*,
Even though it's a Russian word.

И доживу, и выживу, и спросят:
Как били головою о топчан,
Как приходилось мерзнуть по ночам,
Как пробивалась молодая проседь…
Но улыбнусь. И что-нибудь сострю
И отмахнусь от набежавшей тени.
И честь воздам сухому сентябрю,
Который стал моим вторым рожденьем.
И спросят: не болит ли вспоминать,
Не обманувшись легкостью наружной.
Но грянут в памяти былые имена —
Прекрасные — как старое оружие.
И расскажу о лучших всей земли,
О самых нежных, но непобедимых,
Как провожали, как на пытку шли,
Как ждали писем от своих любимых.
И спросят: что нам помогало жить,
Когда ни писем, ни вестей — лишь стены,
Да холод камеры, да чушь казенной лжи,
Да тошные посулы за измену.
И расскажу о первой красоте,
Которую увидела в неволе.
Окно в морозе! Ни глазков, ни стен,
И ни решеток, и ни долгой боли —
Лишь синий свет на крохотном стекле,
Витой узор — чудесней не приснится!
Ясней взгляни — и расцветут смелей
Разбойничьи леса, костры и птицы!
И сколько раз бывали холода,
И сколько окон с той поры искрилось —
Но никогда уже не повторилась
Такое буйство радужного льда!
Да и за что бы это мне — сейчас,
И чем бы этот праздник был заслужен?
Такой подарок может быть лишь раз.
А может быть, один лишь раз и нужен.

I will live and survive and be asked:
How they slammed my head against a trestle,
How I had to freeze at nights,
How my hair started to turn grey …
But I'll smile. And I'll crack some joke
And brush away the encroaching shadow.
And I will render homage to the dry September
That became my second birth.
And I'll be asked: "Doesn't it hurt you to remember?"
Not being deceived by my outward flippancy.
But the former names will detonate in my memory —
Magnificent as an old cannon.
And I will tell of the best people in all the earth,
The most tender, but also the most invincible,
How they said farewell, how they went to be tortured,
How they waited for letters from their loved ones.
And I'll be asked: what helped us to live
When there were neither letters nor any news — only walls,
And the cold of the cell, and the blather of official lies,
And the sickening promises made in exchange for betrayal.
And I will tell of the first beauty
I saw in captivity.
A frost-covered window! No peepholes, nor walls,
Nor cell-bars, nor the long-endured pain —
Only a blue radiance on a tiny pane of glass,
A lacy winding pattern — none more beautiful could be dreamt!
The more clearly you looked, the more powerfully blossomed
Those brigand forests, campfires and birds!
And how many times there was bitter cold weather
And how many windows sparkled after that one —
But never was it repeated,
That upheaval of rainbow ice!
And anyway, what good would it be to me now,
And what would be the pretext for that festival?
Such a gift can only be received once,
And once is probably enough.

И за крик из колодца "мама!"
И за сшибленный с храма крест,
И за ложь твою "телеграмма,"
Когда с ордером на арест, —
Буду сниться тебе, Россия!
В окаянстве твоих побед,
В маяте твоего бессилья,
В похвальбе твоей и гульбе.
В тошноте твоего похмелья —
Отчего прошибет испуг,
Все отплакали, всех отпели —
От кого ж отшатнешься вдруг?
Отопрись, открутись обманом,
На убитых свали вину —
Все равно приду и предстану,
И в глаза твои загляну!

For the cry from the well of "mama!"
For the crucifix torn from the wall,
For the lie of your "telegrams"
When there's an order for an arrest —
You will dream of me, Russia.
In the accursedness of your victories,
In the anguish of your impotence,
In your bragging and carousing.
In the nausea of your hangover —
Why does fear break through?
All has been mourned, all have been sung to rest —
Who do you flinch from all of a sudden?
Though you deny it, take refuge in illusion,
Put all the blame on those who have been killed —
I will still come and stand before you
And look into your eyes.

Bakhyt Kenjeev

Бахыт Кенжеев

Bakhyt Kenjeev was born in 1950 in Chimkent, Kazakh-
stan and graduated from the Chemistry Department of
Moscow State University. In 1970 he was a founding mem-
ber of *Moskovskoe vremia* (Moscow Time), an informal
group of poets which included Aleksandr Soprovsky,
Sergey Gandlevsky, and Aleksei Tsvetkov, among others.
He was first published in 1972 in *Komsomol'skaia pravda*.
After several other publications, Kenjeev's poetry moved
out of the country and into the pages of the émigré press.
The author himself followed in 1982, when he joined his
wife in Montréal, Canada. Since then he has published
two books of poetry in the United States, four in Russia,
and one bilingual collection in his native Kazakhstan. His
work has been translated into English, French, German,
and Swedish. Kenjeev also writes fiction (his four novels
were published in Moscow by the journals *Znamia* and
Oktiabr') and critical essays. After several years at Radio
Canada International and in a foreign trade company, Mr.
Kenjeev now works as a translator and interpreter for the
International Monetary Fund.

Translations by Nina Kossman

Завидовал летящим птицам и камням,
И даже ветру вслед смотрел с тяжелым сердцем
И слушал пение прибоя и разбойный
Метельный посвист. Так перечислять
Несовершенные глаголы юности своей,
Которые еще не превратились
В молчание китайских мудрецов,
Недвижно спящих на бамбуковых циновках,
И в головах имеют иероглиф ДАО,
И, просыпаясь, в руки журавлиное перо
Берут и длинный лист бамбуковой бумаги.

Но если бы ты был мудрец и книгочей!
Ты есть арбатский смерд, дитё глухих подвалов,
И философия витает над тобой,
Как серо-голубой стервятник с голой шеей.
Но если бы ты был художник и поэт!
Ты — лишь полуслепой, косноязычный друг
Другого ремесла, ночной работы жизни
И бесполезного любовного труда, птенец кукушки
В чужом гнезде, на дереве чужом.

И близится весна, и уличный стекольщик
Проходит с ящиком по маленьким дворам.
Зеленое с торцов огромное стекло
Играет и звенит при каждом шаге,
Вот-вот блеснет, ударит, упадет.
Так близится весна, и равнодушный март
Растапливает черные снега, и солнечным лучом
В немытых зимних окнах зажигает
Подобие пожара. И старьевщик
Над кучей мусора склоняется, томясь.

You envied the flying birds and stones,
your eyes followed even the wind, your heart heavy,
and you listened to the song of the surf,
and the snowstorm's pirate call. So to list
the imperfective verbs of your youth
which have not yet turned
into the silence of Chinese wise-men,
sleeping motionless on their bamboo mats,
and in their heads they have the hieroglyph TAO
and, waking, they take a crane's feather
and a long sheet of bamboo paper.

But if you were a wise man and a bookworm!
You are a commoner of Arbat, a child of god-forsaken basements,
and philosophy soars over you
like a gray-blue vulture with a naked neck.
But if you were an artist and a poet!
You are only a half-blind, tongue-tied friend
of a different craft, the night work of life,
and of the useless labor of love, a cuckoo's fledgling
in somebody else's nest in somebody else's tree.

The spring is drawing near, and a glazier
walks around with his box, from yard to yard.
Seen green from the pavement, all that glass
sparkles and clanks at his every step,
it just about flashes, strikes, and falls.
So the spring draws near, and indifferent March
melts away the black snow, and with a ray
lights up a semblance of fire in unwashed
winter windows. And a junk-man
bends over a heap of garbage, wistfully.

… а что дурак, и умница, и скряга —
все перейдет, и реки утекут
пока в руках у Господа Живаго
переживешь бессонницу и труд,
пока сквозь небо, в страхе терпеливом,
не пролетишь над вымершим заливом,
где музыка, порывисто дыша,
не покидает звездного ковша…
Верши, метель, забытую работу
над брошенной страницей из блокнота
ростовщика, где кляксою мое
лукавое, дурное бытие
распластано… вся жизнь была залогом…
вся жизнь была… в беспамятстве убогом
спит город твой. Погас его гранит.
И мокрый снег ладони леденит.

... and a fool, and a smart one, a miser,
all will pass, and rivers will flow away,
while in the hands of the Living God
you will survive insomnia and work,
until through the sky, in patient fear,
you fly over an extinct bay,
where the music, breathing fitfully,
does not leave the starry ladle ...
Snow-storm, complete the forgotten work,
on an abandoned page from the note-book
of a usurer, where like an ink-blot,
my miserable, sly existence
sprawls ... my whole life was pawned ...
my whole life was ... in wretched forgetfulness
your city sleeps. Its granite is dimmed.
And the wet snow chills my palms.

Уходит звук моей любимой беды, вчера еще тайком
зрачком январским, ястребиным,
　　горевшей в небе городском,
уходит сбивчивое слово, оставив влажные следы,
и ангелы немолодого пространства, хлеба и воды
иными заняты делами, когда тщедушный лицедей
бросает матовое пламя в глаза притихших площадей.

Проспекты, линии, ступени, ледышка вместо леденца.
Не тяжелее детской тени, не дольше легкого конца —
а все приходится сначала внушать неведомо кому,
что лишь бы музыка звучала в морозном вытертом дыму,
что в крупноблочной и невзрачной странице,
　　отдающей в жесть,
и даже в смерти неудачной любовь особенная есть.

А кто же мы? И что нам снится? Дороги зимние голы,
в полях заброшенной столицы зимуют мертвые щеглы.
Платок снимая треугольный, о чем ты думаешь, жена?
Изгибом страсти отглагольной ночная твердь окружена.
И губы тянутся к любому, кто распевает об одном,
к глубокому и голубому просвету в небе ледяном…

Gone is the sound of my favorite misfortune, which even yesterday
burned secretly in the city sky like January's hawk eye.
The muddled word goes away, leaving behind its moist footprints,
and the angels of the not-so-young space, of bread, and of water
are busy with other things, while a puny actor
throws a dull flame into the eyes of the silent courtyards.

Avenues, lines, steps, an icicle not a lollipop.
It's no heavier than a child's shadow, as quick as an easy end,
and yet one still has to impress it upon God knows who:
just let music sound in the frosty threadbare smoke,
in a blocky, plain page resounding in tin,
even in an unlucky death, there's a special love.

So who are we? What do we dream of? The winter roads are bare.
Dead goldfinches hibernate in the fields of the abandoned capital.
As you doff your triangular kerchief, wife, what are you thinking of?
The firmament of the night is surrounded by the curve of a verb's
        passion.
And the lips stretch towards anyone who sings of such things,
towards the blue chasm of the icy sky.

Between Zukofsky and Zhukovsky

J. Kates

In the Grip of Strange Thoughts is not just a collection of poems. It is also an anthology of literary translations.

There are many ways to translate poetry. At one extreme, a translator can choose one or more formal aspects of a poem and reproduce them in his or her own language. The more formal aspects that get reproduced, the more successful the translation. Obviously, a translator cannot reproduce all the formal aspects of the original — the *reductio ad absurdum* of this strategy results in simply reprinting the original poem in its original language. Playful examples of this are the Louis and Celia Zukofsky translations of Catullus, whose distich "Odi et amo" (see note number 9 to Kushner's "As Catullus wrote ...") becomes "O th'hate I move love. Quarry it fact I am, for that's so re queries. / Nescience, say th' fiery scent I owe whets crookeder." But at its most elegant, in the contemporary work of Richard Wilbur or Walter Arndt, the effects are stunning and persuasive. Rhyme and meter are usually the formal aspects most carefully regarded by a translator, followed by attention to overall diction and internal patterns of sound, imagery and rhetoric.

At the other extreme, there is the notion of translating the sensibility of a poem even more than its sound and sense. The foremost American exponent of this in the last generation was Robert Lowell, with his "imitations," but he was preceded by hundreds and has been followed by thousands. Although many Russian readers and writers today are adamant in their espousal of formal fidelity to rhyme and structural patterning, among the most spectacular examples of the more Romantic idea of translation is, early in the last century, the work of Vasily Andreevich Zhukovsky. Zhukovsky introduced many Russian readers to Western European literature through the filter of his own interpretations. It is not easy to recognize in the tight octave:

Отымает наши радости
Без замены хладный свет;
Вдохновенье пылкой младости
Гаснет с чувством жертвой лет;
Не одно ланит пылание
Тратим с юностью живой —
Видим сердца увядание
Прежде юности самой.*

— this freely flowing quatrain of fourteeners by Byron:

There's not a joy the world can give like that it takes away,
When the glow of early thought declines in feeling's dull decay;
'T is not on youth's smooth cheek the blush alone,
                    which fades so fast,
But the tender bloom of heart is gone, ere youth itself
                    be past ...

Zhukovsky regarded fidelity to the sentiment (and perhaps to the cæsura) more highly than fidelity to each image or to the pattern of rhyme. A century later, Boris Pasternak is said to have responded to criticisms of his own versions of Shakespeare by shrugging his shoulders and answering, "Well, he was a genius, and so am I."

We have tried to stay well between Zukofsky and Zhukovsky in our choice of translations for this book, although we have also been concerned to present as wide a spectrum of translating techniques and tones as we can. Some of the translators have stayed very close to the original structure, while others have striven for an equivalency of effect.

An instance illustrated by Zhukovsky's translation of Byron is that Russian is far more at home with easy rhymes than English is — this happens to be an acccident of the history of each language

---

* "A cold world extracts our joys without replacement; The inspiration of passionate youth weakens with the feeling, with the sacrifice of years; We use up not only the blush of cheeks along with vivacious youth — We see the withering of the heart even before youth itself goes."

and of its own poetic tradition. Moreover, Russian poetry in the twentieth century never felt the necessity to cut itself loose from older formal constraints, and therefore, much poetry that is avant-garde in content or effect uses traditional rhyme and meter. The conventional attitude of many Russian readers of poetry can be easily summed up in the judgment of Joseph Brodsky: "[W]e should recognize that only content can be innovative and that for-mal innovation can occur only within the limits of form. Rejec-tion of form is a rejection of innovation. . . . More than a crime against language or a betrayal of the reader, the rejection of meter is an act of self-castration by the author." But some of our transla-tors have made different choices. They have judged that it would falsify the effect of the poems they are responsible for if they ren-dered them with the same formality in English as in the original Russian. Therefore, these translators have set certain rhymes and regularities aside, while maintaining other qualities of sound and sense. In other cases, translators have felt it important to preserve this particularly Russian seeming contradiction.

That said, I should interject here an anecdote from my own translating experience. Once in Moscow I was reading my own poems — all of which begin in strict rhyme and meter, and many of which stay that way — as well as my translations of Mikhail Aizenberg. In the critical discussion that always follows a Russian poetry reading, I explained my reasons for translating the strict forms of the Russian verses into slightly looser structures in En-glish — a practice understood and approved by Aizenberg. But one prominent critic stood up and commented, "That's all very well. You make a good case. But you should try harder."

Since then, I have always tried harder.

Our translators come from all sides, some from the academic study of Russian literature, others from the realm of pure poetry. Judith Hemschemeyer, for instance, is a fine poet who stumbled into the Russian language and translation through her interest in the poems of Anna Akhmatova. She works not just from the Rus-sian texts themselves, but from literal versions of each poem pre-pared by a native speaker. Ronnie Apter and Mark Herman are primarily translators of opera libretti, and are currently engaged in a project translating Okudzhava's verse suitably for song. This necessarily involves one kind of compromise with the original text, just as a different strategy requires another. Lyn Hejinian's translations of Arkadii Dragomoschenko arise from their mutual interest in the function of language in poetry. They have been colleagues and collaborators in theory as well as in practice for more than a decade.

Discerning readers may also notice a difference in tone between the British translators — Peter France, Catriona Kelly, David McDuff, Richard McKane, Michael Molnar, Avril Pyman, Robert Reid and Daniel Weissbort — and the Americans. Ideally, we should have been able to include translators from all over the English-speaking world, because regional accents are important elements in English-language poetry. But we have not had that extravagant luxury.

And there has been variety in editing these translations. There are translators who hold themselves completely responsible for the integrity of their work, and others who prefer to work in a collaborative, editorial dialogue.

It must also be said that translations are not made for readers of the original language. Experienced readers of Russian who let their eyes volley back and forth from the left-hand page to the right-hand page are playing an amusing and a useful game. But we would like to think that we also reach readers for whom the right-hand pages are at most an introduction to the left.

Every translation can be only one reading of a poem. Within a range of accuracy, many readings are possible. The translator's chief responsibility is not to seek to be definitive, but to be hospitable. Readers are invited into the poem, where they can make themselves at ease as suits them best.

The Translators

RONNIE APTER is Professor of English at Central Michigan University. A published poet and a translator of poetry, she is a recipient of New York University's Thomas Wolfe Poetry Award. She is the author of the critically acclaimed book on Ezra Pound's contribution to the translation of poetic forms into English, *Digging for the Treasure: Translation after Pound*. In collaboration with Mark Herman, she has also written eighteen performable opera translations and numerous articles on translation and on opera. Dr. Apter is currently working on a book of translations of the complete poems of the troubadour poet Bernart de Ventadorn, and, in collaboration with Mark Herman, a bilingual edition of the songs of Bulat Okudzhava.

ELENA BALASHOVA was born in Moscow. She now lives in Berkeley, California, where she works in the library of the University of Califonia. She and Lyn Hejinian have worked together as translators since 1985.

SARAH BLIUMIS is a published poet, essayist, and Russian translator. Her poems have been published most recently in *Spoon River Quarterly, Whetstone,* and *Ceilidh.* She translated the complete poems of the Russian poet Bella Dizhur, entitled *Shadow of a Soul* (1990). She has taught as a poet-in-residence in New York schools for Poets In Public Service and teaches poetry writing to adults through Greenwich Continuing Education.

SIBELAN FORRESTER teaches Russian Language and Literature at Swarthmore College. She is a published poet and has also published translations of poetry by Anna Bunina, Sofia Parnok, and Dubravka Oraic, as well as prose by Evgeniia Tur and Davor Slamnig. Translations of poems by Evdokiia Rostopchina, Mariia Petrovykh, Anna Akhmatova, and Marina Tsvetaeva are forthcoming, as is a translation of Irena Vrkljan's lyrical autobiography, *The Silk, The Shears.* She has received an Academy of American Poets Prize (1981) and is the author of a book, *Engendering Slavic Literatures,* co-edited with Pamela Chester (1996).

PETER FRANCE was born in Londonderry, Northern Ireland, in 1935. He went to school in Yorkshire, England and studied French and Russian at Oxford and in France. He has taught principally at the universities of Sussex and Edinburgh, where he now lives. He has written extensively about French literature and edited the *New Oxford Companion to Literature in French*. He is also the author of *Poets of Modern Russian* (1982). As a translator, he has worked from both French and Russian (Rousseau, Diderot, Blok, Pasternak, Brodsky, Chukhonstev), but has devoted himself above all to the translation of Gennady Aygi. In addition to numerous publications in anthologies and journals, his translations of Aygi include *Veronica's Book* (1989), *Salute to Singing* (1995) and the *Anthology of Chuvash Poetry* (1991).

PAUL GRAVES, a graduate of Rice University, is a poet and translator who studied with Joseph Brodsky in the School of the Arts at Columbia University. In addition to Brodsky, he has translated Aleksandr Kushner, Timur Kibirov, Olesia Nikolaeva, Vladimir Druk, and others. He currently resides in Finland, where he teaches English at the University of Helsinki.

DINARA GEORGEOLIANI was educated in Moscow (Russia) and Tbilisi (the Republic of Georgia), where she earned an advanced doctorate. She is a linguist, with extensive experience in English/ Russian translation and scholarship concentrated in comparative linguistics. She worked as a translator for three years in Iran with a team of Soviet scholars. She has published, in Russia, more than ten articles on the history of American film. Presently, she is an Assistant Professor at Central Washington University where she teaches in the Department of Foreign Languages and collaborates with Mark Halperin on translations from Russian/Soviet literature.

MARK HALPERIN teaches in the English Department at Central Washington University. He has taught in Japan, Estonia, was a Fulbright lecturer at Moscow State Linguistic University in Russia, and has returned there as well as serving as an exchange professor at Hertzen University in St. Petersburg, Russia. He has published three collections of poetry, the most recent, *The Measure of Islands*, from Wesleyan University Press. Together with Dinara Georgeoliani, he has published translations from Russian and Soviet-period writers including Alexandr Galich, Daniil Kharms, Vyacheslav P'yetsukh and Andrei Platonov.

LYN HEJINIAN was born in 1941 and lives in California. She has published several volumes of poetry, including *Writing is an Aid to Memory*, *The Guard*, *My Life*, and *The Cell*. She met Arkadii Dragomoschenko while touring the Soviet Union in 1983, and a friendship developed between the two poets, resulting in Hejinian's role as translator and introducer of the new Russian poetry to Americans. She has published two volumes of translations of Dragomoschenko's poetry, *Xenia* and *Description* (both with Elena Balashova).

JUDITH HEMSCHEMEYER is an Associate Professor at the University of Central Florida, where she teaches Creative Writing and Literature. She is the author of four books of poetry and a book of stories, as well as the translator of *The Complete Poems of Anna Akhmatova* (Zephyr Press, 1990).

PATRICK HENRY took his B.A. in Russian at Middlebury College and received his M.A. in Slavic literature from the University of California at Berkeley. He has been translating contemporary Russian poetry and prose for over eight years, and his translations have appeared in *Five Fingers Review* and *Talisman*.

MARK HERMAN is a literary translator, technical translator, chemical engineer, playwright, lyricist, and actor.

JOHN HIGH was born in Baltimore, Maryland. He is a founding editor of the *Five Fingers Review*. His own books include *Ceremonies, Sometimes Survival*, and the *lives of thomas: episodes and prayers*. He has received awards from The Witter Bynner Foundation of Poetry, Arts International, and The National Endowment for the Arts. A book of his selected works translated by Nina Iskrenko, *along her thighs*, appeared in Moscow in 1993. High's translation

422

(with Patrick Henry and Katya Olmsted) of works by Iskrenko, entitled *The Right to Err,* was published in 1995. He has also translated other Russian poets ranging from Osip Mandelstam to Ivan Zhdanov. He taught as a Fulbright Fellow at the Moscow State Linguistics University from 1991 to 1994, and now resides with his family in the San Francisco Bay Area.

GERALD JANECEK, a native of New York, is Professor of Russian at the University of Kentucky and Chair of the Department of Russian and East European Studies. He received his Ph.D. in Slavic Languages and Literatures from the University of Michigan in 1972 and specializes in avant-garde Russian literature of the 20th century. His books include translations of Andrei Bely's *Kotik Letaev* (1973) and *The First Encounter* (1979), *The Look of Russian Literature* (1984), and *Zaum: The Transrational Poetry of Russian Futurism* (1996). He has also published articles on contemporary Russian poetry, as well as translations of Nekrasov, Prigov, Rubinstein, Ocheretyansky, Aristov, and Aygi.

J. KATES is a poet and translator who lives in Fitzwilliam, New Hampshire. He has translated a great deal of modern French poetry (including Robert Desnos, Ivan Goll and Jean-Pierre Rosnay) as well as Russian. In collaboration with Stephen A. Sadow, he is the translator of Ricardo Feierstein's *We, the Generation in the Wilderness* (Ford-Brown, 1989).

CATRIONA KELLY is Reader in Russian and Fellow of New College, University of Oxford. She is a specialist on Russian literature and cultural history, whose books include *Petrushka, the Russian Carnival Puppet Theatre* (1990), *A History of Russian Women's Writing, 1820-1992* (1994), and *An Anthology of Russian Women's Writing, 1777-1992* (1994). Among the writers she has translated are the poets Olga Sedakova, Elena Shvarts, Anna Prismanova and Anna Barkova and the novelists Leonid Borodin and Sergei Kaledin.

NINA KOSSMAN was born in Moscow in 1959 and emigrated to the United States in 1993. She is the author of *Behind the Border* (1994, 1996). Her poetry has appeared in a wide spectrum of Russian,

American and British periodicals, and her fiction won a Unesco / PEN Short Story Award in 1995. Her translations of Russian poetry have appeared in several anthologies, and a book of her translations of Tsvetaeva, *In the Inmost Hour of the Soul,* was published in 1989.

DAVID McDUFF was born in 1945. He is a writer, critic and translator of Russian and Scandinavian literature. In addition to Irina Ratushinskaya, he has translated Brodsky, Tsvetaeva, and Mandelstam, among others. His most recent publications are translations of Andrei Bely's *Petersburg* and Bo Carpelan's *Urwind.* David McDuff lives in London.

RICHARD McKANE was born in 1947 and received his degree in Russian from University College, Oxford in 1969. He has published several volumes of translations of Akhmatova, Mandelstam, Gumilev, Voznesensky, and other Russian poets, as well as translations of Turkish poetry. He is a member of English PEN and an interpreter from Turkish and Russian for the Medocal Foundation for the Care of Victims of Torture. He lives in London with his daughter, Juliet.

PHILIP METRES is studying for his Ph.D. in English literature at Indiana University, Bloomington. His poems and his translations of Gandlevsky and other Russian poets have appeared in numerous periodicals, including *Glas, Modern Poetry in Translation, Visions International,* and *Spoon River Poetry Review.* He has recently completed the translation of *Celebration: Selected Poems of Sergey Gandlevsky.* He would like to thank Dmitry Psurtsev for his invaluable advice and guidance in translating these poems.

MICHAEL MOLNAR's translations from Russian include poetry by Arkadii Dragomoschenko, Viktor Krivulin, Aleksei Parshchikov and Elena Shvarts, published in *Child of Europe* (edited by Michael March, Penguin, 1990) and prose by Igor Klekh, Svetlana Vasilieva, Zufar Gareev, Viktor Lapitskii and Olga Novikova in *Description of a Struggle* (edited by Michael March, Picador and Vintage, 1994). He has edited and translated a selection of Elena Shvarts' poems,

424 *Paradise* (Bloodaxe, 1993). He works at the Freud Museum in London, and has also edited Freud's diary notes. He has written various articles on translation and on Freud.

KATYA OLMSTED worked in Moscow as the director of Russia's first American Cultural Center. She was born in San Francisco, where she completed her B.A. in Russian Studies at San Francisco State University in 1986. She also studied at the Pushkin Institute in Moscow as part of her degree. Her translations of Russian poetry with John High have appeared in the anthologies *Third Wave, 20th Century Russian Poetry: Silver and Steel*, and in journals including *Talisman, Glas: New Russian Writing, Poetry Flash*, and others.

AVRIL PYMAN was born in England in 1930. She received her Ph.D. in Modern Languages from Cambridge University. She lived in the Soviet Union from 1959 to 1974. Dr. Pyman has translated Pushkin, Lermontov, Fet, Aleksei Tolstoi, and others. She is the author of editions of works by Blok, Bulgakov, and Evgenii Shaits, numerous articles, a two volume biography of Aleksandr Blok (1979, 1980), and *A History of Russian Symbolism* (1994). She is now Reader in Russian at Durham University.

F. D. REEVE's modern oratorio, with music by T. L. Read, was performed in 1998 at London's Barbican Centre as part of the Inventing America series.

ROBERT REID is Senior Lecturer in Russian Studies at Keele University. His principal research interest is Russian romanticism, and his publications include *Problems of Russian Romanticism* (1986) and *Pushkin's 'Mozart and Salieri'*. He regularly translates Russian poetry, including works by Brodsky, Sedakova, and Dolina. He recently completed a monograph on Lermontov's *A Hero of Our Time* (1997).

MAIA TEKSES, born in 1962, has always lived in and around Philadelphia, except for several extended trips to the former Austro-Hungarian empire and the former Soviet Union. She has published a few of her translations from Central and Eastern European languages in small magazines now defunct. Tekses writes under several names, and teaches school to earn a living. She became interested in Aleksandr Tkachenko's work after seeing other translations, which left her interested but unsatisfied, in print.

CAROL UELAND received her Ph.D. in Slavic Languages and Literatures from Columbia University in 1995 and is now Associate Professor of Russian at Drew University. She has published a book of translations, *Apollo in the Snow: Aleksandr Kushner, Selected Poems 1962-1988* (1991) with the poet and translator Paul Graves. She has also collaborated with Paul Graves on translations of Vladimir Druk, Timur Kibirov and Olesia Nikolaeva.

DANIEL WEISSBORT edits the twice-yearly journal *Modern Poetry in Translation*, out of King's College, London University. He himself still teaches at the University of Iowa, where he directs the MFA Program in Translation. He has published poetry, translations of poetry (mostly from Russian), and edited anthologies of poetry and a collections of essays on the translation of poetry. His most recent publication is a collection of poems: *What Was All The Fuss About*, Anvil Press, UK. In 1999, Carcanet Press will publish his comprehensive translation of the poetry of Nikolay Zabolotsky.

MICHAEL VAN WALLEGHEN is the author of four collections of poetry: *The Wichita Poems* (1975); *More Trouble with the Obvious* (1980); *Blue Tango* (1989); and *Birds Stalking* (1994). *More Trouble with the Obvious* won the Lamont Award for 1980. Other awards include a Pushcart Prize and two fellowships. Mr. Van Walleghen is Professor of English at the University of Illinois.

Notes

A Union of Lone Wolves

1   1. A Union of Lone Wolves: "Soiuz odinochek" first appeared in *Obshchaia Gazeta* No. 50 (178), 19-25 December 1996, p. 10.

2   2. Monatyrsky: Andrei Monatyrsky (b. 1949) Semyon Faibisovich (b. 1949) Eric Bulatov (b. 1933) and Oleg Vasiliev (b. 1951) are visual artists associated with the Moscow Conceptualists. The other names in this essay are poets and writers. Zinovy Zinik (*The Mushroom Picker*, St. Martin's Press, 1986; *One-Way Ticket*, New Directions, 1995) now lives in London; Leonid Ioffe in Israel.

Introduction

7   3. Sinyavsky: Andrei Donatovich Sinyavsky (b. 1925), who, using the pseudonym "Abram Tertz," wrote works that were published abroad, and was imprisoned from 1965 until 1971. In 1973 he emigrated to France.

9   4. Futurists: Futurism was a major avant-garde artistic movement in early twentieth-century Russia.

9   5. Oberiuty: An avant-garde literary group ("The Association of Real Art") in Leningrad, 1927-1930, that centered around Daniil Kharms, Aleksandr Vvedensky and Nikolai Zabolotsky.

14   6. Third Rome: Moscow as the Third Rome reflects a theological and cultural perception that assumes a continuity of the Roman Empire from Rome itself through Byzantium (the Second Rome) to Russia.

Okudzhava

19   7. Okudzhava: There are several recordings available of Okudzhava's songs, including the popular "Oh, Nadya, Nadyenka" and "To me, Muscovites." The music is available in two volumes of Okudzhava songs selected and edited by Vladimir Frumkin and published by Ardis.

23   8. Scythians: A reference to a 1918 poem by Aleksandr Blok (1880-1921), "Scythians," which affirms an Eastern nature for Russians in contrast to Western Europe. "Yes, we are Scythians! Yes, we are Asiatics!"

Kushner

41   9. As Catullus wrote: *Carmina Catulli* li, "Ille mi par esse deo uidetur ... "

41   10. Nets: The first (1908) book of poems by Mikhail Kuzmin (1875-1936).

41   11. We hate and love: An allusion to Catullus' distich *Carmina* lxxxv, "Odi et amo, quare id faciam, fortasse requiris / nescio, sed fieri sentio et excrucior."

41   12. sleepless poems: by Innokenty Annensky (1856-1909), whose book *The Cypress Chest* is arranged into twenty-five triptychs. Annensky suffered from insomnia.

45   13. S. R.: A member of the Socialist Revolutionary Party, a group outlawed by the Bolsheviks after the October Revolution.

45   14. Chiniselli Circus: The circus building (built in 1877) on the banks of the Fontanka Canal in St. Petersburg.

45   15. the blockade: the 900-day siege of Leningrad (now, as before the Soviet era, St. Petersburg) in World War II by the Nazi army, which lasted from September 1941 until January 1944. The definitive book on this epic defense that is one of the defining events of the city is Harrison E. Salisbury's *900 Days: The Siege of Leningrad*, Da Capo Press, 1969.

Sosnora

51   16. gaslamp, drugstore, / street: These lines echo well known lines in a 1912 poem by Aleksandr Blok, "Noch' ulitsa, fonar', apteka," which ends: "You will die — you will start again from the beginning. / And repeat everything as in the old days: / Night, an icy ripple on the canal, / A drugstore, a street, a streetlamp."

51   17. Mniszech: Marina Mniszech was a powerful Polish aristocrat who in May 1606 married "the False Dmitry," a pretender who assumed the throne after the death of the tsar, events dramatized in the historical play *Boris Godunov* by Aleksandr Pushkin (1799-1838). Mniszech identified a second "false Dmitry" as her husband in 1607, and he lasted in rebellion until 1610.

51   18. Evgeny and the Neva night: This is a reference to the "Bronze Horseman" by Pushkin. The Neva is the principal river running through St. Petersburg. The name of the river is pronounced with a stress on the second syllable.

51   19. Salieri: A rumor too juicy to die has it that the composer Antonio Salieri (1750-1825) poisoned Mozart out of jealousy of his genius. Among others who have taken up this theme, Pushkin wrote a short play called *Mozart and Salieri*.

57   20. Klodt's monsters: The Anichkov Bridge over the Fontanka (see note 14) is distinguished by four immense bronzes of horses being tamed by muscular young men, statues designed by Peter Karlovich Klodt (1805-1867).

57   21. The Admiralty: This building with its distinctive gilded spire was designed by Andrei Zakharov and constructed between 1806 and 1823. It is one of the landmarks of St. Petersburg's Palace Square.

59   22. Toricelli: Evangelista Toricelli (1608-47) was Galileo's secretary, a physicist, a mathematician, and the inventor of the barometer. A "Toricelli vacuum" is on display in the Academy of Sciences in St. Petersburg.

59   23. Nevsky Prospekt: The principal thoroughfare in St. Petersburg.

Morits

67 24. Anna Akhmatova (1889-1966) and Marina Tsvetaeva (1892-1941) are two towering Russian poets of the twentieth century.

67 25. Zhenya, Andrei, Bella, Novella: These are Evgeny (Zhenia) Yevtushenko (b. 1933), Andrey Voznesensky (b. 1933), Bella Akhmadulina (b. 1937) and Novella Matveeva (b. 1934) popular, public poets of the generation that includes Morits (b. 1937).

Iskander

77 26. Gegard: In Armenia, a church hollowed out of mountain rock.

Rein

99 27. Red Presnya: Krasnaia Presnia is a historic and industrial quarter in western Moscow.

101 28. Piskarevsky: The Piskarevsky cemetery in St. Petersburg is the repository of the mass burials from the Blockade. See note 15.

101 29. remained in Leningrad / the winter of '42: That is, during the harshest winter of the siege of the Blockade. See note 15.

101 30. Fontanka: See note 14.

101 31. Moika: The Moika River runs through St. Petersburg (Leningrad).

101 32. Yusupov Palace: In the classical Yusupov Palace on the embankment of the Moika, the "Mad Monk" Grigory Rasputin was killed in 1916.

101 33. Nicholas / of Lycian Myra: Nicholas, a fourth-century bishop in Asia Minor, known as "the Miracle Worker," had been canonized by the sixth century. The patron saint of sailors and children, his feast day is December 6.

103 34. Rozanov: Vasilii Vasilievich Rozanov (1856-1919) was a powerful thinker and writer of his time.

105 35. Kruzenstern: Admiral Ivan Fedorovich Kruzenstern (1770-1846) was the first Russian to circumnavigate the globe (1803-6). His statue stands near the Academy of Sciences in St. Petersburg.

105 36. This line has also been published in the original Russian in the variant: "Across the Bridge of Kisses I emerge / at the Mariinsky" ("Через мост Поцелуев я выйду к Маринке...").

105 37. Nikolsky Cathedral: The eighteenth-century Cathedral of St. Nicholas in St. Petersburg. See note 33.

105 38. a student / fastening an axe to the lining of his coat: Raskolnikov, in Fedor Dostevsky's novel *Crime and Punishment*, carries an axe in this fashion.

105 39. Derzhavin's door: Gavrila Romanovich Derzhavin (1743-1816) was an innovative poet and one of the fountainheads of Russian literature. He lived at Number 118 on the Fontanka embankment.

105 40. Nekrasov: Nikolai Alekseevich Nekrasov (1821-78) is one of the best known poets of the nineteenth century. See also Note 81.

430

105 41. Delvig: Anton Antonovich, Baron Delvig (1798-1831) a poet, was the contemporary and friend of Pushkin.

105 42. Zhukovsky: Vasily Andreevich Zhukovsky (1783-1852) was a poet and translator associated primarily with the Romantic literary movement in Russia. See "Between Zukofsky and Zhukovsky" in this book.

105 43. Neva, Admiralty: the Neva River, and the Admiralty building that stands on its bank. See notes 18 and 21.

107 44. Nevsky: See note 23.

109 45. Petrograd: the name briefly (1914-1924) given to St. Petersburg before it became Leningrad.

Bobyshev

113 46. Kronstadt ice: Kronstadt, a seaport icebound much of the year, had long been identified with mutinies and revolutionary upheavals against the prevailing Russian régime, most recently against the Bolsheviks in 1921, an insurrection that was harshly put down under Trotsky's direction.

115 47. Chaliapin: Fedor Ivanovich Chaliapin (1873-1938) the celebrated operatic bass, lived abroad after the Revolution and died in Paris in 1938, where he was buried next to his wife. A few years ago, their grave was opened and the remains of Chaliapin disappeared. They turned up finally in Moscow at the prestigious cemetery of the Novedichy Monastery, where he was reburied at the behest of the state.

117 48. "Well get up then ...": The poet weaves into stanzas ten through twelve quotations from the Russian lyrics to the opening of the *Internationale*, the anthem of international Communism and of the Soviet Communist Party.

Akhmadulina

129 49. Tarusa: A city on the Oka River, south of Moscow.

131 50. Oka: See note above.

131 51. *There's no free will ...* : An allusion to Aleksandr Pushkin's 1834 poem "Pora, moi drug, pora! Pokoia serdtse prosit." See also D. A. Prigov's poem in this volume, p. 261, "Dialogue No. 5."

Tkachenko

159 52. Kursky train station: This major railway station in Moscow serves trains to and from the southeast.

163 53. Dynamo Stadium: This is the stadium of the Moscow Dynamo football (that is, soccer) team, on which the poet played.

Sapgir

175 54. Psalm 137: The Hebrew and Protestant editions of the Book of Psalms are numbered differently from the Russian Orthodox and Roman Catholic versions, so what is numbered Psalm 136 in the Russian becomes Psalm 137 in the King James Version used here.

175   55. O nori ... Veyli bayon! ... O levi ... Tzion: This language is meant to   431
sound like the Hebrew of the Psalms, but without actual meaning.

175   56. Er singt wie einige Nachtigall: German, "He sings like a nightingale."

175   57. Zerstören!, Vernichten! Vertilgen!: German, "Destroy!, Annihilate!,
Obliterate!"

177   58. Erschießen: German, "Execute [by shooting]."

179   59. Evoë! A cry of Bacchic revelry.

181   60. Has unrolled as if on a screen ... a shoe crunches eyeglasses underfoot:
This whole section is an allusion to the cinematic editorial style of montage of Sergey Eisenstein, with particular reference to the "Odessa Steps" sequence of *The Battleship Potemkin*.

Yeryomin

201   61. Street lamp. Something missing. Drugstore: See note 16.

Stratanovsky

207   62. Herostratos burned down the temple of Diana at Ephesus, one of the
Seven Wonders of the Ancient World, solely in order to achieve fame. The destruction worked: Who now remembers the names of those who built the beautiful temple?

207   63. "Black Stream" is a landmark within present-day St. Petersburg, but once a stream-bank on the outskirts of the city, where Pushkin was fatally shot in a duel in 1837.

207   64. tomamatoes: a word play in the original.

209   65. Evgeny: the hero and victim of Pushkin's "Bronze Horseman." See note 18.

211   66. underground ... Dostoevsky: This is an allusion to "Notes from Underground."

Sedakova

217   67. Demodocus: In Homer's *Odyssey*, Demodocus is the singer of the
Phæacians (Book 8).

221   68. "Fifth Stanzas:" There are excellent explanatory notes to this poem in
An Anthology of Russian Women's Writing, 1777-1992. See our bibliography.

225   69. a Mediolanian glimpse of paradise: An allusion to St. Augustine's conversion (Confessions VIII, 8-12) which occurred in a garden in Milan.

Shvarts

229   70. O rosa mystica: (Latin) O mystic rose.

231   71. Marsyas: Marsyas was a satyr who engaged in a musical contest with
Apollo. He was flayed for his hubris.

Prigov

261   72. There is no happiness on earth: See note 51.

Dragomoschenko

267 73. Little Prince Ivan: The hero of many Russian folktales.

275 74. the Siren is gold on the bough: In Russian mythology, the siren — a bird with the head and breast of a woman — descends from heaven to earth, bewitching humans with its singing.

Iskrenko

293 75. It snowed & snowed: Quoted from Boris Pasternak's poem "Winter Night."

295 76. the Pirquet reaction: An archaic term for a tuberculin test.

295 77. Shchors: Nikolai Alexandrovich Shchors (1895-1919) was a commander in the Red Army and a hero of the Civil War. He died in battle.

Shcherbina

301 78. Pioneer: The Young Pioneers were the youth organization of the Communist Party.

303 79. koumiss: A fermented milk drink of Central Asia.

305 80. Suvorov: Field Marshall Aleksandr Vasilevich Suvorov (1729-1800) was known for a heroic crossing of the Alps in 1799.

Nekrasov

309 81. not that Nekrasov / and also not the other one: For Nikolai Alekseevich Nekrasov (1821-78) see note 40. Viktor Platonovich Nekrasov (born 1911) is a well known contemporary novelist. What the two writers have in common, besides their surname, is a down-to-earth, "realistic" approach to literature.

Gandlevsky

329 82. Ordzhonikidzerzhinsky: A humorous, acerbic conflation of the names of two Soviet revolutionary heroes, Grigory Konstantinovich Ordzhonikidze (1886-1937) and Felix Edmundovich Dzerzhinsky (1877-1926) whose statue was summarily upended by protesting crowds during the 1991 failed coup.

329 83. Drugstore, a line of folks, a shiner: See note 16.

329 84. Today it's my turn: a quotation from Pushkin's *Eugene Onegin*, Canto 8, stanza xlii, line 14.

331 85. Old Arbat: The Arbat is a celebrated ancient, modern, enduring street in Moscow. The Old Arbat is distinguished from the New Arbat.

331 86. Drevlan: According to Russian legend, this town was burned down by pigeons carrying flaming straw.

331 87. Chita, Suchan, Karaganda: Prison camps.

331 88. Yauza: The Yauza is a river running through and north of Moscow. "The onset of the industrial revolution ... rendered it a grimy wasteland 'emblazoned by factory waste in all colours of the rainbow,' in the words

of a 1917 city guidebook. Little has changed to this day." (Robert Greenall, **433**
An Explorer's Guide to Moscow, Zephyr Press, 1995) p. 180.

333 89. MEI: A youth camp organized by the Moscow Energy Institute.

333 90. Omsk to Osh: that is, from Siberia to Kirghizstan, the breadth of the old U. S. S. R.

333 91. Simonov: Konstantin Mikhailovich Simonov (1915-1979) was an officially approved, sentimental poet (among his other writing accomplishments) of the Soviet Union especially in the 1940s and 50s.

333 92. "Remember, Alyosha": "You remember, Alyosha, the roads of Smolensk province," is the first line of "Smolensk Roads," a 1941 poem by K. M. Simonov (translated by Jack Lindsay and published in *Soviet Literature*, no. 6, 1967, p. 143).

333 93. Plyatt: Rostislav Ianovich Plyatt (b. 1908) was a celebrated actor with a large, imposing figure.

333 94. Enchanted Traveler: This is a reference to a story about a runaway serf by the prose writer Nikolai Semenovich Leskov (1831-1895).

333 95. Pamir: A brand of cigarette depicting on its package a shadowy figure on a mountaintop.

335 96. Shostkino: A Soviet film studio, of which the poor quality stock is rapidly disintegrating.

335 97. black-bookers / from Cracow and Salamanca: literally, sorcerers, magicians. In the parlance of the labor camps, those convicted of disseminating anti-Soviet literature.

Bek

345 98. Vodnoy Stadium: A stadium for water-sports near the Moskva River.

349 99. Dynamo Stadium: see note 53.

Nikolaeva

357 100. Women's Day: It is traditional for women to gather for a women-only party on International Women's Day, March 8.

Popova

371 101. The Lion Bridge: One of the small, graceful bridges of St. Petersburg.

Kekova

383 102. Lilith: In Hebrew mythology, Adam's first wife, who was later characterized as a demon, a succubus, and a thief of newborn babies.

383 103. Susannah: See "Daniel and Susannah" in the Apocrypha, where Susannah is a virtuous woman spied on in her bath and falsely accused of adultery.

387 104. Ben-Hinnom: The valley of "the son of Hinnom" (see the books of Joshua, 2 Kings, 2 Chronicles and Jeremiah) lies just south of Mt. Zion.

434   *Ratushinkaya*

401   105. Mandelstam's swallow: "The Swallow," a 1920 poem by Osip Mandelstam's (1891-19) begins, "I have forgotten the word that I wanted to say."

401   106. Boris Leonidovich Pasternak (1890-1960).

401   107. Marina Tsvetaeva: See note 24.

401   108. Tyutchevian waters: poet Fyodor Ivanovich Tyutchev (1803-73) renowned, among other things, for his natural descriptions.

Kenjeev

409   109. Arbat: See note 85.

409   110. a child of god-forsaken basements: "One important word [in the Russian] is дитё [child] rather than the neutral (or slightly poetic) дитя. It reminds the reader of Dmitry Karamazov's famous dream, where he questions the entire meaning of life. (Why is the baby crying, he asks: почему плачет дитё) Hence the word is an allusion to the idea of the cruelty of life." [B. K.]

409   111. A glazier / walks around with his box: "a staple of urban life in Russia in the 1950s. Essentially, so was the junk man. The former would wander around town with a huge box packed with window glass, the latter with a huge sack. Both would usually be followed by excited kids. The window guy was just plain fun, the junk guy would offer cheap toys for old things. They are understandably juxtaposed in the poem." [B.K.]

411   112. all will pass, and rivers will flow away: An allusion to Ecclesiastes 1:7.

411   113. in the hands of the Living God: The reference here is to Hebrews 10:31, "It is a fearful thing to fall into the hands of the Living God."

411   114. my whole life was ... : "a vague indication that we are dealing with essentially a love poem. An avid poetry reader might recall two lines [35-36] from Tatiana's letter to Onegin: 'All my past life has had one meaning — / That I should meet you ...' " [Note from B. K. — The lines quoted here from Tatiana's letter in Chapter Three of Pushkin's *Eugene Onegin* are in the translation by Babette Deutsch.]

Between Zukofsky and Zhukovsky

417   115. judgment of Joseph Brodsky: This comes from pages x-xi of the essay "Poetry as a Form of Resistance to Reality," translated by Alexander Sumerkin and Jamey Gambrell, which introduces Tomas Venclova's *Winter Dialogue*, Northwestern University Press 1997.

BACKGROUND OF RUSSIAN POETRY AND REFERENCE:

Bristol, Evelyn, *A History of Russian Poetry*, Oxford University Press 1991.

Brown, Edward J., *Russian Literature Since the Revolution*, Harvard University Press, 1982.

France, Peter, *Poets of Modern Russia*, Cambridge University Press, 1982.

Janecek, Gerald, *The Look of Russian Poetry*, Princeton University Press, 1984.

Kasack, Wolfgang, *Dictionary of Russian Literature since 1917* (translated by Maria Carlson and Jane T. Hedges) Columbia University Press 1988.

Ledkovsky, Marina, Charlotte Rosenthal and Mary Zirin, *Dictionary of Russian Women Writers*, Greenwood Press, 1994.

Makin, Michael (editor) "Alternative Chronicles of Russian Poetry, Essays by Mikhail Aizenberg," *Russian Studies in Literature*, volume 32, number 2, spring 1996.

Mirsky, D. S., *A History of Russian Literature from its Beginnings to 1900*, Vintage, 1958.

Terras, Victor, *Handbook of Russian Literature*, Yale University Press, 1985.

OTHER ANTHOLOGIES:

Erofeyev, Victor, editor,*The Penguin Book of New Russian Writing*, Penguin 1995.

Glad, John and Daniel Weissbort, editors, *Twentieth-Century Russian Poetry*, University of Iowa Press, 1992.

Goscilo, Helena, editor, *Lives in Transit: Recent Russian Women's Writing*, Ardis, 1995.

Johnson, Kent and Stephen Ashby, *Third Wave*, University of Michigan Press, 1992.

Kelly, Catriona, editor, *An Anthology of Russian Women's Writing, 1777-1992*, Oxford University Press, 1994.

Moss, Kevin, editor, *Out of the Blue: Russia's Hidden Gay Literature*, Gay Sunshine Press, 1997.

Smith, Gerald, *Contemporary Russian Poetry*, Indiana University Press, 1993.

Todd, Albert C. and Max Hayward, editors, *20th Century Russian Poetry: Silver and Steel*, Doubleday, 1993.

GENERAL INTELLECTUAL AND CULTURAL BACKGROUND:

Boym, Svetlana, *Common Places*, Harvard University Press, 1994.

Gerhart, Genevra, *The Russian's World: Life and Language*, Harcourt Brace & Company, 1995.

Gessen, Masha, *Dead Again*, Verso, 1997.

Solomon, Andrew, *The Irony Tower: Soviet Artists in a Time of Glasnost*, Knopf, 1991.

SOME ENGLISH-LANGUAGE LITERARY MAGAZINES
WITH FEATURES IN CONTEMPORARY RUSSIAN POETRY:

Five Fingers Review, numbers 8/9 and 10, edited by John High, 1991.

Glas: New Russian Writing (continuing) edited by Natasha Perova and Arch Tait, Moscow.

The Literary Review, volume 34, number 3, edited by Thomas Epstein, Fairleigh Dickinson University, 1991.

Modern Poetry in Translation, nos. 10 and 11, edited by Daniel Weissbort, King's College London, 1997.

Negative Capability, volume viii, numbers 1 & 2, edited by Jay Higginbotham, 1988.

Nimrod, volume 33, number 2, edited by Francine Ringold, Arts and Humanities Council of Tulsa, Oklahoma, 1990.

World Literature Today, volume 76, number 1, edited by Djelal Kadir, University of Oklahoma, 1993.

Указатель Стихотворений

Colophon

In the Grip of Strange Thoughts was designed and produced
by Dan Carr & Julia Ferrari at Golgonooza Letter Foundry &
Press, Ashuelot NH, with assistance from Gahlord Dewald. The
digital types are Lazurski, from ParaType International of
Moscow & Monotype Dante.
The Cyrillic was designed by Russian calligrapher
Vadim Lazurski, and originally cut in metal
under the direction of Giovanni Mardersteig who also
designed the Dante types. These two typefaces, designed
to work together, were first combined to print
Alexandr Pushkin's *The Bronze Horseman,*
at the Officina Bodoni in Verona Italy. The original version of
Lazurski was known as Pushkin, for this reason. Our thanks to
Emil Yakupov of ParaType,
Robert Bringhurst & Burwell Davis who helped obtain the
digital Lazurski font from Moscow for this book.

DATE